Absolute impact

the drive for personal leadership

Matthew May

PELOTON
PUBLISHING

LOS ANGELES

LOS ANGELES

Peloton Publishing
9234 Deering Avenue Los Angeles, California 91311
Tel: (818) 882-6231   Fax: (818) 700-7774
e-mail: info@pelotonpublishing.com

Ordering Information
Peloton publications are available through most bookstores and online booksellers. They can also be ordered direct from Peloton Publishing. Special discounts are available on quantity purchases by corporations, associations, and other organizations. For details, contact the "Special Sales Department" at the Peloton Publishing address above. For information on academic use / course adoption please contact Peloton Publishing.

Absolute Impact™ is a registered trademark of Aevitas Learning

Publisher Cataloging-in-Publication Data

May, Matthew.
Absolute impact: the drive for personal leadership / Matthew May
p. cm.
Includes bibliographical references.
ISBN 0-9729794-0-9 (pbk. : alk. paper)
1.Leadership.   2. Success—Psychological aspects.   3. Conduct of life.   I. Title.
BF637.I4 .M39 2003   158.4—dc21
2003091590

Images by Wildside Press and Ecclecticollections
Printed and bound in the United States of America on acid-free paper

Dedication

To all the everyday heroes in my life.

To my father, who taught me at an early age that *"all things change, and we must change with them."*
Rest high on that mountain.

The Penalty of Leadership

In every field of human endeavor, he that is first must perpetually live in the white light of publicity. ¶ Whether the leadership be vested in a man or in a manufactured product, emulation and envy are ever at work. ¶ In art, in literature, in music, in industry, the reward and the punishment are always the same. The reward is widespread recognition; the punishment, fierce denial and detraction. ¶ When a man's work becomes a standard for the whole world, it also becomes a target for the shafts of the envious few. ¶ If his work be merely mediocre, he will be left severely alone – if he achieves a masterpiece, it will set a million tongues a-wagging. ¶ Jealousy does not protrude its forked tongue at the artist who produces a commonplace painting. ¶ Whatsoever you write, or paint, or play, or sing, or build, no one will strive to surpass or to slander you unless your work be stamped with the seal of genius. ¶ Long, long after a great work or a good work has been done, those who are disappointed or envious continue to cry out that it cannot be done. ¶ Spiteful little voices in the domain of art were raised against our own Whistler as a mountebank, long after the big world had acclaimed him its greatest artistic genius. ¶ Multitudes flocked to Bayreuth to worship at the musical shrine of Wagner, while the little group of those whom he had dethroned and displaced argued angrily that he was no musician at all. ¶ The little world continued to protest that Fulton could never build a steamboat, while the big world flocked to the river banks to see his boat steam by. ¶ The leader is assailed because he is a leader, and the effort to equal him is merely added proof of that leadership. ¶ Failing to equal or to excel, the follower seeks to depreciate and to destroy – but only confirms once more the superiority of that which he strives to supplant. ¶ There is nothing new in this. ¶ It is as old as the world and as old as the human passions – envy, fear, greed, ambition, and the desire to surpass. ¶ And it all avails nothing. ¶ If the leader truly leads, he remains – the leader. ¶ Master-poet, master-painter, master-workman, each in his turn is assailed, and each holds his laurels through the ages. ¶ That which is good or great makes itself known, no matter how loud the clamor of denial.
That which deserves to live – lives.

This text was written by Theodore F. MacManus and appeared only once as an advertisement in the Saturday Evening Post on January 2, 1915. Copyright © by the Cadillac Motor Company. Reprinted with permission.

Appreciation

No one succeeds alone, certainly not I.

In acknowledgement of the efforts and influences of those who have made this book possible, I wish to extend my heartfelt appreciation:

To my colleague and compadre, Dr. Mike Morrison, Dean of the University of Toyota – our work over the past half decade has helped greatly to catalyze my thoughts.

To the unnamed countless individuals in dozens of client and partner organizations who have unwittingly provided me two decades of learning laboratories, yielding profound insight into personal excellence and the human working condition.

To my professors at The Wharton School from whom I learned to think critically, and to view leadership as something much more than directing the performance of others.

To my professors at The Johns Hopkins University from whom I learned to love the questions, and to view education as something much more than the simple accumulation of accepted knowledge.

To my wife Deva, for introducing me to heraldry and the Renaissance, for enduring my extended preoccupation, and for granting me the luxury of early morning and late night solitude.

To my parents, for giving me a love of the library.

To my early draft reviewers, for invaluable input.

To the Mbox boys, for making me look good.

Contents

In seeking a symbol to represent the spirit of **Absolute Impact**, I chose the *fleur-de-lis*, the quintessential icon of the Renaissance, a time of European cultural rebirth experiencing the greatest growth in arts and sciences in the history of human endeavor. Commonly found in heraldic crests, it was one of the most highly regarded marks among those of nobility. The *fleur-de-lis* (French for "flower of light") is derived from the lotus (a.k.a. lily or iris) flower. The three leaves are believed to symbolize faith, wisdom, and valor.

Preface

At some point in life, we will all reflect on a most important question regarding our life's work: *Have I made the most of what I have to offer the world?*

Whether one's work is parenting or presiding, the ability to lead oneself toward a positive answer to this deceptively simple question is of paramount importance, for it stands at the very heart of making a difference. An unequivocal "yes" is a true personal triumph; yet, it is a victory few ever truly realize. In fact, most people avoid confronting the question entirely until it is far too late in life to change their circumstances.

Consider this*:

• *Most people (71%) would rather be doing something else with their life*
• *Most people (73%) spend most of their day (6 out of 8 hours) distracted in their work*
• *Most people (77%) feel they don't/can't bring their true self to work*

Beyond prompting the questions of how and why so many so often end up on the wrong path in work and life, these results reveal a disturbing situation in which personal excellence is withheld from one's work. Reversal is of unquestionable importance, and anyone attempting such a compelling personal renaissance must face rather daunting questions about the role of work in life.

My intent in writing **Absolute Impact** is to raise these very issues, and in so doing talk about leadership in a new way – a much more personal way. I believe leadership must move beyond simple effectiveness and directing the performance of others to become more about making the most of our unique abilities to positively impact the lives of those with whom we are connected in work and life – ultimately leading ourselves to truly meaningful accomplishment. In my view, the ability to lead oneself in this manner is the defining prerequisite to leading others – it is indeed *personal* leadership.

This, in turn, requires an uncommon level of self-knowledge – insight rarely found except among highly impactful people (those we deem leaders). Yet, "success secrets" urging adoption of some amalgam of visible practices – techniques attributed to, or held in common by, noteworthy individuals – have yielded little in the way of standout, standup performance. Reasons? First, because these 'cookbook' approaches simply don't dive deep enough (it is the process that yields the original recipe that holds the key). Second, because most of what works for others is generally mismatched to our unique constellations.

Over the past two decades, I have studied high impact individuals using a much different approach. Viewing common denominators as a concept best left for mathematics, I searched for *variation* within the species itself, discerned patterns in a continuum of variation, delineated the dimensions of common

*(Based on a nationwide poll conducted by Aevitas Learning)

uniqueness, and devised a model thusly. My discovery: three distinct, self-driven factors (*not* techniques) that account for nearly all of the variance in personal impact, regardless of one's walk in life. These factors in tandem suggest a readily accessible and rather timeless pathway – one, it turns out, that is supported not only by one of the greatest thinkers of all time (Plato), but also by more contemporary thinking on human nature.

Absolute Impact thus posits a uniquely different route: a universal means by which we chart our own course through life in what amounts to a lifelong quest to discover, deepen, and direct that which truly drives us. The goal is not necessarily to embark on a radically new path in life, but to investigate how we might bring more of who we are to our current, everyday experience. You must be of two minds to embark on this exploration – one of curiosity, the other of challenge – as there are two lanes to travel: thought and action.

From this point forward, consider yourself a journeyman leader. But beware, traveler, for there is no map (that would miss the point). You must learn your way as you *make* your way. Like any epic odyssey, travel into unfamiliar and unknown territory is required. My role will be simply to help facilitate the process by moving you beyond concept to application, past explanation to demonstration. I have included a section at the end (*Artenza's Tools*) to further aid you in your efforts to lead yourself toward absolute impact. I apologize in advance for not offering pat answers. None exist.

My desire is to elevate and challenge your thinking. I aim to do so by offering you a unique and enjoyable read founded in research, science and philosophy, and using dramatic dialogue as the propelling literary device – complete with all the lyricism, alliteration and symmetry I could muster. Instead of the typical single viewpoint offered by most books, there are four – each represented by a different character, each with a distinctly different worldview. My bet is that you will identify with at least one of them.

A final thought: now more than ever, we need excellent leadership at every level in our society – in our families, communities, institutions, and organizations. In a world where certainty and stability have yielded to a myriad of predominantly disruptive forces and a truly frightening speed of change, this need is one not easily met. However, some things must stand firm to both guide and inform us in times of great change. These are the absolutes. This is the territory of ***Absolute Impact.***

I hope – and indeed believe – you will find the experience of reading ***Absolute Impact*** both entertaining and enlightening.

Matthew May
Westlake Village, California
November 2002

Introduction

*Out of Plato come all things that are still written
and debated by men of great thought.*

Ralph Waldo Emerson

Plato had it right 2500 years ago.

Advancing the notion that there are few new ideas after Plato, I humbly defer to that most profound thinker of antiquity, from whose philosophies virtually all other study can arguably be derived. Even those notable thinkers taking issue with Plato find themselves defending and comparing their ideas to his.

Absolute Impact pays homage to Plato, who wrestled with the issues of personal excellence in leadership long before anyone else, and whose seminal ideas and high concepts are as relevant today as they were then. Anyone familiar with this classical master will recognize his dialectic methods reflected in the book. I have selected key ideas from Plato's major works that lend support to my approach, and included them throughout in the form of framing quotes.

A bit about Plato and his relevance to **Absolute Impact**:

Plato (427 - 347 B.C.) *Greek philosopher*

Plato was consumed with the fundamental, philosophical problem of working out a theory for the art of living and knowing, and he felt that knowledge was a living, interactive force.

Plato saw his task as that of leading humanity to a vision of some sense of the highest good – of defining and pursuing the *good* life beyond merely the *successful* life. A good man was a just man, with justice defined as each person doing their work according to their nature. According to Plato, when we develop our talents and flourish, the results are a good life – for the individual and the society we live in. So to understand justice, one must understand goodness, which in turn demands the pursuit of truth.

Plato's method of philosophical inquiry, taught to him by his teacher, Socrates – whose wisdom we know of only through Plato's written dramatic dialogues in which Socrates figures centrally (Socrates never wrote anything) – consisted of challenging people and working them through a series of questions. This "Socratic method" – or *dialectic* – eventually gave rise to the idea that truth must be pursued through dialogue and query. Plato founded "The Academy" in 385 B.C. to formalize this pursuit. The Academy would become, in its time, the most famous school in the classical world, with Aristotle its most famous pupil.

Plato was convinced of the ultimately harmonious structure of the universe, and his goal was to show the rational relationship and alignment between the soul, the state and the universe. In what is perhaps his best-known work, the *Republic*, Plato embarks on a long discussion about how an ideal state might embody the four great virtues: *temperance, justice, courage,* and *wisdom.*

This led him to ponder the issue of personal excellence in leadership: who should be considered to lead the ideal state? Plato utilizes epistemology, metaphysics, and ethics in order to answer this question, concluding that knowledge, learning, and judgment are the fundamental requirements. Implied in this conclusion is the idea that without any one of these, true leadership will elude. Believing that only those adhering to certain moral absolutes ought to be counted as leaders, Plato observed that the best-suited would undoubtedly shy from the distinction, recognizing that leadership requires relentless testing of one's character – rigor few would actively seek.

By today's standards, Plato aims uncomfortably high for most. And, detractors argue, what does epistemology, metaphysics, and ethics have to do with leadership? If he were alive today, Plato would say that epistemology is the study of knowledge, and seeks to answer the question: *What do we think we know?* Metaphysics is the study of what is real, and seeks to answer the question: *What is the current situation?* Ethics is concerned with living a virtuous life, and seeks to answer the question: *What is the right thing to do?* Plato undoubtedly would argue that these are the very questions that must absolutely guide any leader. Too, these are the same issues every leader must face in the defining moments of adversity, when critical actions must be taken, forcing decisions requiring reflection and reexamination of our very being. They are, in fact, the questions of life.

Finally, Plato classifies human beings based on their innate strength and intellect. In the famous *Allegory of the Cave*, Plato utilizes a "divided line" analogy to illustrate "four faculties of the soul" – what might best be defined as states of mind, or intellects: *perception, conviction, understanding,* and *reason.* These four intellects relate to, and are aligned with, the four cardinal virtues. According to Plato, all humans seek knowledge to some extent in all four areas – with a natural tendency toward one presiding over the other three. This tendency in turn influences the best use of one's natural gifts, ideally resulting in fulfillment of the pivotal roles in society: *agency, propriety, diplomacy,* and *philosophy.*

In **Absolute Impact**, each of the characters represents one of these four unique mindsets, enabling a universal treatment of the key issues. The character of Artenza (agency) embraces the virtue of *courage* and represents *perception;* the character of Dutamis (propriety) embraces the virtue of *temperance* and represents *conviction;* the character of Trutorio (diplomacy) embraces the virtue of *justice* and represents *understanding;* and the Prince (philosophy) embraces the virtue of *wisdom* and represents *reason.*

Maximus represents all those seeking maximum impact in work and life, and the Court might be any organization. And now to our story…

Part One

Setting

Our drama takes place one evening in a mythical, provincial Court in which a fading Prince and his three most trusted Courtiers (advisors) meet for a final summit in the Pantheon to discuss and debate the challenges facing the Prince's young heir, Maximus, in leading himself toward a bright future of truly significant accomplishment.

DRAMATIS PERSONAE

The Prince: *A visionary leader, master of strategy and ruler of the highest ranking Court in the Province — a man of vision and reason*

Dutamis: *A conscientious Courtier, gifted administrator and Minister of the Interior — a man of service and **duty****

Trutorio: *An ideological Courtier, virtuous advocate and Chancellor of Diplomatic Affairs — a man of spirit and **truth****

Artenza: *An impulsive Courtier, brilliant tactical commander and General of the Provincial Army — a man of action and **artistry****

(* Emphasis added to aid character memory)

Questions

*In which the Prince challenges his Courtiers
to embrace the power of proper inquiry*

In the highest ranking Court of the most powerful principality in the
Province, the aged and ailing Prince summoned his three most trusted
Courtiers to the Pantheon for a final summit.

Upon their arrival, the Prince warmly embraced and acknowledged
each advisor in turn.

"Trutorio, my most trusted emissary…you have kept our course true,
our purpose unified," he said to the first.

"Dutamis, my most trusted administrator…you have kept our gates
secure, our economy productive," he said to the second.

"Artenza, my most trusted general…you have kept our influence
strong, our expansion robust," he said to the third.

The Courtiers replied in unison: "We simply follow your lead and
humbly serve your vision, Liege."

The Prince nodded in acknowledgement of his Courtiers' deference,
and began to speak in earnest.

"My friends, I fear my time is near, and I have a most urgent matter to
discuss with you. When I tell you of the topic, I am certain you will agree
it is appropriate that we meet here, in this great hall of heroes."

Naturally, the Courtiers were distressed to hear the Prince speak of his imminent demise, for they each had served at the Prince's side for their entire careers.

"How may we serve you?" they asked.

"In the following way," replied the Prince. "As you well know, my son Maximus will ascend to the crown of this Court when I pass. He is young and will need guidance. I wish to enlist your help to ensure that he will realize as much from his life and work in the Court as possible – as I have from mine – and, in so doing, lead the Court to a new generation of success."

The Courtiers immediately began to protest. "But my Prince, surely we cannot guarantee…"

But the Prince silenced them with a wave of his hand. "Patience," he smiled.

"You see," continued the Prince, "I am soon to join the ranks of those whose images adorn this hall. In this my final season, I am compelled to reflect deeply on a most important question regarding my life's work: *Did I make the most of what I had to offer the world?*"

The Prince went on. "It is a deceptively simple question, one with many and complex dimensions – of self and significance, of calling and cause, of potential and performance, of meaning and mastery, of purpose and possibility, of leadership and legacy – in sum, a question of absolute impact. These thoughts consume me, Courtiers! Moreover, I am certain I am not alone in this. That is to say, although we each travel upon a track through life as unique as our thumbprint, each of us will someday wrestle with this most humbling of questions, just as I have – some perhaps sooner than others, but certainly all as elders facing the twilight of life."

The Courtiers leaned forward, anxiously awaiting the answer, for they knew the Prince was right. The Prince paused to savor the anticipation before continuing.

"Colleagues, I am happy to report that I can answer in the unwavering affirmative. My advanced state of age affords me a momentary lapse in the fine art of humility to say that mine has been a life well lived!" The Prince smiled, feigning bombastic pride.

"To be quite earnest," he continued, "I have led a truly extraordinary life – one of great vitality and deep meaning for me. I do, however, have one thing more I wish to accomplish. And therein lies the conundrum."

The Courtiers looked at once relieved, amused and confused. The Prince smiled at their quandary.

"Come and sit with me at this roundtable," beckoned the Prince.

And so it was that the Prince and the Courtiers began their discussion of grave magnitude.

"You see," began the Prince, "in order that Maximus lead others, he must first learn to lead himself. In truth, I fear chance will rule his destiny. Maximus is not unlike you or me – or anyone else, for that matter – in the following way: the confines of his path have been determined, but the content has not."

The Courtiers paused to contemplate this thought, for the Prince's proffer was deep and perplexing.

Dutamis spoke first. "I am not certain I understand what you mean by 'confines of his path,' Sire."

The Prince was pleased, for he saw that his challenge had sparked the very flame of debate he sought.

"Most everyone is invested in an established course from which dramatic departure can be difficult," replied the Prince. "Maximus is to be the Prince of this Court. He will rule the Province, live in this villa, command the legions, and be charged with the prosperity of the Province. Can he realistically abandon any of these aspects without negatively affecting others?"

Artenza, too, had doubt. "With all due respect, is not the content of his path preordained to be identical to your own?"

"It is a mistake to separate the leader from the act of leadership, the contributor from the contribution, the achiever from the achievement – which the pundits are so wont to do," replied the Prince. "You are a highly accomplished Courtier, as is Dutamis, as is Trutorio. Have you all embraced identical philosophies, mirrored each other's moves, or employed the same techniques within your position?"

We will all someday reflect on a most important question regarding our life's work:

Did I make the most of what I had to offer the world?

Finally, Trutorio commented. "Maximus is of royal birth, my lord, and surely you are not suggesting he is like either a commoner or, for that matter, a Courtier."

"Rank and title – and in this case privilege – are of no consequence to the matter at hand," replied the Prince. "They are neither necessary nor sufficient to adequately address the issues as I will present them to you. Doesn't everyone, regardless of station, face the same question of content in leading their life and conducting their work?"

The Prince saw that his Courtiers were still somewhat frustrated, for their questions had been met with yet more questions.

"My friends," he continued, "there are no easy answers to such a complex problem. Only the questions. It is the questions that drive us all – each of us, without exception. And, this is an excellent theme with which to launch our discussion. Allow me to demonstrate."

The Prince paused to gather his thoughts, for he sought to extract a moment of learning.

"Courtiers, what manner of query propelled you to complete your day?" asked the Prince.

The Courtiers promptly responded in turn.

"What were my deadlines?" answered Dutamis.

"What were my obligations?" answered Trutorio.

"What were my objectives?" answered Artenza.

The Prince smiled as the Courtiers realized they had each responded in character with a different question.

"Good," acknowledged the Prince. "Each of you quite unique, no? Now, let us take it one step further. What issues frame the conditions of success in the position of Courtier?"

This time the Courtiers reflected a bit more before answering.

We cannot separate the leader from the act of leadership

"What is my responsibility?" replied Dutamis.

"What is the real significance of my role?" replied Trutorio.

"What is the desired outcome of my actions?" replied Artenza.

Again the Prince smiled. "Excellent. Again, to each his own. From my own perspective, I would add the challenge: *what is it that I must master?*

"Now," he continued, "it is clear that these questions can easily consume the majority of our waking time, true? But is there not yet another, more purposeful depth of inquiry to which we can descend – a tier of query beyond the mandate of the day?"

The Courtiers looked at each other, momentarily baffled by the Prince's challenge. They turned back to the Prince.

"You see, gentlemen," continued the Prince, "as I face my own mortality, it is quite clear to me that we all live our lives in constant and continuous pursuit of answers to questions that occupy our minds – forever learning, forever in search of knowledge at many levels. And while we are generally successful in answering the questions we ask, we often either don't ask the right questions, or don't give the right questions much thought."

"But what are the right questions?" asked Trutorio.

"That is one in itself, Trutorio!" replied the Prince. "And it is precisely that question which we must discuss first."

The Prince hesitated ever so briefly, then in a most serious tone asked: "Courtiers, what must one know in order to lead a good life of absolute impact – a life rich in a tapestry of calling, cause and conquest?"

The Courtiers were silent while they considered the Prince's most perplexing question.

"A deep and difficult question, indeed," said Dutamis.

We live our lives in constant pursuit of answers to questions – though we are generally successful in answering the questions we ask, we often either don't ask the right questions, or don't give the right questions much thought

"We would need to know what you know."

"We spend precious little time on this question, it is true," said Trutorio. "There is much we don't know."

"Most are not inclined to broach the subject, for it is a weighty one, to be sure," said Artenza. "Perhaps it is the fear of the unknown!"

"You see my point," observed the Prince. "And although for each there would be a different answer, it is exactly this larger and more significant issue we must pursue, for it is one of universal relevance. In it lies the personal odyssey that will yield a positive answer to the question we all face in the end. We must consciously reach beyond the simpler questions of daily existence. I submit to you that life has addressed a most important question to each of us, the pursuit of which drives a lifelong quest that defines us as unique individuals – a personal alchemy of power, purpose, and potential. I believe it identifies the essence of who we are and what we have to offer the world."

The Courtiers appeared eager to speak, but the Prince held them off to continue his thought.

"At its source, it is an energy quite primal – something we find so deeply compelling, so personally forceful, that we cannot ignore it without risking our authenticity, vitality and creativity. Call it what you may – passion, soul, bliss, heart, drive, spirit, fire – the label is irrelevant. What is important is to realize that this element of human nature is fundamental to our ability to become the person we were born to be, enabling each of us to determine the content of our respective steps through life and, ultimately, to direct our real destiny and leave a noble legacy."

Suddenly, an excitement filled the air, and the Courtiers rose to the exchange. They now understood where the Prince was going.

Trutorio was the first to speak. "Block it, and we block our life's truest course, our work's most excellent end."

"Just so," replied the Prince, nodding.

Artenza spoke next, anxious to forge ahead. "Our immediate objective, then, should be to help Maximus to find and follow that which truly draws him, for it holds the key to his real potential and creative best."

Before the Prince could reply, Dutamis joined in the discussion, which was now becoming lively.

"Honorable associates, I would agree that your esteemed counsel seems like so much common sense. But it cannot be that easy or simple. Were that it was, our Prince would not have called upon us," stated Dutamis.

"I'm not sure I quite follow you," said Artenza.

Dutamis was patient in his reply. "The context of our discussion is that of our life's work, correct?"

"Correct," replied Artenza.

"Well, is there anything more vital and vexing?" probed Dutamis. "Do we not spend the majority of our waking lives in our work? Haven't our work and personal lives merged to become a cohesive whole, the boundaries so blurred that it is impossible and indeed pointless to separate the domains? Might we only be rationalizing to think our chosen work doesn't deeply impact the entire spectrum of our life? Isn't it through our work that we engage the world, express our creative ability, enable our prosperity, enjoy our just rewards, and enrich our lives fully? Does anything reveal more about us as unique individuals than our work? For these many reasons, isn't our work then a critical and fundamental determinant of our ability to lead ourselves to meaningful impact, to make the most of what we have to offer?"

"All true," agreed Artenza.

"And," concluded Dutamis, "I suspect that while there are some who seem to know with unerring clarity what it is they are meant to do in this world – and how to do it – most don't manage well the process of finding and following the proper path through work and life that would enable each to realize the deeply gratifying impact the Prince has. It is the design and delineation of the means by which one – specifically, Maximus – may do so that is our goal here, and I believe our Prince has charged us with tackling this most difficult challenge."

There is nothing more vital and vexing than the challenge of discovering and conducting our life's work – our work is a critical determinant in our ability to lead ourselves to meaningful impact

❧

While there are some who seem to know with unerring clarity what it is they are meant to do in the world — and how to do it — most don't manage well the process of finding and following the proper path through life that would enable each to realize true impact

❧

"Well said," agreed the Prince, standing up to walk and talk.

"Alas," he continued, "as I walk the streets of our Province, I look into the faces of our constituents and see the same wrong questions in their eyes. It is as if their lives are no more than a tedious collection of hours and days with no unity beyond mere sequence. I am dismayed to think that most will go to their graves without answering a question so basic, it is posed to all those seeking audience with the Court: *why are you here?*"

The Courtiers chuckled as they recognized the truth in the Prince's observation, and nodded their heads in concurrence.

"I hate to be the one to add complexity to an already difficult issue," interjected Trutorio, still smiling, "but I believe yet another danger exists beyond that of which we have spoken."

All eyes were on Trutorio. He took a deep breath and continued.

"Assuming one is of the mind to ask the right questions, is there not the danger of private mendacity – a peril of counterfeit answers and deception of self?"

The others looked a bit unsure, but remained silent.

Trutorio continued. "Are there not many and powerful competing claims on us, on our identities? There is certainly no dearth of those all too eager and willing to tell us how we should construct our lives, irrespective of our true aspirations, and, more often than not, in ways that are undoubtedly not authentic. If we succumb, might we not follow a road that leads to material success, but leaves us in want of deeper meaning and fulfillment in the final analysis?"

"Excellent questions," observed the Prince. "I believe that our tremendous human capacity to adapt to the very pressures you cite often prevents us from reaching the core of our true identity. But I believe we are saying the same thing – false answers amount to answers to the wrong questions. Chasing someone else's definition of success can only lead to the one question we wish to avoid ever having to ask, namely: *is there nothing more to life?"*

"True enough," concluded Trutorio. "No power exists in pursuing only that which others project for us."

"Of course, you are quite right," added Dutamis, who had been quietly contemplating the exchange. "I know of a particular merchant in the piazza who feels himself a hostage by his own hand. As you say, he has a loathsome regard and silent hatred for his wares. Moreover, I believe he despises himself because his life means little more to him than the fleeting glee of topping his coffers. Dreadful."

"An unlived life, to be sure – the ultimate return from one's work must always be the intrinsic reward which that work brings," agreed Trutorio. "The peril surrounding questions here is overwhelming. Our own questions can be our demise. We must ask the right ones to escape the wrong ones!"

Artenza spoke up. "All is not lost. As you mention it, I know of many accomplished individuals in our Province who took an initial wrong turn, so to speak, before finding the right road: Baldesar, the sculptor, was trained as a magistrate. Greco, the musician and composer of great works, was first a physician. Our most prolific inventor, Treviso, started his career as a printer. Our most learned scholar, Cerrio, was slated to be a blacksmith by his family."

"But that is what makes the challenge ever so much more difficult, Artenza," said Dutamis. "It is the one luxury young Maximus does not have!"

"As don't most with any degree of responsibility for others," added Trutorio. "And even if they do, the move is still a difficult one, and the aim must still be

Our tremendous human capacity to adapt often prevents us from reaching the core of our true identity and deepest desires

genuine. Our charge is to assist Maximus in finding the real richness in life – that which comes from making the most of all that he has to personally offer the world through his work and given role as sovereign Prince, for it is this that will mark him a noble leader on a number of levels. If the means we employ help Maximus, they should be ever more successful with those who might not be so confined."

"And if he is unable to find that which drives him truly, he will be poorer for it," said the Prince. "But I would argue that one need not necessarily leave their current path for a new one – although such a course might very well be the way for some, even many. The true test is in keeping our senses keenly attuned to every opportunity to bring more of our unique power to bear on our present experience. I find the challenge to be one shared by all."

Artenza, ever seeking the action item, was eager to move on. "We must then discover the process that will enable Maximus to do just that – to consciously pursue the right questions with accessible and self-directed strategies – to lead himself toward real impact."

"Yes, that is our project," replied the Prince. "And our time runs ever so short."

The Prince stopped to gaze solemnly into the eyes of his Courtiers before continuing.

"Gentlemen, if I know anything at this point, it is that life is a constant quest for authentic answers to the deeper questions of self and work – a courageous journey of challenge and curiosity in which we *learn* the way as we *make* our way. I am convinced that if pursued properly, the answers will come. And if there is such a thing as magic in life, it lies in that space between – in the attempt."

Turning his attention to the matter directly at hand, the Prince focused his thoughts toward Maximus.

"Most worrisome to me is that like so many others,

Life is a constant quest for authentic answers to the deeper questions of self and work – the magic lies in the pursuit

Maximus has not entertained these questions in a truly significant way. As Artenza has so rightly put it, we must define the process by which he can do so — the ways and means to discover and direct himself toward a destiny of his own design — not ours or anyone else's. Courtiers, it is a supremely daunting task!"

"He must believe something inside him is superior to circumstance!" exclaimed Trutorio.

"It is the sole reason we have so few strong leaders, so few valiant followers!" exclaimed Dutamis.

"Few are those that are of a mind to accept the challenge until it is far too late!" exclaimed Artenza.

"And," continued the Prince, "no one succeeds alone. It takes strength and maturity to ask for help, and I'm not certain Maximus is of such a mind at this point in his life. I have chosen you three for the wise counsel you have given me these many years. I am certain that, as leaders in your own right, you have clarified these questions for yourselves, each in a most unique way. Your paths have been singular and noteworthy."

"We will be honored to accept this charge, Prince," said Dutamis, characteristically.

"We will serve this great cause with solidarity, Prince," said Trutorio, characteristically.

"We will achieve the goal at best speed, Prince," said Artenza, characteristically.

The Prince concluded by saying, "And now let us take a break from our debate, for the real work lies ahead. We shall resume in short order."

As the Courtiers rose to leave, the Prince said, "In the interim, it is worthwhile for you each to reflect on that which has lit your way, for we will need all of your wisdom to continue."

As they walked out of the Pantheon, the Prince called out to them.

"Remember, Courtiers, how and why so many so frequently end up on the wrong path through life has everything to do with the nature and dimension of their questions. The questions beget the quest!"

Guidance

*In which the Prince challenges his Courtiers to
identify the pathway to absolute impact*

The Prince stood in the center of the Pantheon as he once again
welcomed his Courtiers. He stopped them, gesturing around the
room at the images and statues adorning the space.

"Before you sit," said the Prince, "look around you at those honored in
this magnificent hall. What is it that you see?"

"Noble crusaders," replied Trutorio.

"Courageous soldiers," replied Dutamis.

"Brilliant champions," replied Artenza.

"Yes, quite an august group, are they not?" asked the Prince. "Generals,
scholars, warriors, athletes, zealots, artists, philosophers, diplomats,
writers, missionaries, scientists, poets, provosts, chamberlains, even a
prince or two – all who have made a noteworthy mark on our Province."

The Courtiers concurred with a unanimous murmur of agreement.

"We have not known these paladins personally, so what is it that we find
so compelling about them?" asked the Prince.

"The deep significance of their great achievement moves us," replied
Trutorio.

"Their legacy of contribution suggests a future we can hope and hunger for," replied Dutamis.

"The virtuosity and genius of their acts inspire us," replied Artenza.

"All true," agreed the Prince. "The key, though, is to have the right heroes, correct? We must move beyond the level of momentary public glamour, for the mantle always fades to reveal whatever true good has been rendered. When we embrace the deeper issues of profound wisdom and meaningful accomplishment, we are left with the real question, the one that is before us now: *what enables the hero to be heroic?*"

"For that matter, the leader to lead?" added Trutorio.

"The soldier to sacrifice?" joined in Dutamis.

"The champion to win?" chimed in Artenza.

The Prince smiled, warmed by the enthusiastic exchange. The energy of the discussion escalated even higher.

"Yes!" cried the Prince. "What is the license of their legend?!"

The Courtiers grew silent, for although they had spent time during their brief sabbatical reflecting on the arc of their own enterprise, they knew the Prince had given more thought to the issue.

"To get at the answers," the Prince went on, "we must look beneath the recorded achievement, for it is there that our pathway resides. We have already said that we cannot separate the achievement from the achiever, so we must delve below the surface to the very genesis of power. To examine only technique or tactic would be pointless and superficial, for what works for one may not work for another. The act itself gets us little."

Artenza had his doubts. "But what of lessons we have learned in battle and beyond? The best of practices we have laboriously recorded? Methods of masters?"

"Valuable knowledge, indeed," replied the Prince. "But let the way of he who created the practice be

*What enables
the hero to be
heroic?*

*The champion
to win?*

*The leader to
lead?*

our target for study. Are these techniques created by others, although incorporated into our own exercise, of any true advantage? Is not the advantage now spent, and the practice now standard procedure?"

Trutorio added further insight. "Artenza, you know as well as any that what you know and do can be copied, but who you are cannot. Learning a master's technique does not ensure one of becoming a master."

Dutamis, too, lent his sage. "It would seem that the true pathway to standout, standup performance lies deeper than the visible manifestation of the practice that yields the accomplishment – much closer, as Trutorio suggests, to the center of one's person."

The true pathway to standout, standup performance lies deeper than the visible manifestation of deed or method

"You're saying that while a certain method in the hands of one may be magic, it may be only mediocre at best in the hands of another – that a deeper reason exists to explain why a given action works for that performer. To this I can agree," stated Artenza. "We must search beyond method to the more enduring elements, and allow the individual to put them in play in a manner befitting his uniqueness."

"Quite right, I am certain of it!" replied the Prince. "Therefore, as we know little else of these heroes, let us pay tribute and respectfully acknowledge the apparent achievements and visible deeds well done, but progress from there."

The Prince pressed his point. "It is obvious to all that what separates the Pantheon denizen from the everyman is the sheer magnitude of impact in their achievement. But since no two have taken identical roads, let us move past obvious commonality of degree to examine the more interesting question of what differentiates them each from the other. It is far more fascinating and difficult to note the variations within the group itself. I submit that to trump the superficial musings of those who claim to know the secrets, we must shun their approach of merely listing a cornucopia of common denominators – such a concept is best suited for mathematics, not people. Rather, we must discern patterns in a continuum of variation, delineate the dimensions of common uniqueness, and construct our model thusly."

The Prince stopped momentarily to read the faces of his Courtiers. Seeing that they understood, he continued with a question.

"As you look around you and draw upon history for reference, what made their journey to impact unique, different from the others even within their class?"

Artenza was the first to speak. "For some, it was the dimension of the obstacle and their ingenuity in overcoming it!" he exclaimed.

"For others, it was the constancy to their cause and sheer clarity of their quest," added Trutorio.

"For still others, it was the depth of their effort and the masterful use of their abilities in their endeavors," concluded Dutamis.

"Bravo!" rejoiced the Prince. "Now, let us employ this wisdom even further."

To Artenza he challenged, "Don't we all face obstacles in our respective circumstances that rival the heroic achievements of our icons, differing only in objective scale and scope, but no less of a challenge to us?"

To Trutorio he challenged, "Don't we each need a place to come from as well as to go to – a cause and a quest of our own to pursue – an origin and destination to mark our journey lifelong?"

To Dutamis he challenged, "Don't all of us seek the vigor and vitality of matching our talent to challenges we deem worthy of our attention and ability – achievements of which we can be proud?"

This time, the Courtiers immediately saw the power of the Prince's inquiry.

"It is clear to me now," said Trutorio in a hushed tone. "The hero is not a special kind of person. Rather, each person is a special kind of hero."

"A special kind of contributor," added Dutamis.

"A special kind of achiever," added Artenza.

"And there it is," whispered the Prince. "The very heart of this notion of *absolute impact* that I have been carrying with me – certain, consummate, categorical – built upon the combined uniqueness of our most illustrious icons, yet applicable to all within our walls. Think of it, Courtiers! We cannot *not* have impact in work and life; the issue is ultimately one of quality and quantity. Our actions always have impact – they must land somewhere on someone, for we do not live in isolation. And with every act, the result is either helpful or hurtful, accepted or rejected. To the extent that we help, that our way is accepted, we are followed willingly. Therefore everyone, regardless of their station or situation, is in a position to truly lead – lead themselves as well as others – in their work, and in their personal lives, and to do so with uncommon excellence."

The Courtiers were quiet as they pondered this new revelation.

"True is it not?" prompted the Prince. "Think of the individual in your life who has had the deepest impact on you – someone you have known and who has touched your life in some meaningful way – a personal hero, if you will."

With a quick wink, the Prince added, "Excluding your illustrious leader, of course. Who is it?"

The Courtiers smiled at the Prince's levity.

"A family member," replied Dutamis.

"A teacher," replied Trutorio.

"A friend," replied Artenza.

"And by our definition, truly leaders all," stated the Prince. "Individuals that have undoubtedly prompted profound change in you – that you have willingly followed, listened to, and learned from."

The Prince went further to ask, "And the reasons you hold this person above all others? What were the transformational qualities that made these individuals so impactful, so personally meaningful to you?"

The Courtiers were thoughtful. Dutamis spoke first.

"Respectfulness, trustworthiness, selflessness."

The hero is not a special kind of person – each person is a special kind of hero

"Authenticity, purpose, integrity," added Trutorio.

"Strength, courage, vitality," replied Artenza.

The Prince nodded his understanding. "Knowledge, wisdom, intellect – the list goes on, correct? If we sat here long enough, we would eventually exhaust the virtues. The point is this, gentlemen: we all have, and need to have, heroes – larger-than-life heroes as well as personal, everyday heroes. The qualities that exemplify their status are much more accessible than we think. It is a matter of clearly establishing and managing the personal path upon which we should trek. While the road itself will be unique, the *process* for constructing and following it is universal, I am certain of it. It is leadership at a most personal level! Speaking from experience, it's not instinctive, it's not easy, and it cannot be taught. It is, however, something that everyone, and certainly Maximus, can *learn*. It is indeed a challenge of learning lifelong in tenure."

"Learning to find our own answers to our most difficult challenges," added Trutorio.

"Learning to navigate our own way through life and lead ourselves toward excellence as we define it for ourselves," added Dutamis.

"And I believe we have all we need to begin our design," stated Artenza, again eager to forge ahead.

The Prince smiled, and replied, "Yes, Artenza, we have all we need. And since you are most anxious, you may lead us! What shall be our pathway?"

Excited to launch the project, Artenza began.

"I favor your idea that we are all journeymen and wayfarers in life, that each of us walks a path of our own construct. If you will allow me, I will configure my introductory thoughts in this metaphor. Agreed?"

The others all nodded their assent.

"Please continue," urged the Prince.

Artenza answered with a challenge of his own.

The qualities that exemplify our chosen heroes are much more accessible than we think

"To my mind," he posed, "the question then becomes: *what guides our personal journey toward impact?* If it is like any other journey in structure, three elements act in concert to do so – the origin, the destination, and some means of navigating travel between the two. This trio enables the construction of a uniquely individual path. The difference here is that while we do not have specific coordinates, neither do we do need them for our task at hand."

"Meaning?" asked Dutamis.

"That it is not for us to define a route for Maximus," replied Artenza. "Great achievement has no road map. Rather, it is before us to conceive the means by which he may chart the trail by his own hand."

"Certainly no single definition exists for our life's work," concurred Trutorio. "As leaders we will each define our work uniquely, play our part distinctively, and seek different ends through various means."

"And," added the Prince, "what simple prescriptive definitions do exist lack the depth to render them relevant to the challenge now before us. That is why I have called forth your collective counsel. No generic formula for uncommon achievement exists that would enable all to realize the desired degree of impact from the same program."

"Precisely!" exclaimed Artenza. "Our task, then, is to identify the points of a universal process by which the everyman may establish a clear path and make their way along their own road to impact! Therefore, we must begin by first arriving at a way to ascertain our capacity for travel – the methods of transport and means by which we will negotiate and navigate our way. Certainly we cannot even begin to talk of further strategies until we have addressed this issue."

"What do you suggest?" asked Dutamis.

"Simply this," replied Artenza. "That our brightest guiding beacon lies not in the stars above, but rather

Great achievement has no road map

deep within us. It is the primal force of energy we spoke of earlier – the instinctive drive that alone holds the key to unlocking our creative best. We may never understand it completely, but we can certainly find it and follow it! We do so through the very best leading indicators we have: our inherent gifts of self – our native aptitudes and unique intellect – traits of both nature and nurture from which spring our individual patterns of special talents and values. From these we get all of our personal strength, and strength enables every other virtue. Without strength, we will never realize our full potential. We must first and foremost learn to recognize, understand and use our gifts to our best advantage; test them to their limit with worthy challenges that lead us to venture out into unknown territory; and, finally, sharpen them to mastery and apply them creatively to achieve and advance.

"Colleagues, it is this before all else: to release our personal energy through creative engagement in meaningful work, we must learn to *govern our gifts!*"

A thunderous silence filled the Pantheon.

The Prince was beaming. "I have chosen wisely," he said. "You have hit upon it, Artenza. Clues to our calling, our métier, the work we were born to do – our real zone of power – reside in the knowledge of our natural sources of strength. I commend you!"

"Most unique," admired Trutorio. "Others would have us first envision and decide upon some distant and imagined destination, but this is of little relevance if we have not, or know not, the means to reach it. Cheers!"

"Intrinsically logical," added Dutamis, "yet by no means conventional. In fact, it is the very antithesis of the established approach found in our institutions, which would have us build breadth over depth, tending to our vulnerabilities first. This is easy to understand, for by nature, we focus on weakness simply to protect ourselves. But mere survival is no longer the issue,

Our greatest source of power lies in our ability to fully capitalize on our native aptitudes and unique intellect

⚜

To release your personal energy through creative engagement in meaningful work, you must learn to **GOVERN YOUR GIFTS!**

correct? We wish to build the highest levels of personal performance, and who can deny that our greatest chance for remarkable achievement lies not in the limitations of our deficiency, but in the strength of our genius? Most excellent!"

The Prince gestured around the Pantheon. "As we look to these grand masters of their respective games, can we see the wisdom of Artenza reflected in their mark?"

"Indeed we can," replied Trutorio. "I do believe Dutamis said it best earlier – it is in the depth of their effort and masterful use of their strength in their endeavors."

With a smile he added, "Every hero shines with the light of his own brilliance."

"It is only our gifts of self that we have to offer the world, the means to achieve any desired end," agreed Dutamis. "I see in this cornerstone a rich vein of potential, one to be deeply mined, for many learning challenges abound within it."

"Yes," said the Prince, "and we will come back to this point in much greater detail, for I, too, see many strategies to employ in this arena. But let us move on to what we might think is yet another guidepost to our pathway. Once we have laid the foundation, we will return to build the framework. Agreed?"

The Courtiers nodded their assent.

Trutorio chose to take up the challenge next. "It seems to me, in keeping with the metaphor Artenza has employed, that if we have the means of navigation, the next challenge would entail the determination of one's point of origin, figuratively speaking – one's center of reference, one's place to come from, as it were."

"Your thoughts?" asked Dutamis.

"Well, we are free to choose any origin we wish, so the power lies in the choice we make," replied Trutorio, thoughtfully. "I believe that the most important choice we can make is the choice to serve others well."

He paused a moment before continuing, allowing the thought to fully land on the others.

"I am of the opinion that while any activity which engages our gifts fully will have meaning for us, deeper fulfillment lies in our ability to share those gifts to the highest benefit of others. I submit that true leadership requires us to balance our own private desires and interests with the requirements of those in our charge. This choice – the choice of contribution – is the essence of a purposeful life. It requires us to commit to moving beyond ourselves, our own interests, our egos. We are naturally self-centered, but our capacity to serve others remains unbound. We cannot live only for ourselves, for we are all connected to others, to *each* other. Each will select a unique intent, for each has unique gifts. But we all must commit to focusing outside ourselves – learning to do so builds trust, fosters positive feelings, and creates the powerful connections needed to advance and enhance our impact. Therefore, I submit that to make the most positive difference in the lives of others, we must learn to *share our strengths!*"

"Raison d'être!" exclaimed the Prince. "It is not simply what we do, but our very reason for being – the passionate dance between ability and nobility, art and cause! It is here that we will have the greatest positive impact, for our efforts will be directed outward, toward others. It is here that we begin to create the legacy of leadership that will outlive us. Such is my intent and desire to help Maximus – to ease, enrich and elevate his experience."

"I can certainly see how our chosen contribution must be our point of provenance," added Dutamis, excitedly. "It is an act of constant and conscious deliberation to devote our drive toward something outside ourselves, and to commit to it forever. It is not a specific mission to be accomplished or a definitive goal to be achieved, but rather a genesis. Pursuing this deeper purpose – this personal cause – keeps us centered. It is our personal Polaris to guide us indefinitely!"

"Yes," confirmed Trutorio. "To wit, my own aim is to use my gifts to keep the virtues of the Court true and our intentions unified. I have given myself to that

Our greatest source of fulfillment lies in our choice to employ our gifts to the highest benefit of others

⚜

To make the most positive difference in the lives of others, you must learn to

SHARE YOUR STRENGTHS!

commitment, for it is how I serve the Prince, the Court, and his vision of the Province – how I put my strengths into play for the highest benefit of all. My work shall never be finished! I shall do whatever is necessary – reinvent myself, take on new roles, change my tactics, accept new projects – to ensure unwavering constancy to my cause."

"This adds a necessary component to the governance of one's gifts, certainly!" added Artenza. "We will never tap into the deepest well of our ability until we set ourselves to some noble aim, for it is purpose that channels strength. I believe more talent has been laid to waste from a lack of central guiding purpose than from any other cause. The true heroes never cease in their quest for the greatest good – it is a timeless challenge!"

Trutorio turned to the Prince and took a serious tone.

"You realize that the requirement for Maximus here is that he must lead a life not mainly centered on his own desires and needs, but one that integrates larger interests. He must seek to achieve that rarest of blends – the *juste-milieu* between *what's in it for me?* and *how can I help?*"

"Fully," said the Prince. "But by doing so, he will be rewarded with remuneration of the highest nature. By serving in the manner suggested, he will begin to build the positive relationships and experiences that will lift both his and the Court's performance to the next level. We shall revisit this challenge to explore it in more depth, I assure you. In the interest of completing our foundation, let us move to the final vector."

Dutamis took his turn eagerly. "It is of course the challenge of devising a track that guides our trajectory toward all that we desire to become and achieve – the destination – the most visible leg of the journey."

Dutamis rubbed his chin and tapped his temple.

"This part of the pathway is not a destination in the traditional sense of the word: it is not a fixed endpoint, but rather a continuous extension of our expectations. It is the mountains we climb – the ascension to the summit of one such peak prompts movement toward yet another, *ad infinitum*. It is the dissonance created between the goal and its achievement that spurs the advancement and momentum we seek. Let us not forget that the journey is lifelong in course and it is the everlasting quest that in part defines us as leaders."

Pausing ever so briefly, Dutamis continued, albeit somewhat more tentatively.

"Having said that, I must admit that I am to some degree hesitant to continue, for my ideas run slightly counter to the prevailing motivational wisdom surrounding dreams, goals, and indeed the entire realm of pursuing possibility and achieving one's vision."

This piqued the interest of others, for it was most out of character for Dutamis.

"Fresh insight into this admittedly well-trodden area is most welcome!" cried the Prince.

"Dare to defy!" urged Artenza.

"Challenge the convention!" coaxed Trutorio.

Buoyed by the enthusiasm of his colleagues, Dutamis paused to gather his thoughts before moving on.

"Now, we are told at an early age that we can be anything we want to be, that nothing is impossible, and we continue to be told this throughout our lives. But — and here is where I depart from traditional thinking — I believe this more often that not demoralizes and leads to disappointment in life, for we fail to separate pure fantasy from truly achievable dreams that play to our power and that are tied firmly to our deepest purpose. We simply have not learned how to dream effectively!"

The others leaned in to hear more, for this was most definitely a new take on an old maxim.

Dutamis took a deep breath and continued his polemic.

"There is perhaps no more consistent practice known to us that leads to higher performance, accomplishment, and positive change than that of setting ambitious goals that capture our imagination and desires," he said.

"But," he then warned, "there is an art and science to divining a new future — to setting one's sights properly — to marking our mission with clear and compatible objectives that transcend immediate reality to the domain of belief, and to overcoming the obstacles that may block their achievement. We must do so with a full view to our forte and focus."

"Say more!" urged Artenza.

"Gladly," Dutamis replied.

"You see, in order to achieve what we want out of life, we must first imagine what is possible given our unique gifts and framed within our

Our greatest source of achievement lies in our capacity to create and commit to a clear and compelling view of the future tied firmly to our power and purpose

⚜

To create a new reality and accomplish all you envision, you must learn to

ANCHOR YOUR AMBITION!

purpose. This is the critical nuance to constructing a compelling picture of the future that can effectively guide one's campaign. Such clarity enables us to then set bold goals that require us to stretch, to reach beyond what we *know* for certain we can achieve to what we *believe* we can. Because the reach is beyond our immediate grasp, it will force us to think creatively, plan carefully, and act decisively – and to constantly learn.

"By nature we underestimate our real potential, but there is almost no limit to what we can achieve once we are clear about who we are and what we have to offer, and commit ourselves to dreams that incorporate both by design. To create a new reality and accomplish all that we envision for ourselves, we must learn to *anchor our ambition!*"

"Hail the irony!" cried the Prince. "To reach beyond reality, we must be realistic! We create our future only with focused foresight tethered in principle to calling and cause! Anything else is simply wishful thinking – ideas and illusions adrift on a sea of fancy without power or purpose! This element of continuity and alignment is the vital linkage others have missed, and it provides the necessary final guideline!"

"It would seem we have arrived at the key challenges to realizing absolute impact," said Trutorio. "Taken separately, they are undeniably solid strategies that may surely lead one to a certain modicum of success. But taken in tandem and employed in sum, they suggest a more powerful and synergistic continuum, a pathway leading to uncommon achievement, personal excellence, and inspired performance."

"I find this triumvirate process quite compelling beyond its universality," commented Dutamis. "I find it difficult to even think of the three points separately. Certainly we cannot even begin to talk about sharing our strengths until we understand them; we cannot anchor our ambition without first understanding that to which we must anchor; and there can be no realization of true impact without a means to move with our gifts."

"It is indeed through governing our gifts, sharing our strengths, and anchoring our ambition – in essence, masterful work done for the right reasons toward a signficant end – that we have the best opportunity to make the most of what we have to offer the world," agreed the Prince. "The neverending pursuit of impact so absolute in nature will brand one a true leader."

Suddenly, Artenza produced a slate from the folds of his tunic and began to scribble furiously. The others watched with avid curiosity. When he was finished, he proudly revealed his work with great excitement and animation.

"We can represent our pathway as an equilateral triangle – the strongest of all geometric constructs – each cornerstone given equal weight and importance, inscribed in a circle symbolizing the continuous nature of the lifelong journey to impact!"

The others looked on at Artenza's artistry with wonder, and a reverberating applause erupted.

"Thank you, one and all," said Artenza, smiling and taking a slight bow.

When the din died down, the discussion resumed.

"It occurs to me," noted Dutamis, "that our triad has application beyond the individual! Would not the Court as well as Maximus realize a higher degree of growth and success following the logic of this pathway – by focusing on furthering our collective and core strength, purposefully creating the highest benefit for all in our Province, and striving toward a well-aligned and inspiring vision of tomorrow?"

The Pantheon was quiet as the Courtiers turned to see the Prince's reaction to this latest insight.

We can make the most of what we have to offer the world by governing our gifts, sharing our strengths, and anchoring our ambition – in essence, masterful work done for the right reasons toward a significant end

"So it would seem," smiled the Prince. "Courtiers, I stand proud and warm of heart, for this construct is so elegant in its simplicity and strength, and, as you say, with broad application. I am truly convinced that this model represents a universal and timeless pathway upon which all may challenge themselves. I could not be more pleased."

The Prince hesitated, then said, "But to conceive a brilliant strategy is one matter, to execute it brilliantly is quite another. We must consider Maximus, and all those who would make the attempt."

"You speak of the practicum," observed Artenza.

"We have debated and discussed the *why*, designed the *what*, and we must now develop the deeper *how*," added Trutorio. "It is the specific learning challenges and component strategies in each keystone we must pursue further."

"Quite correct," replied the Prince. "To render our pathway as something more than academic exercise, philosophical treatise or conceptual model, we must become utilitarian!"

"It will help us immensely in our efforts to guide and assist Maximus on his journey," noted Artenza. "We must strive for the application."

"I have yet another concern," stated Dutamis.

The others waited for Dutamis to continue.

"It is this," continued Dutamis. "We have said that managing this pathway is at the heart of our ability to lead ourselves to meaningful achievement. What measures will we use to enable us to know if we are firmly on the road to such true and total impact?"

"An important consideration," replied the Prince. "I believe the answer lies in the manner in which we delineate the critical requirements in each of the three key challenges. I am confident in our ability to arrive at a means to monitor our progress by virtue of the

To realize absolute impact, all three self-driven strategies must be executed brilliantly – the key lies in the deeper 'how'

specificity of our design."

The Prince rose from the roundtable.

"Gentlemen, the hour grows late, and we still have much work to do. Let us take yet another brief recess to recharge our energy, for the hardest part lies ahead. Upon our return, we will approach each of our three strategies in order. I wish to sincerely thank each of you for your wisdom and insight into this most difficult of projects. It means more to me than you can ever know!"

"It is our honor, Prince," replied the Courtiers, and they began to walk out of the Pantheon.

The Prince stopped them with a final word.

"Courtiers, as you gather your ideas for the next phase of our effort, a final question."

The Prince waited a moment, then asked: "To whom are *you* a hero?"

The Prince's question gave the Courtiers pause, and they looked at each other searchingly as they resumed their exit.

The Prince called after them. "A hint, Courtiers – look behind you!"

Part Two

All things will be produced in superior quantity and quality, and with greater ease, when each man works at a single occupation, in accordance with his natural gifts, and at the right moment, without meddling with anything else.

Plato

Govern Your Gifts

In which the Prince and his Courtiers discuss the challenge of releasing personal energy

The Prince welcomed the Courtiers back to the roundtable, and began by saying, "Courtiers, to resume, a question: do you view your work as a chore, commodity, or calling?"

"If by *chore* you mean work I view simply as a means of survival pay per diem, of merely making a living – a laborious task I relegate myself to that neither engages nor interests me, my answer is *calling*," replied Trutorio.

"If by *commodity* you mean work I perform mostly for the opportunities of reward, advancement and status – a means to another professional end that I would easily trade up for something more or better, my answer is *calling*," replied Dutamis.

"If by *calling* you mean work of true service and significance that transcends chore and commodity to stand on its own as the ultimate end in itself – the work I believe I was meant to do and cannot imagine my life without, my answer is *calling*," replied Artenza.

"There is nothing we'd rather do or be!" they cried.

"You have confirmed my presumption, naturally," stated the Prince. "However, the inquiry provides the necessary and proper perspective in our debate addressing the challenges inherent in our first pathpoint – that of governing one's gifts."

"The goal here being the ability to help Maximus find his real work – the work he was born to do, within his given role of sovereignty," observed Dutamis.

"The work that plays to his personal strengths – work that enables him to reach his full potential," added Artenza.

"The work that expresses his unique identity – work that centers on his deepest drive," added Trutorio.

"Precisely," replied the Prince. "And I am of the mind that it is the first of all challenges to discover the true work we are meant to do. I fear most in our Province would rather be doing something else with their life. We cannot let that fall upon Maximus. We must ensure that he continually moves toward a view of his work as a genuine calling, for anything less will result in a negative answer to the question that sparked our project in the first place!"

The Prince paused. "Initial reactions before continuing?" he asked.

Trutorio spoke first. "I think most people are indeed searching for their calling, not merely a chore."

Dutamis was next. "I believe most people have a vocation of some sort, but it is in one's gifts that clues to a calling reside."

Artenza concluded by saying, "I think our choice of work is a very deep, difficult, and determining decision, and it has everything to do with the source of our strength."

The Prince nodded, then began to tell a story.

"My weekly visit to the Court physician earlier today bears stark testimony to the dynamic of this hierarchy of perspective regarding one's work. As I passed through the infirmary, I chanced upon three workers diligently swabbing the pavers. *'What are you doing?'* I inquired. *'Mopping the floorboards – it is an exhausting chore,'* said the first. *'Sanitizing the corridor – bonuses are paid for the cleanest halls,'* said the second. The third said proudly, *'I am helping to heal the sick and infirmed within these walls – they cannot get well without my antiseptic!'*"

The Courtiers were silent, for they were struck by powerful message in the Prince's anecdote.

The Prince forged ahead. "So you see, gentlemen, neither stature nor function is of any consequence to the view of one's work. When we feel our work is a calling, we perform a substantially different role, and for a substantially different reason!"

"We can only hope that the Court physician views his work as a calling!" cried Trutorio.

"Can you imagine the difference in the level of care delivered if he viewed his work as merely a chore or commodity?" queried Dutamis.

"The search for remedy would be greatly impaired!" exclaimed Artenza.

Continuing on, the Prince said, "To your points, gentlemen, let us look further into the various scenarios implicit in this simple continuum. What might we expect from those who view their work as merely a means of daily economic survival – that is, just a *chore?*"

Remembering the Prince's story, the Courtiers made their replies.

"Little in the way of meaning, mastery, or motivation about their toil," began Artenza.

"Little in the way of productivity, performance, or passion about their task," added Dutamis.

"Little in the way of effectiveness, engagement, or effort about their travail," concluded Trutorio.

"Agreed," concurred the Prince.

"In this saddest of scenarios," he went on, "individuals unwittingly forego their life's truest course to make a living. Their very livelihood undermines their ability to put their natural power into play. They tap little if any of their true potential. The hue and cry of this contingent is the lack of apparent opportunity, but I believe most in this category simply choose to view their work – and work in general – in the most narrow of lights. They rationalize that deeper yearnings are best left to avocation, that work cannot possibly be stimulating, that work is meant solely to provide sustenance, and that all work is menial and tedious labor. Thus, they resign themselves to the dismal drudgery and stifling mediocrity of work without passion – a restrictive

Neither stature nor function is of any consequence to the view of one's work as a true calling

⚜

Deeming our work a true calling, we perform a substantially different role for a substantially different reason

view at best, for it ignores the core of what they have to offer. Again, the right questions are not pursued."

The Prince turned to Artenza. "Artenza, as our first pathpoint was your contribution, what say you?"

Artenza remained silent for a moment, then replied thoughtfully.

"The point and force behind governing one's gifts is to proceed from strength, not weakness, and to bring more of our unique constellation to bear on our present enterprise," he noted. "If we cannot transcend the notion of work as simply survival, we move from weakness – and while we shall indeed survive, we will not truly live. The survival mentality can suffocate and eventually defeat the natural inclination to use one's talents, if – and only if – we let it!"

The Prince turned to the others. "Thoughts?"

"It is difficult," agreed Trutorio. "Life without work is not possible, yet when our work is not borne of our natural gifts, we die inside. I can think of no greater self-infliction than to work against our gifts."

"While it might well appear to some as threatening economic survival to follow their true strengths, doing so is the very foundation upon which rests our verve and vitality!" exclaimed Dutamis.

"All true," agreed the Prince. "And the degree to which the lost potential affects the performance of the group or organization to which the individual belongs is immeasurable, but surely staggering."

The Prince resumed his line of query.

"And what of the person who views his work in the admittedly larger yet still limited sense of a *commodity* – an occupational waystation on the track to something better? What might we expect in this scenario?"

"I can envision a much higher degree of productivity and performance," offered Artenza.

"I can envision a much higher degree of effort and

Deeming our work merely a chore, we resign ourselves to dismal drudgery and stifling mediocrity

effectiveness," added Dutamis.

"I can envision a much higher degree of motivation and mastery," submitted Trutorio.

"Again, correct," confirmed the Prince.

"However," he continued, "in this most common scenario, while performance can reach the heights of technical competence, the ultimate return and reward is not the satisfaction the work itself brings – the motivation is not intrinsic. Rather, external reward is the driver – position, power, status, wealth, prestige, material possession, acceptance and approval…the very issues Trutorio warned us of earlier. Ever higher accumulation of these become the goal, for the deeper meaning is missing. Energy invested in an endless cycle of getting and spending ravages the individual's native power. The insidious feeling of perhaps being miscast in the role pervades – not only do the limits of the work not expand beyond the rigid description of the position, but the outlook is one of constant vigil for something better, something more. The vast majority of the day is spent in distraction – boredom, anxiety, or busyworking. Maximum engagement eludes, for one's abilities and values are not optimally matched to the challenge and role. Eventually, the issue of meaning is called into question as the fruitless search for the perfect position becomes the realization that such is but an illusion."

"The genuine desire for the work itself is not in their heart," added Trutorio. "They have not discovered their deep and authentic drive. The spirit does not work with the hand and mind – high art is lost."

"Achievement in this case is judged by status and salary," offered Artenza. "Their work in life is not the ultimate enticement it should be."

"I fear the peloton of professionals populate this plateau," commented Dutamis. "Their work is simply a form of glamorous slavery from which eventual escape

❧

*Deeming
our work a
commodity,
we ravage our
native power
in pursuit of
something
more or better*

❧

is sought. This only begs the question *why* – when isn't it those among us who discover their true work and in that work flourish that in essence find real freedom?"

"I believe a reasonable explanation exists for this predominant and prevailing circumstance," noted Trutorio. "We have a well-entrenched enemy that must be confronted to effect the escape to which you refer."

The others turned to Trutorio, awaiting his reasoning.

"By way of explanation, allow me to recount a story of a curmudgeon who lives near me, whose house overlooks a large grassy field where children used to play each day after school," he began.

Having enjoyed the Prince's earlier anecdote, the others welcomed the new tale told by another.

"The children's play was noisy, and thus bothersome to the crotchety old man, who sought only quiet to pass the day. Not owning the land, he knew he could not very well command them to stop, so he crafted a clever ploy. He approached the children with a surprising offer, telling them that since it gave him great pleasure to watch them play, he would pay each child three pennies for each day they did so. Naturally the children were shocked, for no one had ever paid them for something they loved so much, only dreadful chores. The old man kept his promise, and gave each child three pennies for five days in a row. On the sixth day, however, he informed them that he was running low on funds, and so his payment could only be two pennies each."

"What happened?" asked Artenza, sensing the old man's strategy.

"Most simply shrugged indifference, since it was, afterall, play," replied Trutorio. "On the eighth day, though, the old man told them that he could only pay two pennies; and on the tenth day, he apologized that he had no more money at all to give them for playing."

"What then?" pressed Dutamis.

"The children shouted and shrieked!" answered Trutorio. "They were so disappointed and angry at the old man, they vowed they would never again play in that field."

"The curmudgeon's ulterior motive worked!" cried the Prince.

"Yes," said Trutorio. "He had stolen from them the very thing they loved most to do, unbeknownst to them."

"By our own hand, the enemy!" cried Dutamis. "It is in our institutions, our culture as a whole – employing reward as a primary motivational mechanism! If we are not careful – consciously and courageously so – we become easily manipulated like so many rats after cheese in a maze!"

"A pervasive and powerful opponent, to be sure," continued Trutorio. "Attaching such monetrary or material reward to desired performance is commonly viewed as the most effective means of conditioning, controlling, and conforming. Yet it stifles our creative expression and shunts our natural energy – to wit, Trutorio's story of the old man and the children!"

"We have met a nefarious foe that can block the discovery of our true métier!" exclaimed Artenza.

"Only if we let it," advised the Prince. "And we have come back to revisit the very challenge upon which our project centers. As Trutorio's fine story so rightly illustrates, we cannot realize our full power without being in the position to experience profound joy in the work itself – where the work does not seem like work, where the work is it's own reward, and where the work is such that we would perform it free if circumstances so permitted. This is indeed the view of our work as our *calling*. What then is the expectation in this scenario?"

"The very highest levels of effectiveness, effort, and engagement!" cried Dutamis.

"The very highest levels of motivation, meaning, and mastery!" cried Trutorio.

"The very highest levels of passion, performance, and productivity!" cried Artenza.

"Indeed!" cried the Prince. "The very highest levels of everything!"

"In this most desired of scenarios," he continued, "we operate within our zone of natural power. Here, our innate talents are fully employed, our values fully activated. We expand our role without giving it a second thought – defining the work differently, being much more resourceful and resilient, easily seeing opportunities to improve and innovate that others don't, continually wanting to know more about our field of endeavor, intuitively setting objectives to seek ever higher levels of performance, and feeling connected to, and an integral part of, something larger than our private agenda."

The goal of governing our gifts is to become maximally and creatively engaged in work that expresses who we are, thus realizing the enormous impact that derives from calling forth the very best of our strengths

"The key to all of which is governing our gifts!" cried Artenza.

"Hear! Hear!" cried Dutamis and Trutorio.

"And can we rest until we are assured Maximus views his work in this manner? Dare we imagine the consequences of his viewing his work as something short of this tier?" challenged the Prince.

"Certainly not!" cried the Courtiers in unison.

"We must guide him in his efforts to move ever higher on the continuum from *chore* to *calling!*" exclaimed the Prince.

The Pantheon became silent, for the Courtiers knew only too well what was to follow.

The Prince smiled at his Courtiers and challenged, "Now then – *how?*"

Artenza swallowed hard, took a deep breath, and stepped forward.

"As this challenge is one I put forth, I have given the component strategies the best of my attention. If you will permit me, I will offer them in an initial outline, with the proviso that we will dissect and debate each in greater detail. Are we agreed?"

"Agreed!" said the others unanimously.

"Very well," said Artenza. "To refresh, the goal of governing our gifts is to be maximally and creatively engaged in work that truly expresses who we are, thus realizing the enormous impact that derives from calling forth the very best of our strengths. I see five critical self-directed elements inherent in our ability to do so, moving from self-knowledge to aligned action to maximal capitalization – resulting in progressively deeper impact. Each builds on the previous, and they are best executed as a comprehensive approach."

At that point, Artenza produced his tablet, and began writing his points as he outlined each.

"From the outset, we must recognize, identify, clarify and indeed fully understand the seminal qualities that provide the basis for our personal power. As we have said, these are the dimensions of our native aptitudes and unique intellect – our individual pattern of talents and values. Together they serve as the best leading indicators of our personal center – our core drive and deepest of needs, as we have discussed. Simply put, we cannot begin to govern our gifts without first thoroughly comprehending them. Colleagues, the four of us will need to define and come to some consensus on these characteristics in the course of our discussion."

On his slate, Artenza wrote:

Source your strength.

"Once we fully comprehend our gifts of self, we must then focus our energy on aligning action with that knowledge and understanding. To do that, we must learn to do two things well. The first is to concentrate on transforming our talents into performance – pursuing, developing, and exploiting the most positive influence of our natural abilities while decreasing the potentially detractive influence of our limiters."

On his slate, Artenza wrote:

Play from power.

"The second is to make consistent choices based on our personal values, ensuring that they too become a source of active strength. Our talents and values must be aligned within our work, for the combination of the two will guide us closer to the roles in which we best belong. Working against our values will only weaken and prevent us from moving nearer to our calling, even if our talents are fully exercised. Additionally, and equally as important, we must learn to stand on our most deeply held values, fully utilizing them as we develop a process of sound judgment in making choices and decisions."

On his slate, Artenza wrote:

Manage what matters.

"Once our talents and values have been clarified and strategies executed to put both into play, we can turn our attention to maximizing the impact of our gifts.

"We will need to learn to do two things concurrently, employing twin strategies centered on a crescendo of challenge and virtuosity. The first is to optimize our engagement and build our depth by pitting our strengths against escalating levels of suitable and worthy challenge, taking intelligent risks that test our boundaries and carry us into territory of an uncertain and ambiguous nature. We will never know our highest potential without testing the limits of our current capability – continually redefining our personal bounds. It is here we will experience the greatest growth and development in our gifts, gaining the means to maintain our vitality with full investment in, and connection to, the here and now."

On his slate, Artenza wrote:

Lean into limits.

"At the same time, we must embrace continuous learning, improvement and innovation – gaining the knowledge and techniques that support our strengths, represent key areas of interest, and enable us to meet our challenges. Here we seek to not only hone our talents, but to apply our brilliance in the drive to become true masters of our game – wizards in our area of expertise. To enter the company of masters, we must first acquire the requisite existing knowledge and expertise through education and experience. We couple that with the new and equally, if not more, important knowledge we discover through challenging convention and exploring possibility within the framework of our gifts. By combining the old and the new, we can achieve innovative breakthroughs designed and engineered through the application of our natural creativity."

On his slate, Artenza wrote:

Move toward mastery.

Artenza rested his tablet, sat down and waited for the reactions of the others.

Slowly, then gathering great decibel and tempo, applause filled the Pantheon.

"This is *your* gift, Artenza," remarked the Prince proudly.

"Your clarion call cannot be denied. Could we achieve as much impact in our attempt to govern our gifts omitting even one of these strategies? Nay! Let us then drill down into each of these learning challenges in singular fashion, with a view toward arriving at a solid pentacle pathpoint."

And so it was that the Prince and his Courtiers plunged into their discussion of how Maximus might learn to release and leverage his personal energy.

Govern Your Gifts

Source Your Strength

Play From Power

Manage What Matters

Lean Into Limits

Move Toward Mastery

Source Your Strength

———◆———

Let there be four faculties in the soul — reason answering to the first, understanding to the second, conviction to the third, and perception to the fourth.

Plato

"I submit that our starting point should be to clarify further our definition of *gifts*," began Artenza, launching the debate. "Might there not be an issue surrounding the inclusion of values in the category of gifts?"

"If there is, it is a silly and academic one," replied the Prince. "While I am certain there are those who would argue the point that talents are innate, while values are not — a claim I gladly take issue with — the distinction is irrelevant to our discussion. Whether by nature or nurture — and I would argue that both are involved — our talents and values are given to us. Both are enduring and unique. Most importantly, by the time we reach the working age, both are most definitely set. One is a gift of aptitude, the other of character — but they are what they are, and part of who we are. I maintain that who we are — who Maximus is — will not change in any significant way, so we need not trouble ourselves on the matter. Let us move on to further defining each."

The Courtiers were once again struck by the Prince's simple but solid reasoning.

"I believe we should begin with the concept of *talent*, for I am of the mind that it is much harder to both define and identify," stated Dutamis.

"I would agree," added Trutorio. "Many are those that profess they know where their natural abilities lie, but I would venture a guess that most are quite mistaken, more often than not. We may know a bit better what our talents are not. We certainly have an easier time seeing the strengths and weakness of others!"

"Ah, but why is that?" asked the Prince.

"Perhaps because everyone is endowed with the gift of talent," replied Artenza.

Artenza hesitated, then furthered his thought.

"Perhaps because they are innate and reflexive, we do not need to think hard about our talents — thus we tend to take them for granted," he continued. "Perhaps we falsely presume talent is supposed to involve activity deemed difficult to perform. And perhaps we don't appreciate our own abilities enough – mistaken are we in the thought that talent is reserved for others, or those only of distinction – that *I cannot possibly have talent!* I believe those we interact with often have a better view of our talents, for no two share the same gifts. Others are thus in a good position to observe that which they recognize as something they do not own."

"Let us test your theory!" challenged the Prince.

Turning to Dutamis, he asked, "Dutamis, what do you believe to be Artenza's talents?"

Dutamis turned and gave Artenza an appraising and thoughtful look.

"Artenza is an extremely gifted tactical commander," replied Dutamis. "His talents lie in implementation, quick response, and sparking movement forward. He makes things happen! Too, he is quite naturally artful – a master craftsman, performer and composer. Witness his slate as a constant companion!"

"Artenza, reactions?" asked the Prince.

"Put that way, I would agree with the assessment," replied Artenza. "But it is true I would perhaps have described myself differently. These abilities come quite easily for me, so I can see how I might tend to assume they are easy for all and overlook them as true talents. It seems how we view ourselves is often quite different from how others see us."

"Yes," interjected Trutorio, who had been listening. "We tend to view ourselves more aspirationally – how we'd like to be, more than how we really are."

Trutorio thought a moment more, then turned to Dutamis.

"For instance, I think of Dutamis as a grand master of legislation and logistics, but I venture he doesn't. His ability to focus on the detailed steps and processes required to keep us on track I find wondrous. We owe

We more easily recognize that which we do not own – thus others often have a much better view of the talents we possess and tend to take for granted

him our economic stability, our Provincial security – our infrastructure is virtually invincible. Too, his cautious deliberation, discipline, and diligence in planning and regulation are astounding to me. I am constantly amazed at what he takes on with ease. Witness the miracles he has performed with the Court Guard. I would have to work quite hard to become at best inept at what he is able to do so effortlessly."

"Thank you," said Dutamis. "It is true that I find these enjoyable and easy, now that you mention them. But you are quite right – it would seem that we don't consider our natural inclinations to be talents by virtue of the fact that we own them – and they own us – and we are taught at an early age to value more and thus seek that which we perceive ourselves not to possess. We would be better served to want and seek that which we already have, for if we are not cognizant of our talents, we may unwittingly work against ourselves!"

Dutamis shifted his focus to appraise Trutorio.

"I would love to be able to employ diplomacy with the same flair for language and people that you do – your ability to create harmony among seemingly incompatible positions is uncanny. Your impeccable ethics and advocacy of worthy causes are inspiring and admirable. You are gifted in the ways of patience, nuance, and nurturing others to search for and develop themselves – I am certain we will look to you to lead us in our efforts with Maximus. But in truth, as much as I envy your gifts, I would be a hopeless student if I so much as even attempted to attain such acumen in these areas."

"Thank you, my friend," acknowledged Trutorio.

"And it should now be apparent why you three are my chosen consul," said the Prince. "You three naturally possess gifts that I don't, that I never could! My talents, at least as far as my advanced age permits me to determine, revolve around the investigation

No one is a universal master, nor should anyone try to be

of concepts, theories, strategies, and visions of the morrow. And as you can gather from this very project, I seek to challenge us in our efforts to achieve higher levels of performance. Together, our collective talents combine and complement to become a formidable repertoire. But none of us is a universal master – nor should we try to be. The point is to first discover and understand our talents, so that we may look for the proper opportunities to put them into play, whatever our work."

"How then might we best assist Maximus with this discovery?" asked Artenza.

"Let us first agree upon the criteria by which we define talent, for it is most critical to the outcome," said Dutamis. "Then we must determine where we should look to help him discover his talents."

The others nodded their agreement.

"I would propose that talent is a manifest proclivity toward certain abilities arising out of genetic patterns of aptitude – an amalgam of qualities given to us by nature, as opposed to those gained otherwise," offered Trutorio.

"We cannot learn to be talented in a given realm of activity, in other words," confirmed Dutamis.

"Precisely," replied Trutorio.

"In this sense, talent is but endowed potential," noted the Prince. "Raw at birth, noticeable at a young age, and developed into skill over time through continued exposure to exercise and environment."

"Yes," replied Trutorio. "The pattern of development being dependent upon the degree and depth of these influences, as you suggest."

"And in the context of our discussion, our talents are to be thought of as seminal attributes of self which represent our greatest source of power in actually performing our work," added Artenza.

Talent is a manifest proclivity toward certain abilities arising out of genetic patterns of aptitude – an amalgam of qualities given to us by nature, as opposed to those gained through acquisition

"Most definitely," replied Trutorio. "Also, a social component to talent exists – it must result in roles and skills positively valued by our culture."

"A simple yet robust definition," noted the Prince. "Are we agreed, Courtiers?"

"Indeed!" they replied.

"How then are we to locate our talents?" asked the Prince.

"Certainly we must look beyond exhibition – what we are able to do and what we are presently involved in – for two reasons," began Dutamis.

Our talents are seminal attributes of self that represent our greatest source of power in performing our work, resulting in roles and skills positively valued by our culture

"First," he continued, "I can envision a circumstance in which a certain degree of competence or proficiency in a given activity has been developed through significant training and extensive practice, but does not represent an area of natural ability. Second, we may have undiscovered or dormant talents that have never been lit by exposure or exercise, but that nonetheless remain as a potential supply of power."

"I agree," said Artenza. "As the undiscovered gift is the bigger challenge, let us attack the former instance first. Assuming that our talents reside within the realm of our current endeavors, I submit that they can be found in those activities toward which we naturally gravitate – those that come most easily for us, that we most enjoy, and at which we consistently excel. When we are one with our true nature, this trio becomes the collective calibre."

"I concur that all three criteria are required," affirmed Trutorio. "Anything less would indicate something short of talent, as we have defined it."

"Yes. It may be difficult to distinguish a true talent based solely upon one's visible performance, for example," agreed Artenza.

Dutamis thought a moment, then added: "Thorough examination would be required to understand the level of work and exercise required to attain an observable height of performance in any given area. As I argued earlier, that one has developed proficiency might be indicative of nothing more than a skill that has been acquired through necessity or diligent practice, or both. One who has spent years developing a given skill may be at par with a truly talented novice. Manifest excellence yields only partial insight into the ease of acquisition and execution."

"Which is why we must utilize our triad as the evaluative measures," confirmed Trutorio.

"It occurs to me that we need effective tools to aid us in our immediate efforts to recognize and catalog Maximus' strengths," added Artenza.

"An excellent idea," agreed the Prince. "What do you suggest?"

Artenza thought carefully for a moment.

"Assessment instrumentation consisting of major talent categories rated by our three measures would help significantly," he replied.

"Why complicate matters?" argued Trutorio. "The element of *ease* is facilitated by documentation. Why, a simple list would suffice."

"*Enjoyment* is likewise easily documented," noted Dutamis. "Upon listing favored activities, we can note any underlying patterns of virtue inherent in the given action, if required. A given role or skill may entail a number of component talents."

"For example?" asked the Prince.

"Hypothetically speaking, an acumen for architecture might spring from a native spatial aptitude applied through core abilities in composition and design," offered Trutorio.

"There must be thousands of talents. To do this, we would need to narrow the field – perhaps arrange a system of classification from which we can draw and

⚜

Talent Criteria

✧ *Ease*

✧ *Enjoyment*

✧ *Excellence*

⚜

compare," observed Dutamis.

As this realization dawned on them, they turned to Artenza, who was smiling broadly.

"Tools are my bailiwick, friends!" he exclaimed. "Do you see now why it makes sense to have a grid of talent motifs juxtaposed to our three criteria?"

"Certainly!" they deferred.

"Two matters complicate such a device, however," continued Artenza. "The first is the degree of subjectivity in such an assessment. The second is the source of the categorization itself."

"The measures of *ease* and *enjoyment* do not present quite the dilemma that *excellence* does," offered Trutorio. "*Ease* and *enjoyment* are inherently personal and subjective."

"Agreed," interjected the Prince. "But might we not perhaps elaborate on both?"

"For *ease* we might do well to consider the ease of learning, the ease of performing, and the ease of perfecting," noted Dutamis.

"For *enjoyment* we might consider the same dimensions!" noted Artenza. "Enjoyment of learning, performing, and perfecting a given activity."

"Which brings us to the more objective element of *excellence*," said the Prince. "What then is required?"

"A starting point may be to note that there is an obvious relationship between enjoyment and excellence," said Trutorio. "We focus more energy at excelling at the activities we enjoy most. At the same time, we enjoy more those activities in which we tend to excel. The two reinforce each other. Since enjoyment drives one to practice their talent, and rising ability in turn drives enjoyment ever higher, perhaps one measure is the degree of time and effort spent developing skill within a given activity."

"Perhaps a log of one's efforts over time, then?" offered Artenza.

"In the course of one's attempts – decisions and actions – projections of eventual outcomes may be notated," he continued. "Months hence, when results have become evident and recorded, a review of performance can be made. Comparisons to the projections may be drawn, and deltas noted, in a relatively objective fashion. Over the span of some time, one's strengths – and weaknesses – should become rather apparent. Those instances where outcomes meet or exceed the projected expectations would indicate an area of excellence. Where the results are inferior, limitations are revealed. Accounting for the differential should yield explanations worthy of future regard."

"Bravo!" cried the Prince. "An effective means to not only gauge one's excellence, but to better understand the nature of one's strengths."

"Indeed!" exclaimed Dutamis. "To bolster this journal of personal excellence, we might suggest an objective review of our performance by another – a superior, peer or subordinate?"

"Agreed," said Artenza. "These two methods would surely give us insight into the criterion of excellence."

"Which brings us to the matter of classification," said the Prince. "In truth, I am not as troubled by this apparent dilemma, for I have given it much thought of late. If I am not mistaken, what I have to share with you will put the matter of undiscovered talents to rest as well, for I believe I understand the source of talent."

The Courtiers leaned in to listen attentively as the Prince shared his insight. He began in his usual fashion, challenging the Courtiers with inquiry.

"We begin by simply considering human nature," explained the Prince. "What is it that separates us from the lower life forms?"

"Native intelligence," replied Dutamis, easily.

"Say more!" challenged the Prince. "Exhibited how?"

"In our ability to express complex thought in a myriad of ways," replied Trutorio.

"In our advanced aptitude even in those areas we share with lower forms," replied Artenza.

"Proof!" the Prince parried back. "What unconditional evidence can we reference?"

"Logic, abstraction, and the use of mathematics," replied Dutamis. "Visualization and the use of mental imagery."

"Complex corporal movement and the use of tools," replied Artenza. "Use of words and language to communicate. Creation and interpretation of musical rhythm and melody."

"Awareness and sense of self," replied Trutorio. "Formation of deep and complex relationships with others."

"You didn't need me!" exclaimed the Prince. "To these I would add an awareness of our environment and sensitivity to the natural world around us."

Again setting forth a challenge, the Prince asked: "Consider now this octagon of core aptitudes as you have so smartly identified it: Language. Logic. Imagery. Physicality. Music. People. Self. Nature. Can you think of any single talent, ability, skill or role – in fact any achievement represented by the heroes in this hall – that cannot be categorized under and traced to at least one of these?"

Try as they might, the Courtiers could not.

"What is the commonality?" posed the Prince.

The Courtiers pondered the Prince's inquiry for several minutes, for the concept was new to them.

"Each ... has a system of symbols ... used to express thought," replied Dutamis, thinking as he spoke. "For example, language has lexicons and alphabets, logic has numbers, imagery has pictures, physicality has tools, music has notes, people have gestures and expressions, the self has vivid memory and dream symbolism, and nature has taxonomy."

"All have numerous examples of human prodigy on record," noted Artenza, picking up the trend of thought. "Great works of art, books, music, social movements, athletics and dance, architecture, philosophies, science – all domains of human activity."

"All are in artifact since the dawn of recorded civilization," added Trutorio. "Ancient scrolls, number systems, hieroglyphic renderings, crude implements, simple drums and shakers, great societies, philosophers and prophets, farming."

"Correct, one and all!" applauded the Prince.

"Now then, the abilities and skills we favor call upon one or more these core human aptitudes, which can

The core human aptitudes center on logic, language, imagery, physicality, music, people, self, and nature

develop and combine in countless variations to yield hundreds of talents," said the Prince, continuing.

"We each have a unique blend of this core, the dominant schema of which relate directly to, and perhaps even determine, our equally unique intellect – the latter being a well-defined archetype which can be thought of as a mental prism through which an identifiable pattern and observable array of manifest talents and values comes to light."

"Manifested how?" queried Artenza.

"In how we naturally prefer to utilize our resources and assets – personal and otherwise – to accomplish our objectives," replied the Prince. "They are visible as well in our various forms of intelligent activity and, of primary importance, in the types of roles we adopt."

"What are these patterns?" asked Dutamis.

"Do they recur?" asked Trutorio.

"How do we identify them?" asked Artenza.

"We call upon the wisdom of the ancients to aid us in answering these questions!" replied the Prince.

This piqued the curiosity of the Courtiers.

Seeing their interest, the Prince smiled and said, "Two dozen centuries of study have not changed the revelation that human intellect tends to exhibit in four distinct mindsets. We all have some of each of these four to some degree – but each of us has a dominant theme that determines much of what underlies our outlook and actions. It is here that we will come to discover and recognize not only the domain of our strengths, but also the realm of what likely drives us."

Dutamis looked incredulous. "I am not aware of these!"

"Do tell!" exclaimed Artenza, excitedly.

Trutorio was contemplating the implications. "What does this mean?"

Two dozen centuries of study have not changed the revelation that human intellect tends to exhibit in four distinct mindsets – well-defined archetypes derived from the core set of aptitudes – which act as a mental prism through which an observable pattern of individual talents and values emerges

"Quite simply, that each has a very distinctive set of characteristics and observable behaviors – a clear motif," replied the Prince. "Thus, they become the window to recognizing and classifying our strengths!"

"Share!" cried the Courtiers, anxious to hear more.

"First are those whose gifts are theoretic in nature," counseled the Prince. "Talented in the ways of thinking and conceiving, they were known as the Philosophers, keeping the world challenged, progressive, and inquisitive.

Naturals at strategy and analytics, the theoretic Philosophers of the world keep us challenged, progressive, and inquisitive – driven by a deep need for knowledge and reason

"Naturals at strategy and analytics, they are most in their element when charting long-range plans to achieve improvement, conceptualizing and constructing new frameworks of thought, innovating and designing systems and models, employing rational scrutiny and critical reasoning, maximizing performance, engaging in scientific study and investigative problem solving, architecting and engineering, optimizing structured plans and contingencies, looking far into the future, and establishing hierarchies of command to achieve goals."

"Scholars and sages!" exclaimed Trutorio.

"Pundits and postulates!" exclaimed Dutamis.

"Masterminds and marshals!" exclaimed Artenza.

"Who does this description remind you of?" asked the Prince, with a sly and mischievous smile.

"You, Sire!" cried the Courtiers.

"Indeed," chuckled the Prince. "And of the eight core aptitudes, which do you find most prevalent within this theme?"

"Logic, mostly," replied Dutamis.

"Imagery, surely," replied Artenza.

"Language, certainly," replied Trutorio.

"Agreed," concurred the Prince. "It is the deep need for knowledge and reason that drives this intellect."

"I have not met many like you," said Artenza.

"Understandable," nodded the Prince. "It has been my observation, however anecdotal, that only a very small percentage of our population – perhaps one in twenty – exhibits this intellectual theme in dominance."

"What is another of these patterns?" asked Dutamis, eagerly.

"Next are those whose gifts are empathic in nature," replied the Prince. "Talented in the ways of connecting and relating, they were known as the Diplomats, keeping the world righteous, unified, and authentic.

"Naturals at advocacy and ethics, they are most in their element when creating meaningful relationships, mediating difficult situations, negotiating disparate positions to resolution, facilitating cooperative action to achieve goals, creating harmony between people, inspiring and supporting ideological causes, intuiting deeper motive, building solidarity within groups, instilling strong moral standards, fostering growth and development in self and others, encouraging belief and restoring faith in the good of humanity, building continuity and connectedness through understanding and compassion, pursuing ideals, and maintaining a unity of purpose."

"Partisans and purists!" exclaimed Dutamis.

"Champions and crusaders!" exclaimed Artenza.

"Healers and humanitarians – remind you of anyone in particular?" asked the Prince.

"Trutorio!" cried Artenza and Dutamis, turning toward Trutorio to find him smiling.

The Courtiers were beginning to have great fun with the Prince's game.

"And the dominant aptitudes?" asked the Prince.

"People and self, foremost!" replied Dutamis.

"Language, definitely," added Artenza.

"Again, I concur," said the Prince. "It is the deep need

Naturals at advocacy and ethics, the empathic Diplomats of the world keep us righteous, unified, and authentic – driven by a deep need for significance and truth

for significance and truth that drives this intellect."

"The diplomatic few represent yet another paucity within the population," added the Prince. "However, I would venture a guess that they are twofold the Philosophers in number."

"I see a commonality between these two themes," interjected Dutamis. "They are both concerned with ideas and principles – things relatively intangible, conceptual, and abstract in construct."

"An excellent observation," said the Prince, nodding. "The remaining two mentalities you will undoubtedly find to be more tangible in nature. Likewise, they are much more prevalent – the overwhelming majority of the population is split almost equally between them. The thinkers of antiquity recognized as much over two thousand years ago."

"And the third pattern?" asked Artenza.

"Next are those whose gifts are economic in nature," stated the Prince. "Talented in the ways of providing and protecting, they were known as the Guardians, keeping the world secure, disciplined, and productive.

"Naturals at propriety and logistics, they are most in their element when managing the allocation of assets and resources, establishing and maintaining security and stability through regulation and fair enforcement, constructing safe havens for communities to flourish, employing due diligence and discipline in planning and processing, dutifully superintending and administrating, conducting careful and thorough preparation, creating order through structure and strong standards, ensuring that commitments are kept, preserving conventions and customs, institutionalizing operational protocol and procedure, building infrastructure, and meticulously coordinating details, projects, budgets, schedules, and events."

"Prefects and providians!" exclaimed Trutorio.

⚜

Naturals at propriety and logistics, the economic Guardians of the world keep us secure, disciplined, and productive – driven by a deep need for duty and sanctuary

⚜

"Magistrates and martinets!" exclaimed Artenza.

"Dutamis!" cried Artenza and Trutorio together, without being asked.

Laughter filled the Pantheon as the enjoyment of the Prince's engaging discovery process escalated.

"Core aptitudes?" asked the Prince.

"Logic, predominantly," observed Trutorio.

"With physicality and people in good measure," added Artenza.

"Yes," affirmed the Prince. "It is the deep need for duty and sanctuary that drive this intellect."

"And the last pattern?" asked Dutamis.

The Courtiers turned to Artenza while the Prince spoke, for they knew now that each of them exemplified one of the four spheres of intelligent activity.

"Finally are those whose gifts are kinetic in nature," stated the Prince. "Talented in the ways of executing and implementing, they were known as the Artisans, keeping the world dynamic, vital and responsive.

"Naturals at agency and tactics, they are most in their element when stimulating immediate action to meet the demands of the moment, reading situations and capitalizing on clear and present opportunity, competing and making aggressive moves to better present positioning, enacting *ad hoc* plans, spurring action and acting on instinct, adapting quickly and artfully negotiating changing circumstances, creating spontaneous shifts in direction to achieve variety, adding visual style and flair to enhance image, persuading and influencing others, developing tools and techniques, as well as entertaining, producing, and crafting."

"Expeditors and executors!" exclaimed Trutorio.

"Icons and impresarios!" exclaimed Dutamis.

Artenza stood to take a bow as Trutorio and Dutamis applauded and cheered.

⚜

Naturals at agency and tactics, the kinetic Artisans of the world keep us dynamic, vital, and responsive – driven by a deep need for action and impulse

⚜

"Physicality definitely leads!" observed Trutorio.

"On par with imagery and music!" added Dutamis.

"Yes," agreed the Prince. "It is the deep need for action and impulse that drives this intellect."

Trutorio spoke up. "I must confess that I see myself to some extent in all of these aptitudes and archetypes."

"We must remember that we all have a measure of each pattern, for we are all alike and different at once!" replied the Prince. "All four are needed to realize the full power of human potential – again, the reason I have called upon you three in the past, present, and for the future."

"Knowing these prevailing patterns, as you have just outlined them, illuminates the zone of undiscovered talent!" noted Dutamis. "This will aid us greatly in our work with Maximus and in the design of our evaluative tool."

"The construction of which I will begin forthwith upon our final adjournment," confirmed Artenza.

"I believe we have captured quite nicely the essential dimensions and intricacies of our gifts of talent, but what of the component of values as yet another source of personal strength?" asked the Prince.

"Ah, yes – our valor! Let us first define the ground upon which we will tread," suggested Dutamis.

"Yes," agreed Trutorio. "For our immediate purposes, I propose we separate personal values from the more universal and cultural values."

"Universal values referring to the more timeless and constant virtues of civilization – wisdom, temperance, courage, justice, prosperity, humanity, spirituality, love, and the like?" asked Dutamis.

"Yes," replied Trutorio. "Universal values are those that are more oriented toward definitive end states."

"And cultural values meaning those reflected in the

There is a measure of each intellect in every individual – and all four are needed to realize the full power of human potential

prevailing behaviors, norms, and ideas adopted by and peculiar to a given society or group – reflected in what is rewarded and punished?" asked Artenza.

"Yes," replied Trutorio. "Those that are more based on moral duties derived from principles of right and wrong, good and bad – customs and standards of conduct."

"Personal values, then, referring to the instrumental qualities held to be most inherently worthwhile and intrinsically important by the holder – our private meanings?" asked the Prince.

"Yes," replied Trutorio. "I am speaking of individual beliefs or desires that guide and motivate our actions – those that define the things we prize the most, and, therefore, provide the basis for ranking the things we want in a way that elevates some values over others. Thus, our values determine how we will behave in certain situations. Now, to be fair, we should note that all three brands overlap."

"Stated in that way, the concept of values is not a difficult one to grasp," stated Dutamis.

"Our values give us impetus and latitude to take action," added Artenza.

"And within that action guide us – becoming a kind of internal compass," offered Trutorio.

"Excellent discussion," said the Prince. "Values, then, provide the meaning we assign to the choices and decisions we make. Clarity around our values lends insight into why certain things have great importance and enjoyment for us. Whenever we make important choices or difficult decisions – whenever we are unsure of what to do – we rely on our values. They are the *why* beneath the *what*."

"Is it safe to say we know more of our values than of our talents, because we constantly and consciously act on them?" asked Dutamis.

Our mostly deeply held values – those most innate and core to our identity – tend to be rather stable and aligned to our unique intellect

"Certainly," replied the Prince. "Unlike our talents, which as we have seen are often hard to articulate, our values are indeed usually better known to us."

"In considering their genesis," offered Artenza, "it would appear that some of our values are inherited, some are acquired through experience or influence of others, while still others are consciously chosen."

"From wherever they spring, they are most definitely a key part of our repertoire of gifts," observed Trutorio. "When we describe the characteristics and qualities of those who have had the most impact on our lives, we invariably speak the language of values."

"We can find clues in our heritage and past," added Dutamis.

"In the more dangerous times of our fathers before us, one lived and died by one's values, so it became critical to understand and display them as a means of clarifying for all who you were and what you were willing to die for. Hence our Coat of Arms! To this day we display shields, badges, and crests emblazoned with symbols that herald unique virtues and values as both a distinguishing essence of our individuality as well as a basic source of our strength."

"Which illustrates a critical difference between talents and values," interjected the Prince. "While talent is more of a have or have not proposition, some of our values are more dynamic and can change over time – especially those chosen. Less so with individuals, it is especially true of groups, organizations, and ultimately society, because the environment in which we live and work is always changing, evolving, and developing. I would note however, that our most deeply held personal values – those more innate and thus most core to our identity – tend to be rather stable. It is these values most properly counted as *gifts*."

"I would surmise, then, that these values align around our respective patterns of intellect," suggested Trutorio.

"Correct," said the Prince. "To wit, what naturally matters most to me are values related to concepts, challenge and competence. They are of inherent worth, and need no justification for their importance."

"They relate directly to your talents and drive," stated Dutamis. "My values revolve around responsibility, regulation and refuge."

"Give me adventure, autonomy and aesthetics!" smiled Artenza.

"Inspiration, integrity and involvement!" claimed Trutorio.

"Artenza? Another tool to aid in the clarification of one's values?" asked the Prince, turning to him.

"In this case, we perhaps need only to build upon this quartet of defining qualities – the major headings as we just outlined," interjected Trutorio.

"Such an instrument will become invaluable as we discuss ways in which to put our values into action," added Dutamis.

"Done," promised Artenza, confidently. "As we go, I will note our needs and construct both instrument and exercise, to be submitted on the morrow for general review."

Dutamis looked perplexed. "I find our quadratic categorization of strengths to be not entirely devoid of complexity."

"What do you suggest?" queried the Prince.

"Might it not be helpful to arrive at a more intuitive means to shorthand them?" replied Dutamis. "Perhaps a single word, icon, or idea that captures each?"

"For example?" probed Artenza.

"For myself," replied Dutamis, "the word *home* symbolically sums up a Guardian's gifts quite nicely."

"Excellent!" exclaimed the Prince. "Colleagues?"

"Heart!" cried Trutorio, speaking for the Diplomats.

"Hands!" cried Artenza, speaking for the Artisans.

"And I shall claim *head,"* said the Prince, speaking for the Philosophers.

"Home, heart, hands, head," repeated Dutamis. "Much better – this code I can remember!"

The others nodded enthusiastically.

"Let us then move forward to our next challenge," urged the Prince.

And so it was that the Prince and the Courtiers advanced their project, returning to the topic of talents.

Philosophers naturally value concepts, challenge and competence

Diplomats naturally value inspiration, integrity and involvement

Guardians naturally value responsibility, regulation and refuge

Artisans naturally value adventure, autonomy and aesthetics

Play From Power

————◆————

We are not all alike; there are diversities of natures among us
which are adapted to different occupations.

Plato

"Artenza," said the Prince, turning to him. "May I borrow your slate?"

Artenza looked quizzical, but relinquished his slate to the Prince, who in turn handed it to Trutorio.

"An experiment, one and all," announced the Prince. "Each of you will sign your name to the slate in regular fashion. Quickly now, and think nothing of it."

Each Courtier did so in turn: Trutorio first, followed by Dutamis, and finally Artenza, who returned the slate to the Prince.

"Now then," said the Prince, handing the slate to Trutorio once again, "Switch hands, and repeat the exercise."

The Courtiers were startled. As Trutorio slowly struggled, Dutamis and Artenza began to chuckle. The laughter accompanying the struggle grew as each, in turn, encountered similar difficulty.

"Hopeless!" cried Trutorio.

"Painful!" cried Dutamis.

"Artless!" cried Artenza.

The Prince laughed along with the Courtiers.

"But the point is made, no?" he said, still smiling. "A simple game to illustrate a worthy approach to employing our talents in our work."

The Prince continued. "Signing with your weaker hand required a good degree more energy and concentration, correct? Forced to do so, we could no doubt develop our ability to sign with mediocrity using our weaker hand, but I am certain that the signature would never be as elegantly and effortlessly executed."

The Courtiers immediately grasped the Prince's lesson.

"Energy expended on that which does not play to our strong suit is indeed wasted," observed Trutorio.

"Energy focused on trying to eliminate our natural limitations is indeed wasted," added Dutamis.

"Energy devoted to the convention of developing mediocrity is indeed wasted," stated Artenza.

"Yes, one and all," confirmed the Prince. "It takes far more effort to improve from poor to fair performance than to improve from good to great. Yet, do we not do this very thing in many of our institutions?" asked the Prince. "Remember the trial of Hercules!"

"I remember!" recalled Artenza. "Shall I retell the story?"

"Please do," urged the Prince. "You are the storyteller *par excellence!*"

And so Artenza recounted the legend of the trial of Hercules.

"In his youth," began Artenza, "the hero Hercules was to learn to play the lyre from Linus, the famous music teacher. But Hercules had no interest in music. Linus quickly became frustrated with Hercules. Finally, in a fit of anger, Linus struck Hercules for playing a wrong note. Hercules struck back with his lyre, killing Linus. Yet at Hercules' trial for the murder of his teacher, the judges found him innocent of any crime, guilty only of defending himself."

"And the reason?" prompted the Prince.

"The judges knew quite well that Hercules was not fit for the arts," continued Artenza. "Even as an infant, he had gained widespread acclaim with his feats of strength and mettle. By the time Hercules was to take instruction in music, he had become world reknown as the undisputed champion in a wide range of sports and combat. His talents were clearly athletic in nature, so in the view of the judges, Linus had been foolish in both his desire and attempt to make young Hercules into something he could never become, when the boy's natural strength so obviously lay elsewhere. And that is the story of the trial of Hercules!"

It takes far more effort to improve from poor to fair than to improve from good to great

The others applauded Artenza's rendition with great enthusiasm.

The Prince rose to take the center of the Pantheon again and invited the Courtiers to ponder once more the heroes of their Province.

"Consider these great leaders and their respective grand achievements," said the Prince. "Can you find a single instance in which the day was won without the hand of strength being played to its fullest?"

Alas, the Courtiers could not.

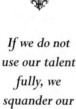

If we do not use our talent fully, we squander our most valuable asset and waste our most precious resource

"And," the Prince asked further, "can you find a single instance in which the achiever acted alone – without any support whatsoever?"

Alas, the Courtiers could not.

"Finally," continued the Prince, "can you find a single instance of universal genius – equal brilliance across the plane of aptitude?"

Alas, the Courtiers could not.

"What then is reasonable to conclude?" asked the Prince. "In the context of our efforts to guide Maximus, what strategies emerge from these observations?"

"Exploitation of singular talents," said Trutorio.

"Agreed," said the Prince. "However, I am curious about your choice of words for what is in essence a concept of capitalization."

"If Maximus has a talent and does not use it, in whole or part, he squanders his most valuable asset and wastes his most precious resource," replied Trutorio. "If he learns to use the sum of it to his highest advantage, he will win a triumph few men ever know – that of satisfaction and meaning. He will move ever closer to a view of his work as a calling."

"Excellent," said the Prince. "Talent is both an asset to be developed and a resource to be utilized. What is involved in such a strategy?"

"Practice!" interjected Dutamis. "The unused talent will atrophy if not exercised daily, like any muscle or nerve. Once we are clear on our realm of potential excellence, we must unleash our power by placing our talents in a position that constantly puts them in play — where they will not only develop continually, but also yield the most impactful results."

"Examples?" shot back the Prince.

"For the theoretic Philosophers, build plans for acquisition of new knowledge and find outlets for exposition of new ideas," replied Dutamis.

"For the economic Guardians, look for opportunities to strengthen processes and institute new standards," he continued.

The others picked up the train of thought.

"For the empathic Diplomats, find causes of interest to become passionately involved in," chimed Trutorio. "Build meaningful mentoring relationships."

"For the kinetic Artisans, delegate tedium, eliminate stagnant time lacking action, energy and movement. Accept high-profile, demanding projects to drive to completion," offered Artenza.

"Well done," said the Prince, approvingly. "The full development of even a single talent is a test of resilience and resourcefulness, and indeed a lifelong endeavor."

"Another thought, Courtiers," continued the Prince, shifting his focus. "Let us ponder what possible barriers you may encounter — what would prevent Maximus from galvanizing his talents as we have just discussed?"

"Perhaps his own reluctance," replied Artenza. "He, like so many others, may feel that it doesn't make sense to focus on areas already strong. It will land on us to guide him."

"Perhaps a feeling that his weaknesses will always overshadow his strengths," added Dutamis. "He, like so many others, may feel preventing failure is paramount.

Once we know our realm of potential excellence, we must unleash our power by placing our talents in a position from which they will not only continually develop but also yield the most impactful results

It will land on us to guide him."

"Perhaps a hesitancy to chase his own talents," offered Trutorio. "He, like so many others, may be convinced he will not discover anything too spectacular. It will land on us to guide him."

The Prince felt reassured. "Need we say more? What other strategies derive from our experiment?"

"Matching talent to task," offered Artenza.

"Ah, yes," affirmed the Prince. "A critical key."

The Prince was quiet for a moment, thinking, then turned to the Courtiers with a new challenge.

"What if sovereignty is not well-suited to Maximus' intellect?" he asked.

Searching for the perfect job is a limited strategy at best – bringing our full power and prodigy to generally suitable position yields far greater impact

The Courtiers grew quiet, each thinking hard, each momentarily stymied. Then, one by one, they lit up with the answer, for the Prince had not fooled them.

"Wrong question!" they exclaimed.

"The challenge is around bringing his brilliance to bear on the role…" started Trutorio.

"…redefining the role in his own terms – crafting it to suit his strength…" added Dutamis.

"…leading both the Court and Province in his own unique way…" finished Artenza.

"Bravo, Courtiers!" cheered the Prince. "You have grasped the essence of it!"

"No recipe for the role of Prince exists, and the perfect job is but pure fantasy," he continued. "Anyone seeking such will find it to be a limited strategy at best. It remains for Maximus to realize his own power and prodigy within the role."

"But what of the minimum requirements that exist for most roles?" asked Dutamis.

"Good question," replied the Prince. "This brings up a final consideration emerging from our experiment."

"That of defusing our deficiency," stated Artenza.

"Yes," replied the Prince. "Suggestions?"

"Know where we have weakness – any sort of action we currently take, or fail to take, that may impinge upon our strength," said Artenza. "Then prevent it from interfering with our potential impact – render it powerless and irrelevant to our performance and effectiveness."

"How?" challenged the Prince.

"Work around it," replied Artenza. "Eliminate or remedy bad habits."

"Know where we have no – or little – talent," said Trutorio. "And waste no effort or energy!"

"How then do we best handle areas of mandatory attention?" challenged the Prince.

"If the requirement is a major or primary component of the position, or one of high visibility, or where excellence is mandated, the fit simply does not exist," replied Artenza. "Natural selection, or deselection as the case may be, aids us here – one generally does not seek a role in which clear inability figures so centrally."

"And if the requirement is a minor factor, or one in which such excellence is not the call – perhaps a specific skill or finite body of knowledge – we can develop the minimal facility necessary to thwart total incompetence," responded Dutamis.

"But most importantly and with greatest impact," interjected Trutorio, "we call upon the talents of others with the strengths required to complement ours."

"Excellent!" exclaimed the Prince. "But let us look closer to see the application."

And with that, the Prince devised another activity.

"Courtiers," he began, "consider our quadrant of intellects. Knowing that we all have some degree of each intellect, what would be your particular ranking of the associated talent themes – in order of decreasing strength?"

We must often develop minimal facility necessary to thwart total incompetence – but calling upon the complementary talents of others with the natural strengths we lack yields far greater impact

The Courtiers thought for a moment, then answered in turn.

"For myself, it is tactics first, of course," said Artenza, "then logistics, followed by strategy, with diplomacy last. I am ever so much better with the concrete than the conceptual!"

"For myself, it is diplomacy first, as we now know," answered Trutorio, "then strategy, followed by logistics, with tactics last. I work best in the space between!"

"We are complements!" realized Artenza. "Mirror images of each other! Where I am strongest, you are weakest. Where I am weakest, you naturally excel!"

"Knowing this creates opportunities for powerful alliances," explained the Prince. "Dutamis?"

"Logistics first, naturally," replied Dutamis, "then tactics, followed by diplomacy, with strategy last. Abstraction is all but lost on me, I'm afraid!"

Finally, the Prince offered his progression: "Beyond strategy, diplomacy precedes tactics, with logistics as my short suit. I thrive on the theory!"

"We are complements!" exclaimed Dutamis. "Our troughs and crests are exact opposites, just like those of Artenza and Trutorio!"

"It is worthwhile to consider our many collaborations over the years," reflected the Prince.

"How many times have Artenza and Dutamis grounded the fanciful notions of either myself or Trutorio in reality?" he began.

"Countless!" cried the Courtiers.

"And how many times have Trutorio and I conceived and inspired the very plans that Artenza and Dutamis implement?"

"Incalculable!" cried the Courtiers.

"Could we have realized even remotely the same level of impact acting alone?"

Those most accomplished and impactful pull their power from but one or two key talents, surrounding themselves with those whose gifts complement their own

"Never!" cried the Courtiers.

"What sense does it make for me to present myself as an expert in matters of propriety?" asked the Prince. "Or for that matter, Dutamis to seek expertise in matters theoretical, Artenza to try his hand at advocacy, or Trutorio to take the tactical lead?"

"None!" cried the Courtiers.

"And so it goes," concluded the Prince.

"The most accomplished and impactful pull their power from but one or perhaps two key talents. They parlay that talent into stellar performance, spending little, if any, time on that at which they know they will never excel, instead preserving their strength – surrounding themselves with those whose gifts complement their own and exploiting talent wherever it may reside. This, then, is what it means to play from power."

And the Courtiers understood.

Manage What Matters

In every one of us there are two ruling and directing principles, whose guidance we follow wherever they may lead; the one being innate desire; the other, acquired judgment.

Plato

"Artenza," said the Prince, "I believe your third stratagem concerning governing our gifts relates once more to the notion of values?"

"Yes," replied Artenza. "Once we have clarified our values, we must go about the business of consciously living by them."

"In our decisions and choices," said Trutorio, continuing the thought.

"In our actions and priorities," added Dutamis.

"Yes," confirmed Artenza. "In all judgments that matter to us, in all that we attach meaning to."

"And in the context of work – how we will pursue it," said Trutorio. "When our values are clear to us, we can more easily identify where we feel we should become involved – where we *belong*. Our values inform our pursuits and guide our urgencies."

"Let us explore further the dynamics involved in managing what matters to us," coaxed the Prince.

"I submit that what most *say* they value diverges widely from what they *actually* value, as can be drawn from their behavior," he continued. "It would take only a list of one's professed work and life priorities in juxtaposition to the resources actually expended in furthering those values to reveal such misalignment. Gentlemen, what matters most must never be at the mercy of what matters least!"

The Courtiers were quiet for a moment, absorbing the Prince's statement.

"I believe you have effectively decimated the popular notion of *life balance,* as I see it," observed Dutamis.

There is no such thing as balance in life, there are only priorities driven by values, and choices made on those priorities – thus, it is the alignment of our choices with what matters to us most that is of critical concern

"There is no such thing in life," replied the Prince. "Those who would purport that one's life must be balanced across a number of seemingly segregated – yet, in truth, wholly inseparable – domains miss the point entirely, and relegate themselves to lives of mediocrity and diminished impact. It is ludicrous to think that some magical formula exists to apportion equal measures of time and energy across the many and varied planes of our vitality. There are only priorities driven by values, and choices made on those priorities – thus, it is the alignment of our choices with what matters to us most that is of critical concern. Misalignment alone is perhaps our greatest source of stress and strife, pressure and pain!"

"To clarify, then, when we speak of values, we are referring to the broad beliefs about that which we intrinsically prize, seek, trust and desire," said Dutamis. "These beliefs, however, guide and motivate our behavior most effectively when we successfully translate them into actionable principles – presiding rules of conduct for ourselves and others, aligned to and derived from our most deeply held values."

"I am of the mind that values can be a source of both strength and weakness," stated Artenza. "From my own perspective, I know that I become anxious when my values and principles are stifled, blocked, or challenged – I would rather fight or leave before abandoning or compromising them! Yet over-adamancy can put me at quite a disadvantage."

"As you mention it," asked Trutorio, "I am wondering which of the two – talents or values – might be the greater source of strength?"

"I can easily envision a circumstance in which one may be in a given position that calls upon one's greatest talent," answered Dutamis. "Yet that position is in an environment that violates one's values. I can't imagine anyone staying under such conditions being able to maintain their satisfaction or productivity."

"In other words, then," smiled Artenza, "values trump talents."

"In most cases, yes," replied Dutamis.

"A difficulty for me arises in that on a day-to-day basis in working with others, we often just assume that values are at play, but rarely do we openly express them, define them, or even question them," replied Trutorio.

"This presents quite a challenge for me as well," agreed Artenza.

"Certainly if we all had the same values, it would be much easier to work together," noted the Prince.

"But," he continued, "since such a wide diversity of values exists, it is absolutely essential that we openly recognize, embrace, and leverage the range of values that can influence decision-making and interactions at every level. The four of us have widely divergent personal values, but together we have forged clear agreement and priority on those that should be shared and core, held high and sacred, to best guide our

⚜

Values guide and motivate our behavior most effectively when we successfully translate them into actionable principles

⚜

collective efforts – and we are stronger for it."

"This singular clarity has provided us a clear line of empowerment to act swiftly, decisively," said Artenza.

"While at the same time inspiring in us ever deeper commitment to the Court," stated Dutamis.

"And effectively eliminating the need to resort to heavy acts of authority – restrictive rule, egregious edict, laborious legislation, or prescriptive policy," finished Trutorio.

"It seems we are momentarily entering an arena of discussion that transcends Maximus' values to those of the Court," noted the Prince.

"Maximus' personal values will most definitely influence those in his charge, and of his constituency," agreed Artenza.

"The Court will be additionally shaped by the values of those he enlists to head his cabinet," added Dutamis.

"It will fall to us to counsel him at both levels, then," noted Trutorio, "in the demonstration of his values through consistent action, and in the gathering of those supporters with whom higher common virtue can be pursued. Without both, a common ethos will elude."

"A difficult but worthy challenge," agreed the Prince. "The common value set will become enduring, and bind the Court in consensus on both the ends and the means to achieve them. Indeed, without a common creed, the Court could not exist."

"And beyond survival, the issue of success," said Dutamis. "We know that the Court's future will rest upon a number of fundamental processes – the key factor in the execution of which is the staff. The issue becomes: what determines the behaviors and decisions of those involved? The answer: clear values!"

"Which begs the question of decision-making," noted Artenza, "specifically, the process itself."

"Your thoughts?" inquired the Prince.

Leadership entails demonstrating values through consistent action, and the gathering of those with whom common virtue can be pursued

"First of all," replied Artenza, "virtually all of our decisions are based on values. Whenever we make a difficult choice, we do so in light of certain values that matter more than others. It isn't an issue of whether or not values – shared or otherwise – come into play. They do."

Artenza paused, then posed his own challenge.

"Here is the dilemma as I see it," he continued.

"Assuming we are clear in our own values, how do we elicit, elucidate and enlist the values of others that may have a stake in an important decision? And, how do we work with perhaps several appropriate and possibly contrary values – in sorting and weighing these values in priority fashion, so that we consistently remain true to those values most important in making difficult choices and driving our decisions?"

The group was silent, for Artenza's test struck the very heart of managing what matters.

Trutorio spoke first. "Building constructive forums enabling those involved to come together to dialogue honestly and learn from each other would help facilitate your first question – much as the four of us have done for many years."

"Yes, but to be quite realistic, talk of values makes many people nervous, to say the least," argued Artenza. "It can become so much contentious discussion."

"Agreed," replied Trutorio. "And it is indeed true that in diplomatic circles, such talk may be used to create some separatist judgment, usually in a negative way. Even at the personal level, are we not often reluctant to openly discuss our values for fear of reprisal in imposing our values on others?"

"The goal of productive dialogue with those whose values seem so different, perhaps opposite, from our own seems like an impossible quest!" cried Artenza, with resigned exasperation.

The challenge facing a leader at any level is to find the higher ground in confronting difficult issues mired in competing and often conflicting values

The Prince, who had been quiet, now spoke.

"This is the challenge facing any leader, at any level – from individual contributor to family head to Crown Prince. For Maximus, and indeed for all of us, the desire to find some higher ground and grace as we confront difficult issues will only grow with the challenge. Values will inevitably compete and conflict. We must all find ways to honor important values and principles while respecting differences and building bridges that bring people together instead of expending valuable energy to drive wedges between them."

"Hear! Hear!" cried Trutorio.

Values-Driven Decisions

✧ *Context*

✧ *Clarity*

✧ *Consequence*

✧ *Choice*

✧ *Communication*

"But," continued the Prince, holding up his hand, "how to do this in a manner that does justice to those values we – and others, if they own a stake – hold as core, and in a way that is both practical and realistic, this is the crux of the matter."

"The need for proficiency in carrying out a cogent process for making hard decisions is thus everclear," offered Dutamis. "The skills in demand here involve understanding and discerning how to manage what matters most – how to choose when a specific decision will honor some values that matter, while failing to honor, perhaps even violating, other values that also matter. This is the domain of judgment."

"We have done this very thing many times in the past, have we not – individually as well as in concert?" asked Trutorio. "What prevents formalization of our collective wisdom?"

"Nothing!" replied the Prince. "Lead on!"

"My thoughts tend toward a facilitative process of exploratory inquiry," replied Trutorio. "May I propose that step one involves establishing context – a clear framework from within which we will operate?"

"Meaning, I assume, the scope and type of issue at stake," clarified Artenza.

"Precisely," replied Trutorio. "What is the nature and domain of our decision? Personal, family, work? Strategy, policy, people?"

"This would narrow the field considerably to focus on those values most relevant," noted Dutamis.

"Yes," said the Prince, "but such labeling may also render us blind or ignorant to the impact on others. We must enumerate not only all facts, but also any assumptions inherent in the current reality."

"Which illustrates the importance of what I propose as the next phase," answered Trutorio. "That of establishing clarity."

"A host of questions leap to mind," said Artenza. "What values – individual and collective – bear on the issue? What is important to consider? Will individuals disclose the values that matter most to them in this context?"

"Has each individual involved been heard and understood?" added Dutamis. "Have all relevant values been identified and explained clearly and specifically?"

"Good!" urged Trutorio. "This naturally leads to a third phase, that of consequence – meaning, of the identified values in play, which are those most important in weight and priority? Which are subordinate?"

"All options to be considered must be identified in the search for the one that honors all or most of our top values," noted the Prince. "It still holds that what matters most must never be at the mercy of what matters least, as we discussed earlier."

"We are left then but to choose well, and we have achieved our objective!" concluded Artenza.

"Almost," replied Trutorio. "If others are involved, we must communicate the decision based upon the values that drive it. Context, clarity, consequence, choice, and finally, communication."

"Indeed, this is a critical but oft-ignored final step," agreed the Prince. "Those deserving of explanation must be identified, and we must be willing and able to be held accountable for any values that could not be honored in the decision. We must defend our process and prioritization."

Pausing briefly, the Prince continued.

"Like Maximus, we must all behave in some manner that demonstrates integrity in managing what matters. We must be clear, deliberate, and reflective – having thought through the rationale in principle for a given choice and its consequences. This marks us leaders at any level – knowing what we believe is important and making judgments authentically based upon it."

And so it was that the Courtiers understood the importance of strong judgment in managing what matters.

The roundtable discussion turned now toward the issue of maximizing the impact of one's gifts.

Lean Into Limits

The first and greatest victory is to conquer yourself; to be conquered by yourself is of all things most shameful and vile.

Plato

"Now then, Courtiers," asked the Prince, "what would you attempt to do if you knew you could not fail?"

The Courtiers contemplated the Prince's unexpected challenge for a long while. Slowly, each in turn realized the hidden meaning in the Prince's question.

"Trickery!" they cried together.

"I see that I cannot fool you," smiled the Prince. "You are quite right, of course – one cannot fail in the *attempt,* only in the *outcome.* And if but the slightest energy is expended, the attempt is made! When the goal itself is *try,* there is no failure, only learning – it is simply that the test precedes the lesson!"

"A mistake of *commission* must then be considered opportunity – a chance to begin again with greater intelligence," observed Trutorio.

"With every wrong attempt discarded, then, we take another step forward," noted Dutamis. "This effectively redefines the common notion of failure."

"A mistake of *omission* – of inaction in going forward – is the real failure," added Artenza.

Nodding his head in agreement, the Prince posed a further test.

"Let us once again dig deeper into the dynamic at hand," he continued. "Courtiers, think of the best mistake you've ever made, and the salient characteristics thereof."

"The *best* mistake?" asked Artenza.

The others, too, were somewhat bewildered by the Prince's choice of words.

Patiently, the Prince explained. "I mean simply that at the time, conventional wisdom advised action contrary to that which you took – yet now in retrospect the act was brilliant by measure of its result."

And so the Courtiers pondered their best mistake.

"Now," continued the Prince, "think of the biggest risk you have ever taken, and the salient characteristics thereof."

And so the Courtiers pondered their biggest risk. As they did, a revelation hit them, and they were eager to speak. But the Prince held them in abeyance.

"Finally," said the Prince, "think of your greatest or most powerful learning experience, and the salient characteristics thereof."

And so the Courtiers pondered their most powerful learning experience. As they did so, their revelation turned to insight.

"Prince, they are all one and the same!" they cried.

"Indeed," affirmed the Prince. "And the qualities present in your experience?"

"A requirement to stretch well beyond perceived capabilities and known boundaries of self," responded Trutorio. "A full commitment of energy, effort, and ability in which time disappeared."

"A feeling of discomfort and unbalance due to the uncertainty of outcome and the ambiguity in process,"

Pushing limits builds efficacy and trust in our own abilities

replied Dutamis. "A feeling of total immersion in the experience."

"A sense of coerciveness of action and urgency of response – a head-on collision with a life situation fired point blank without possibility of postponement," answered Artenza. "A sense of complete exhilaration."

"Excellent," commended the Prince. "For me it was the judgment that something more important took precedence over my immediate alarm."

The Prince then asked: "And what of the impact?"

"Creative breakthroughs quite unimaginable within the familiarity of normal routine," noted Dutamis. "Total redefinition of boundary!"

"Performance gains quite unattainable within the comfort of ordinary effort," answered Trutorio. "Full revitalization of ability!"

"Superlative advancement quite impossible within the complacency of everyday stability," observed Artenza. "Complete reestablishment of par!"

"With these results as proof, how can we possibly deny the power in leaning into our limits and chasing new challenges as a means of maximizing our gifts and building efficacious trust in our own abilities?" asked the Prince, rhetorically.

The Prince was silent a moment longer, then turned to the Courtiers to make his point in solemn fashion.

"If Maximus is not willing to take intelligent risks, if his talents are not constantly matched perfectly to a worthy challenge, if he forever indulges in a fear of failure, if he does not confront tensions head on and stand firmly on his values, he will never experience the highest levels of impact and performance."

"Our greatest growth often occurs when we embrace our discomfort and attempt new challenges," affirmed Artenza.

"We often surprise ourselves when we chance to

If we are not willing to take intelligent risks, if our talents are not constantly matched perfectly to a worthy challenge, if we forever indulge in our fear of failure, we will never experience the highest levels of impact and performance

raise the ante and employ our gifts maximally," offered Dutamis.

"We often underestimate the enormous gains we will realize when we step outside our zone of familiarity and comfort," agreed Trutorio.

"Challenge is the muse of our creative best!" cried the Prince. "I am reminded of the parable of talents in the scriptures I learned as a child. Do you recall the story?"

"I do!" cried Artenza.

"As do we!" laughed Dutamis and Trutorio.

But Artenza was already on his feet. He began to tell the parable of the talents.

"A master about to embark upon a journey entrusts his wealth to his three stewards," recalled Artenza. "His wealth is in the form of talents, each talent being the equivalent of fifteen years' wages for the average laborer. He gives five talents to the first steward, two to the second steward, and but a single talent to the third steward, apportioning the talents to each steward according to their ability."

Dutamis leapt up to continue the story.

"The two faithful stewards risk and invest their talents. Their talents double in worth, and they both are handsomely rewarded with greater responsibility and remuneration by the master upon his return."

Finally, Trutorio stood to render the conclusion.

"But the unfaithful steward buried his single talent in the ground for fear of losing it. The master casts him out, and takes away what little responsibility the steward had to begin with!"

The Courtiers took their seats and looked to the Prince.

"The lesson is clear," counseled the Prince. "To be the very best we can be, we must chance to make mistakes – if we don't make mistakes, we don't make much of anything, certainly nothing of great impact. The wisdom lies in avoiding repetition of our missteps and miscalculations. We must take intelligent risks, fully invest ourselves, knowing that some things will work and others won't. If we do, we will be rewarded with significant achievement. If we don't, we guarantee ourselves an experience void of impact."

Thinking further, the Prince added: "Certainly Maximus will not fully engage his gifts – or his life, for that matter – by desiring only that which is known, certain and safe. In this there can only be accelerating boredom, arrested development, and eventual stagnation."

Trutorio and Artenza nodded their understanding. Dutamis looked perplexed. "How are we to distinguish and define intelligent risk?"

"As challenge in which the considered action falls within the venue of our gifts, yet which may test our strengths beyond their proven limit," answered Trutorio.

"As challenge in which we judge the long-term costs of complacency and inaction to outweigh the immediate costs of acting boldly – a cost-cost analysis, if you will," answered Artenza.

"The requirement, then, is the spirit of challenge," confirmed Dutamis.

"Indeed," replied Trutorio. "It is only when we are beyond our known abilities, in new territory, that the impossible becomes possible by virtue of challenging circumstances calling forth our personal best. How ever shall we possibly know how far we can go without risking going too far?"

"It is true that by nature we impose undue limitations on ourselves – we generally don't know what our potential is until we put our capacity on trial," agreed Dutamis. "This casts a much more positive light on what many – like the third steward – perceive to be a more negative connotation associated with risk."

"Risk and failure are never the direct objectives – learning, challenge and opportunity are," affirmed Artenza. "Risk is merely a subjective description of the leap into uncertainty."

Artenza saw that Dutamis remained unsure.

"By way of illustration, let us momentarily focus on the extreme," he continued. "Think of our most dire situations of catastrophe and adversity – the most

Most of our limitations are self-imposed – we generally don't know what our potential is until we put our capacity on trial

trying of times. Do they not reveal the depth of our character, our resiliency and resolve – in fact, the very best of our strength? Without exception, do they not open up possibility and present new opportunity? And do we not emerge stronger?"

"Of course," replied Dutamis. "But you speak of do or die, not of free choice – of required reaction under duress, not of positive proaction."

"True, and surely we would never seek that which is hazardous in order to experience an equivalent revitalization," confirmed Artenza. "But by pushing our mental confines in the more incremental and positive direction of pursuing ever increasing levels of challenge appropriately set to extend our abilities, we can effect much of the same kind of triumph – growth, change, and development – differing only in scale and scope."

"There must be a bit of art involved in setting the challenge as you suggest," said Dutamis.

"Indeed there is," responded Artenza, thoughtfully. "We disengage if the challenge is either unattainable or too easy. The mark must be set perfectly."

"Yet," offered the Prince, "when we are within our sphere of strengths, the dynamic process of stretching them comes rather naturally; we seek to better and bolster our true gifts almost automatically. Our talents are eager to expand, our values to express. We need only listen and respond. Like water, they seek their own level. We need only get out of our own way!"

"Most interesting!" exclaimed Dutamis. "I have never thought of it in these terms, but this explains the rather fluid nature of our most engaging and energizing experiences – when time flies, focus intensifies, and distraction disappears."

"When heart, will and mind are unified in action," furthered Trutorio.

"When we are one with our gifts – fully present,

When we are within our sphere of strengths, the dynamic process of stretching them comes rather naturally

absorbed in the moment, immersed in our doings," continued Artenza.

"The interesting questions are these," said the Prince. "If by reason and experience we know that constantly pushing the limits of our strengths yields extraordinary results and exhilarating experiences, what deters most from engaging in more of the same? When the staggering loss in potential and productivity is so obviously and directly proportional to the presence of boredom, anxiety, and rote, why do so many speak of a day filled with little else?"

The Prince's questions once again gave the Courtiers pause.

"Perhaps too many are too comfortable with natural languor," surmised Artenza. "The initial energy needed to overcome lethargy and sedentary personal inertia is deemed too taxing."

"Perhaps too many remain unaware of their personal strengths, being informed more of their limitations," proposed Trutorio. "Belief in the preponderance of their own deficiency renders them reticent to advance that which they deem an already dismal proposition."

"Perhaps too many too easily yield to the natural onset of insecurity at the first perceptible shift in equilibrium," guessed Dutamis. "For many, even most, change of any brand is difficult."

Contemplating the Courtiers' thoughts, the Prince offered his own.

"Who among our merry band has not encountered and conquered at least one of these?" he asked.

The Courtiers were silent. The Prince charged on.

"Perhaps, then, the riddle is nothing more complicated than the lack of accessible strategies with which to proactively deal with these all too human inevitabilities – a quandary to which the solution is ever so much easier to develop!"

The Courtiers weighed the suggestion carefully to arrive at the implications for action.

"Thoughts, gentlemen?" challenged the Prince.

"Perhaps we begin with a simple survey of our day…" began Dutamis.

"…identifying the times in which we are most engaged, and those in which we are not…" continued Trutorio.

"…identifying those activities that create energy, and those that steal it," finished Artenza.

"And then?" probed the Prince.

"Understand the characteristics inherent in those activities," started Trutorio. "Such as zeal…"

"…imagination…" added Dutamis.

"…and audacity!" cried Artenza.

"And?" pushed the Prince.

"Consciously build more of each into our doings…" replied Trutorio.

"… into our chosen work projects…" offered Dutamis.

"…into our chosen diversions," added Artenza.

"In so doing replace our status quo with escalating vitality – the effective outcome from adopting the spirit of challenge," affirmed the Prince.

And so it was that the Courtiers understood the importance of leaning into limits as a means of maximizing the impact of one's gifts.

Move Toward Mastery

The learning and knowledge that we have is, at the most, but little compared with that of which we are ignorant.

Plato

"The second of our two complementary strategies – our final in this series – is upon us," pronounced Artenza.

"The drive for mastery, to become the very best of the best in our class," noted Dutamis.

"The pursuit of knowledge to enhance and elevate our gifts of self," acknowledged Trutorio.

At the Courtiers' comments, the Prince stood up and began to pace, deep in thought. Something about their statements seemed to be troubling him. By and by, he stopped, bent down to pick up two stones of differing sizes, and approached the roundtable.

"Courtiers," he began, "imagine that our roundtable represents the universe of all knowledge – ideas and methods both known as well as those yet to be discovered."

The Prince then placed a small pebble on the large roundtable. The Courtiers looked on with curiosity, anxiously awaiting the Prince's exercise.

"Imagine that the pebble represents conventional wisdom – ideas, methods and concepts comprising *generally accepted* knowledge," said the Prince.

The Prince then replaced the smaller pebble with a stone twice as large, and set forth the test.

"This stone represents *all* conscious knowledge – everything we have discovered and documented, incorporating both convention and unorthodoxy. To be fair, the stone misrepresents the dynamic and ever widening nature of this component – but assuming we have momentarily frozen the march of time, what observations and conclusions may we gather from this rather rudimentary analogy?"

"What we know is dwarfed by the sheer immensity of what we don't," observed Dutamis. "We have much to learn."

"We don't know what we don't know," observed Artenza. "The universe of all knowledge is limitless, infinite – endless opportunity and possibility teem within the domain of the undiscovered."

"The bounds of our accepted knowledge are most limiting!" exclaimed Trutorio. "Focusing attention solely on that which is known cannot be considered a truly expansive strategy – if we are not careful, that of which we are certain can confine and constrain us…render us obsolete!"

"Most insightful, and yet most disturbing, is it not?" replied the Prince. "Before we can begin to move toward mastery – to even attempt a process of reversing the prevailing condition – we must first understand how such a situation could possibly come to be."

The Courtiers sat silent, each deep in thought. For a

What we know is dwarfed by the sheer immensity of what we don't – focusing attention solely on accepted knowledge thus cannot be considered a truly expansive strategy

long while, no one spoke. Finally, Trutorio broke the stillness.

"The dilemma lies within our institutions," he said, in a most solemn way. The others looked surprised, for this observation was rather unexpected.

"How so?" queried Dutamis.

"We breed conformity of thought!" replied Trutorio. "We relegate learning to the reign of a rigid and pedantic educational system designed to produce satisfactory accumulation of knowledge, for the most part neglecting critical thinking and applied creativity, when in truth both are necessary."

"It is this very conformity you decry that preserves our established standards of performance," argued Dutamis. "They provide our baselines of comparison, even our most treasured traditions."

"True, but also perpetuate and propagate our greatest misconceptions," interjected Artenza. "Too, these standards of which you speak do not even approach a level of excellence – they result in little more than passable adequacy. I agree with Trutorio – we are often so adamant about what we know and believe to be true that we lose our view of what is possible."

"I too would agree that our traditional approach to learning is limiting," joined the Prince. "It has enabled but a token of understanding in the grand universe of possibility. In these times of change, it is the learners who will flourish in the new world order, while the knowers are magnificently prepared and equipped for a world extinct. The great end of education must be to go beyond merely filling our minds with the knowledge developed by others to disciplining ourselves in the use of our own ingenuity. In truth, I have long dreamt of a new approach."

"It is indeed fact that our academics give higher priority to completing curriculum than to developing skill in proper inquiry," admitted Dutamis. "It seems we inadvertently suppress natural curiosity by placing primary emphasis on securing the right answers, rather than on pursuing the right questions."

"That is not to say the work of others – and the dominant world view – is without value," said Trutorio. "Quite to the contrary. It provides the necessary foundation upon which the mansions of genius are built. It is mandatory knowledge to be digested as a proxy for experience – to be tested through our own experimentation and exploration."

"It seems that we are in essence redefining learning, the conventional view of which looks at knowledge more as a static quantity to be consumed," concluded Artenza. "You realize, of course, that this will mandate a redefinition of mastery, which is generally – and all too easily – synonymous with competence."

"True," agreed the Prince. "While no argument exists for not staying current on the ever-expanding measure of established knowledge – we must do so to remain competitive and relevant – equating competence with mastery is a view too limited for our purposes. It is the requisite entry ante, but it does not distinguish!"

And with that, the Prince began to pace once more, speaking as he moved about the roundtable.

Our learning must become centered on leveraging our natural curiosity and disciplining ourselves in the use of our own ingenuity – placing the primary emphasis on pursuing the right questions rather than on securing the right answers

"Courtiers," he began, "if I told you that there are no new ideas under the sun – that everything we know now and will know in the future is already in existence – what would be your debate?"

The Courtiers eagerly rose to argue the Prince's rather preposterous claim.

"What of our many miraculous breakthroughs in the sciences?" challenged Dutamis.

"What of our many wondrous works in the arts?" challenged Artenza.

"What of our many far-reaching advances in the humanities?" challenged Trutorio.

The Courtiers settled back, quite confident they had defeated the Prince's somewhat radical thought.

To Dutamis, the Prince responded: "Has there been a single breakthrough the operation and effect of which had not always been there, waiting only to be observed and documented?"

To Artenza, the Prince responded: "Has there been a single creation the capacity and material for which was not pre-existing, waiting only to be imagined and envisioned?"

To Trutorio, the Prince responded: "Has there been a single thought the truth and significance of which was not already born, waiting only to be interpreted and inspired?"

The Courtiers sat stunned, paralyzed by the truth of the Prince's undeniable proof. As the realization came over them, they slowly began to speak, each in turn.

"The citrus has always gathered mold," said Dutamis, "the ability of which to rid us of deadly disease has always been so – waiting only for the scientist to devise the medicinal application."

"Great blocks of marble and granite have always adorned the hills," said Artenza, "waiting only for the sculptor to wield his chisel."

"The basic tenets of humanity have always prevailed," said Trutorio, "waiting only for the demagogue to voice the mantle of meaning."

"You see, gentlemen," finished the Prince, "we do not *create* new knowledge; rather, we *reveal* it through experiencing, experimenting and exploring."

Dutamis looked perplexed.

"What then is the role of mastery?" he asked.

"Why, this very revelation!" replied the Prince. "The true master moves beyond the level of paramount proficiency in a given discipline to become a conduit through which flow ideas naturally aligned to his respective gifts and field of focus."

The Prince produced a coin from his tunic and held it up as he continued to speak.

"Imagine two sides to the coin of mastery," the Prince explained. "On one side we find the traditional view of compulsory competence – technical excellence and subject matter expertise, the pinnacle of which resides among the ranks of those commanding the highest levels of existing understanding and technique in a given discipline.

We do not _create_ *new knowledge – we* _reveal_ *it through experiencing, experimenting, and exploring*

True mastery moves beyond compulsory command of a given discipline to become more about ingenuity, keen observation, and problem-solving – using our talents to pioneer the frontiers of knowledge and skill, bringing in and making accessible ideas and methods that perhaps seem impossible to comprehend in the current realm of everyday awareness

"On the other side, we find the more transcendental notion of creative spirit. This definition of mastery takes us to the core of our inventiveness, surpassing the obligatory mastery of content to become more about ingenuity, keen observation and problem-solving – using our talents to pioneer the frontiers of knowledge and skill, bringing in and making accessible to everyone ideas and methods that perhaps seem impossible to comprehend in the current realm of everyday awareness. Mastery at this level becomes centered on innovating breakthroughs in our domain of excellence."

The Prince gestured toward the Pantheon's honored leaders.

"Consider all those we have decorated – are they not all true masters in this light? Have they not all indelibly changed their respective games – questioned convention, defied tradition, challenged orthodoxy? Have they not all expanded the marked confines of their disciplines to bring forth powerful new advances relevant to all?"

As the Courtiers gazed at the heroes and icons, they recognized the common quality of impact to which the Prince referred.

"Witness their voicing of new truths and principles," noted Trutorio.

"Their development of new standards and practices," joined Dutamis.

"Their design of new techniques and tools," added Artenza.

"By this definition, then, true mastery is revealed not through complexity of intellect or elevation of thought, but in the ability to deepen our understanding of the world around us," said Trutorio.

"Everyone has the potential for this type of mastery!" exclaimed Dutamis, excitedly.

"Yes!" cried the Prince. "Our work is no less a canvas because we do not paint! Our voices are no less powerful because we do not give them air! Our hearts are not barren of song because we compose no notes!"

The Courtiers swelled with pride at the Prince's inspirational speech.

"To be clear, then, all knowledge is there already, only for us to discover through investigation…" added Dutamis.

"…imagination…" continued Artenza.

"…and inspiration," finished Trutorio.

"Yes," said the Prince, "and our awareness of this phenomenon makes ingenuity – that is, creativity in our individual exploits…the application of our gifts toward true mastery as we have defined it – ever so much more accessible!"

"Gentlemen, *life* is our lesson," he continued. "It is one the nature of which is passionately pursuing the ideas and questions that consume us, and of expanding and adapting ourselves to an ever-changing world. It is a constant and conscious expedition to push beyond the boundaries of what we know in fact."

"To look at the world with fresh eyes through the lens of our talents and values," agreed Dutamis. "To keep our minds alert to receiving the ideas whose time may have come."

"To never stop questioning," agreed Trutorio. "Is it not for this very reason that curiosity itself exists?"

"We most certainly enter the world that way," noted Artenza. "As children we are nothing if not complete learners and perpetual interrogators!"

"Irony!" cried the Prince. "The paradox is undeniable! It is this aevitas process of possibility which we must master! True mastery has no peak, no finish line! True mastery demands the humility of the novice, the spirit of the apprentice, the energy of the dilettante!"

⚜

True mastery demands the humility of the novice, the spirit of the apprentice, and the energy of the dilettante

⚜

"The child's ardent imagination applied with the scientist's capacity!" cried Artenza.

"Replacing the child's '*why?*' with the master's '*why not?*'" cried Dutamis.

"Replacing the child's pure play with mature playful invention and the wonder of '*what if?*'" cried Trutorio.

"So now then," said the Prince, offering the knowing smile the Courtiers now recognized only too well, "what shall be our strategies to aid Maximus in his pursuit of such mastery?"

"To think distinct!" replied Artenza. "Challenging conventional wisdom and pursuing his original ideas."

"To think prime!" replied Trutorio. "Pursuing the ideal and aiming for what's optimally possible given his unique gifts."

"To think smart!" replied Dutamis. "Conducting investigation of the highest order and solving problems in scientific fashion."

"Most excellent!" praised the Prince.

The Prince and Courtiers then began to elucidate each strategy in turn.

"The first order then is to challenge one's own view of matters," asserted the Prince. "If we cannot alter present circumstances, we can certainly change our sense of it. Make no mistake – the greatest deception Maximus may suffer is from his own untested opinions, assumptions and beliefs."

"This will require an approach of constantly gaining new and different perspectives from a wide network of knowledge sources – and of continuously reframing issues," noted Dutamis.

"This will require an incessant transformation of both fundamental preconceptions and commonly held wisdom," added Trutorio.

"This will require an aggressive effort to become

True mastery entails questioning conventional wisdom and pursuing our original ideas, aiming for what's optimally possible given our unique gifts, and solving problems scientifically

independent of the influence of public opinion," said Artenza.

"We must employ a serial query to guide the process," said the Prince. "Beginning with: does he hold beliefs and employ methods for which he has no experiential validation?"

"From whence do they come?" continued Trutorio. "How is it he believes them to be true?"

"Why does he maintain them?" added Dutamis.

"What knowledge would cause him to change his views, his techniques? Is there another way? A better way?" finished Artenza.

"These provide an excellent template," affirmed the Prince. "But practically speaking, how are they best executed? I do not imagine this to be without difficulty – challenging one's own way does not come naturally. What discipline might we impose to aid the process?"

The Courtiers were quiet for a time, processing the Prince's prompt.

"He must be exposed to the beginner's mind," replied Trutorio, after a while. "Therefore, these questions best come not through a Courtier or peer, but from a true novice seeking to move toward mastery."

"What do you suggest, then?" asked Artenza.

Trutorio thought for a long moment, searching for the appropriate solution.

"I have found mentoring to be most valuable in this arena," he answered. "Placing a young journeyman under the tutelage of Maximus is a natural mechanism for us to consider. The purity of inquisition and curiosity of a neophyte learner seeking Maximus' lessons will be at once rigorous and rewarding for him, at the same time keeping the presence of new eyes in the fore."

"Brilliant!" cried Dutamis.

"An excellent strategy!" praised the Prince.

Our greatest challenge in achieving mastery may come in testing our own opinions, assumptions and beliefs

"One which I shall employ for myself!" exclaimed Artenza.

"We have now provided a foundation for the pursuit of the ideal," stated the Prince. "What next?"

"In keeping with our strategy of moving from a position of power," began Trutorio, "our inquiry shifts from one of challenging present paradigms to one of targeting possibility in maximizing the impact of our gifts."

Pursuing what's ideally possible brings out our creative best, draws on our strengths, and represents a fundamental departure from the simplistic approach of analyzing immediately available options

"Meaning, what is the best I can be in my work?" offered Dutamis. "How good can I truly become? What is the best way to perform my work given my unique talents?"

"What is my ultimate competitive edge – my best kept secret – and how can I exploit it optimally?" added Artenza. "When and how am I most innovative? What is most unique about how I perform my work?"

"Seeking blue sky in this manner brings out our individual best in creative thinking and imagination, for it increases our knowledge of self and draws on our strengths," noted the Prince. "Any technique which does so will likewise increase our inventiveness.

"This is a fundamental departure from the typical and certainly more simplistic approach of perusing and selecting from existing options," he continued. "The latter, of course, being more of a passive inventory of immediately available alternatives and answers, and thus a sub-optimal, non-differentiating tactic falling short of proactive mastery and impact."

"Which leads us to the final strategy – that of solving problems and creating opportunities for improvement and innovation by employing a structured, systematic, scientific learning process," stated Dutamis.

"Thoughts before proceeding?" asked the Prince.

"I think too many fail to grasp the basic truth that learning precedes all improvement, all innovation," observed Trutorio.

"It seems obvious that we cannot continue to employ the same old techniques and expect to achieve substantially different results!" exclaimed Artenza.

"Implicit in this approach is the need to be aware of how we learn, and how we act on newly acquired knowledge," added Dutamis.

"Speaking for myself and Guardians everywhere," he continued, "I know that I look to build upon that which I already know – seeking the historical foundations and practical usage – recalling past experience, remembering details and information, and procuring the necessary and available resources and material."

"I am more experiential, and I presume this is true of most Artisans," stated Artenza. "I want to touch, see, and do – seeking the physical involvement and relevant application – scanning for visible outcomes, grasping the situation, and determining what I can enact immediately and how, putting new knowledge to work without delay."

"Diplomats like myself look for threads of meaning," added Trutorio. "I want to understand the connections and points of continuity – seeking the ideal state given the forces at play – focusing on the relationships and building the bridges that result in collaborative advancement."

"And Philosophers place emphasis on the rationale," said the Prince. "I want the framework of logic behind the concepts – seeking to foresee future implications and the grand schematic – analyzing possibilities and contingencies, designing the optimal avenue for achievement."

"Maximus will need to understand and leverage these learning styles," finished the Prince, "for although our Pantheon had seen its share of meteoric innovations, they cannot be replicated, as they cannot be taught and learned. However, those resulting from a learning-centered problem-solving process can be!"

"What does this process look like?" asked the Artenza.

"Practically speaking," answered Dutamis, "it is a continuous cycle entailing a focus on what we deem to be an important problem or challenge, and discovering the opportunities within it. This in turn demands a significant amount of time spent trying to formulate the problem in depth before attempting to solve it, and the consideration of a wide variety of alternatives before committing to a specific direction.

We must be prepared to make a multitude of attempts, often without success. Finally, we will arrive at the desired solution and development of new capability."

"Needed, then, is a thorough and precise process of hypothesizing, investigating, diagnosing, testing, and analyzing," summarized Artenza.

"Beginning with a proper initial framing of the problem," explained the Prince. "Solving difficult and complex problems many times rests in the ability to conceive a unique theory, with the key to breakthrough in thinking often found in how the problem is framed. There is nothing so practical as a good theory!"

"Next," continued Dutamis, "we must gain thorough understanding of the myriad of factors at play, collect the necessary evidence, and then push beyond obvious symptoms to identify, assess, evaluate, and diagnose underlying causes."

"This would naturally lead us to the generation of many ideas of how to solve the problem or meet the challenge – resisting the temptation to settle for the first apparent solution," stated Artenza, moving to the next point. "And from my experience – short of the rare flash of genius – it is nearly impossible to have a good idea without having many ideas!"

"It is here we must call upon talents of others to capitalize on their unique thought processes in order to exhaust and optimize the search process," interjected Trutorio.

"Meaning?" asked the Prince.

"The integrative thinking of those with the natural prowess for matters of ethics and advocacy," replied Trutorio. "The Diplomats among us!"

"The sequential thinking of those with the natural prowess for matters of logistics and propriety," added Dutamis. "The Guardians among us!"

"The applicative thinking of those with the natural

Solving complex problems requires the systemic thinking of the Philosopher, the integrative thinking of the Diplomat, the sequential thinking of the Guardian, and the applicative thinking of the Artisan

prowess for matters of tactics and agency," added
Artenza. "The Artisans among us!"

"The systemic thinking of those with the natural
prowess for matters of strategy and theory," added the
Prince. "The Philosophers among us!"

"Precisely!" confirmed Trutorio. "We must then, and
only then, select and test the best idea. All the while
tinkering and tailoring, revising and refining, evaluating
and enhancing!"

"The net of which is the discovery of new knowledge
to be shared and transferred – feeding it backward
and forward through dialogue, documentation, and
education," concluded the Prince.

"Oh yes, and with the firmly entrenched mediocrity
of convention close on our heels!" smiled Artenza. "I
know whereof I speak!"

The others laughed, recalling Artenza's history of
both breakthrough and disappointment in his lifelong
pursuit of new and better tools of trade, always at the
mercy of the critics.

"But nonetheless becoming the very best of current
thought!" smiled the Prince. "New knowledge gained
through learning, now to be tested by others in the
same spirit of innovation and mastery we have ourselves
embraced and employed. It is the circle of learning!"

The Prince became quiet, collecting his thoughts.

"Courtiers," he concluded, "I believe we have much
to be proud of. Our collective efforts to explore the
inner strengths of self have yielded a most critical
consequence – the means to pilot the rough waters
of work and life. And by Artenza's hand, we shall
have tools for the trip. The odyssey now becomes
manageable! We have detailed how Maximus is to guide
himself in governing his gifts: he will know where to
look for his talents and values, what to look for, how
to identify them, how to put them into play, and how

*The discovery
of new
knowledge
must be
shared and
transferred
– feeding it
backward
and forward
through
documentation,
dialogue, and
education*

to maximize their impact in his work. In the course of our discussion, we have defined the nature of one's true work, outlined a powerful judgment process, and redefined failure, learning and mastery – and, in so doing, detailed a forceful framework for expanding capability with clear bias toward action."

The Prince stood with arms extended to encompass all three of his roundtable associates.

"You are to be congratulated!" he cried proudly.

The Courtiers beamed, basking in the glow of the Prince's praise.

The Prince stepped back from the group to say: "A respite is well deserved, for much work is still before us. Let us rest briefly, and reconvene in short course."

The Courtiers began filing out of the Pantheon, thankful for the chance to clear their heads. As they neared the doorway, the Prince called out to them.

"Courtiers!" he cried. "A parting thought for reflection…if you could learn anything at all, what would it be?"

The Courtiers paused briefly, knowing the Prince did not expect an immediate answer. As they resumed their leisurely exit, he called out another challenge.

"Whatever your answer – what's stopping you?"

Govern Your
Gifts
Source Your Strength
Play From Power
Manage What Matters
Lean Into Limits
Move Toward Mastery

Absolute
Impact !

Anchor Your
Ambition

Share Your
Strengths

Each citizen should play his part in the community according to his gifts.

Plato

Share Your Strengths

In which the Prince and his Courtiers discuss the
challenge of focusing outside oneself

The Courtiers returned from their brief sojourn to find the Prince already on his feet and pacing about the Pantheon, head bowed contemplatively, once again deep in thought.

"Courtiers," the Prince began, "I have used my rest time to reflect upon our next challenge – *vita brevis*, you know! I am looking forward to our impending deliberation with great relish, for it is this that is perhaps the most heady of our charrette. However, I shall yield the floor to the gentleman of diplomacy."

Turning to Trutorio, the Prince asked, "Trutorio, we are now to your element – how do you wish to proceed?"

"I propose first a debate to aid us in framing the issues involved in realizing the very deepest sense of significance and purpose that results from making a positive difference in the lives of others – the essence of which is a commitment to a contributive cause connected to something outside of, and larger than, ourselves," replied Trutorio, succinctly.

Artenza and Dutamis were quiet, absorbing Trutorio's proffer. The Prince wore the smile of wisdom.

"No easy challenge, this," he cautioned. "The difficulty for most lies in the seeming absence of a definitive first step in the discovery process, which is further inhibited when we exaggerate our importance, deny our real potential, or minimize our strengths. Yet solving this challenge is unavoidable if we desire authentic fulfillment."

"Contemplating one's higher purpose can indeed be a daunting endeavor," observed Dutamis. "We must necessarily broach the subject of our very reason for existence, which for many can be a difficult wrestle."

"Only fear prevents us!" retorted Trutorio. "Are there not countless among us who exist in quiet desperation, afraid to truly live, to deeply consider the meaning of their lives, to step into their higher purpose and at least attempt to positively impact the world?"

"I admit to feeling uneasy at times when posed the question of my ultimate significance," confessed Artenza. "I am best when in pursuit of a clear objective or immediate opportunity – yet in truth those goals always want for continuity, connectivity and cause."

"I find the concept itself neither evasive nor elusive," averred Trutorio. "In a very general sense, our life's purpose is quite simply to share our strengths to the highest benefit of others to whom we are connected in life, thus enriching their experience as well as our own. We are all coming from this same center – it is how we express it that is distinguishing and unique. Each one of us contributes – indeed *must* contribute – something very special and very unique in the name of creating and constructing positive communion."

Trutorio took a moment to consider his own ideas.

"I would restate my position that the most important choice we make is the choice to serve," he continued. "However, I wish to open this view up for broad debate before conceiving the various component strategies, for several reasons...not the least of which include expanding my personal perspective, and exploring factors and facets inherent in the challenge of sharing our strengths. Where is the power in serving? What are the ramifications of contribution? What are the

⚜

In a very general sense, our life's purpose is quite simply to share our strengths to the highest benefit of others to whom we are connected in life, thus enriching their experience as well as our own

⚜

demands of such commitment?"

The others gathered their initial thoughts to engage in Trutorio's case. The Prince was first to the floor.

"This commitment to cause – this core ideology – is one in which our roundtable is well versed," he began. "We each know what it means to move beyond the level of simply rendering a service to become part of creating something we intrinsically care about – as you say, Trutorio, something outside of, and larger than, ourselves. We each live and breathe this far deeper and more transcendental meaning of service – of embracing service beyond self in all matters relevant. Our Court, our Province, indeed the entire land stand as clear evidence! We each understand the power and purpose it provides, the nature of which enables us to endure the sacrifice that real commitment may entail. This we know is the antidote to the oft-lamented poison of the darker side to prevailing unchecked egocentric individualism."

And with that, Artenza rose to expound his views, pacing and gesturing in high energy, ever the showman.

"Let us be clear, gentlemen, that the issue is not one of scope or scale, for we may serve one, some, or many – through the smallest act of kindness or most noble feat of sacrifice. Rather, it is an issue of simple humanistic mandate, a clarion call to action in the absolute. We have been given the worldly power and energy to think and to create, and to so much as even entertain a notion that no intent to better our fellows is required, is to think the unthinkable! Could it possibly be that we have no purpose here other than the accidental, miraculous, magnificent combination of so many particles of matter? Nay!"

Artenza appeared to the others to be just warming up to his ebullition.

"Even those who denounce higher reason cannot deny that we do not, and cannot, exist alone – that we

True service to others is not an issue of scope or scale, for we may serve one, some, or many – through the smallest act of kindness or most noble feat of sacrifice

thrive together, that we cannot escape impacting others. Is not every real thing whole onto itself, yet part and parcel to something larger? The issue moves well beyond the charitable concepts of *me helping you* or *us helping them,* for even these reveal simplistic, separatist views! All must realize the undeniable fact that we are all connected and exist in this universe together, with few if any degrees of separation. Our actions emanate as cause and return to us as effect. Therefore, if we are not helping, we are hurting! No middle ground exists on this issue!"

The others looked wonderingly at Artenza, moved by his eloquent and impassioned perorative.

Artenza took his seat, looked to the others, smiled and shrugged. "I've been saving that."

"Cast in this light, can we deny that we have all come this far on the shoulders of others, propelled by the fury of *their* commitment?" asked Dutamis. "Have we not received much from those who count *us* in their charge? Our path eased by others, is not our goodwill toward them mandatory? Is it then not only a conscious choice but also an obligation to exert ourselves earnestly and responsibly to give as much both in return, and in going forward? Do we not, in fact, owe this reciprocity to the future? And by committing in similar fashion, will not the best of fates likewise accompany us?"

"These are indeed the component issues as I see them," said Trutorio. "The reciprocal power of contribution, the connective power of cause, the focal power of commitment."

"As a most practical matter," proposed the Prince, "our Court and Province are indeed built upon the service rendered by others. Consider the acts of those in this hall – forsooth, our roundtable! Where would we be without Artenza's results? Dutamis' security? Trutorio's ideals? What of our collective efforts to develop people – and in the immediate sense Maximus – for the future?"

The Prince grew quiet, and spoke softly as he continued his thought.

"As I look around me today, I see that contribution takes many forms and means many different things – a helping hand, an encouraging word, an appreciative eye. This is the heart and soul of purpose, gentlemen, to this we must agree.

"The simple requirement is but to leave our world a bit better than we

*Contribution,
which takes
many forms
and means
many different
things
– a helping
hand, an
encouraging
word, an
appreciative
eye – is the
heart and soul
of purpose*

found it, to ease the path of another, if only a little – to play our part in the grand unfolding of the future. We need only to consider the dismal alternative in order to understand the power and necessity of serving our brethren in such a manner."

"What could be more powerful than having every individual in the land sharing their strength to improve the collective experience?" asked Trutorio. "Meaning and fulfillment actualized!"

"I cannot imagine a world without such veritable contributions," offered Artenza. "Anything less than every soul answering both the private and public call is tantamount to shameful waste."

"Certainly no well-intentioned argument against our proposition can be held as valid," stated Dutamis. "However, we must be cognizant of the difficulties therein."

"The higher road is never the easiest," confirmed the Prince. "The demands are innumerable – perhaps it is why more don't live a purposeful life. First is the demand of constant and continuous recommitment to consciously stay on our path. Next is the demand of discomfort – doing what needs to be done rather than succumbing to mood or fleeting desire, we often wind up in situations where what we need to do seems nearly impossible to sustain."

The Prince appeared to have a flash of recollection. "To wit, the perils of Prometheus! Do you recall the myth?"

"The mentor of man!" cried Trutorio.

"The giver of fire!" exclaimed Artenza.

"The father of civilization!" hailed Dutamis.

"A selfless champion, benefactor and teacher who dared defy – and indeed endured – the mighty wrath of Zeus to help mankind," agreed the Prince. "Shall we revisit the story?"

"By all means," replied Dutamis. "No better fable exemplifies the costs and requirements of committing to a contributive cause."

And so the Courtiers took turns retelling the myth of Prometheus.

"Zeus and the gods of Olympus had rid the world of the Titans," began Dutamis. "Only two sons of the terrible mortal giants were left on earth. One was Prometheus. He was kind of heart. At that time, man still lived in caves without fire – cold and hungry. Man had little in the way of creature comforts – he ate raw food, without utensils!"

The Courtiers began playacting the story, having fun with the drama.

Artenza picked up the storyline. "Prometheus saw this and thought, *'Man must have fire. I will help him.'* But Zeus – selfish ruler that he was – forbade Prometheus to bestow man fire."

Artenza gave his best impression of Zeus. *"Never! Fire is not for man. If he had it, he might grow wise and strong as the gods themselves. He must never have it!"*

"But it was the dead of winter, and Prometheus saw man living like the animals," added Trutorio. Then in his best voice of Prometheus: *"I shall give man fire!"*

"Prometheus went to the horizon," continued Dutamis. "As the sun rose from the sea, he touched a reed to the flames, and the reed caught fire. Prometheus entered one of the caves of man. *'See this wonder?'* he said. Then he piled stones for a hearth, laid wood upon it, and touched the reed to it. And man was warmed. He came to know heat and light."

"Prometheus helped all to have fire," retold Artenza. "Men came from everywhere to learn from Prometheus how to build fires, cook food, and make tools. His gift of fire turned caves into homes."

"But! When Zeus found out, he was furious," said Trutorio. "He had Prometheus seized and taken to the top of a high mountain, where he was shackled to a rock."

"And the worst of it," said Dutamis, "was that Zeus sent a great eagle each day to tear the flesh from Prometheus and eat his liver, which healed every night. Zeus sentenced Prometheus thusly until he returned fire to the heavens. But Prometheus endured, suffering this cruel torture and bearing his pain without complaint. He lay there for ages. Many times he grew weak and weary, and was tempted to do as Zeus had ordered."

"But when he looked down upon mankind, he saw fire helping them, and he regained his strength, never losing faith in his eventual release," continued Artenza.

"After many years, Hercules happened upon him," concluded Trutorio. "Hercules shot the eagle with his bow and arrow, unshackled Prometheus from the mountain, and set him free."

The Prince rose to exact the lesson.

"It is clear, is it not?" he asked. "Those who choose to share their strengths to ease the way for others often do so at the cost of making their own lives more difficult. Yet it is this heroic choice – this courage to sacrifice self-interest in the name of commitment to a worthy cause – that defines the lasting legacy of a leader."

A hush fell over the Pantheon.

"It is quite clear to me," said Trutorio, in a most grave tone, "that it is not enough for Maximus to become the best Prince in the Province. He must become the best Prince *for* the Province."

The Prince was smiling as the Courtiers exchanged knowing glances, all in full cognition of what was to follow.

"Yes," he whispered, a sparkle in his eyes. "How?"

The Courtiers looked to Trutorio.

"It is upon me," offered Trutorio, slapping his knees and taking to his feet. "Artenza, may I borrow your tablet?"

Artenza obliged enthusiastically. "By all means!"

"I shall outline the component strategies in a summary fashion, just as Artenza did before," began Trutorio. "Understanding, of course, that each requires deeper examination to become useful."

The others nodded their agreement, familiar now with their template for debate.

"Very well," began Trutorio.

"To refresh, the goal of sharing one's strengths is

Those who choose to share their strengths to ease the way for others often do so at the cost of making their own lives more difficult

⚜

It is not enough that we become the best at something, we must become the best for something to make the most positive difference possible in the lives of others, given our unique gifts – and in so doing realize the deep satisfaction that derives from such service. I see five critical self-directed elements inherent in the ability to do so, moving from self-knowledge to aligned action to maximal capitalization – resulting in progressively deeper impact. However, I must tell you that in truth they are integral components of a cohesive whole. One without the others yields us little. It is for the sake of our discussion only that we might justify their separation."

The others nodded their understanding.

Trutorio then took Artenza's tablet, and began writing his points as he outlined each.

"At the outset, we must definitively clarify – indeed fully understand – the specific nature of our chosen contribution, for it is this that truly moves us.

"To segue from our earlier discussion, it is the commitment to serving well that is a critical dimension to one's view of their work as a calling. Recall that by governing our gifts we discover the kind of work we are designed to do – what we are able to do, how we are best able to do it, and what intrinsically matters most – thus engaging our natural artistry in the most powerful way. But the true artist toils not only to create, but to move and inspire others with his strokes – to permanently bestow the world with his creation – a shift in focus toward contribution that inspires him to invent himself, to become one with the world through what he has created!

"Thus, the challenge now centers more on aspects of social integration – drawing a direct connection to opportunities in need of our gifts. We must look up and out from our individuality to find the touochpoints of commonality – expressing our strengths through a noble aim that benefits others.

"Feeling that our work matters in the grand scheme

The goal of sharing one's strengths is to make the most positive difference possible in the lives of others, given our unique gifts – and in so doing realize the deep satisfaction that derives from such service

of things can only come from this focus on contribution, for it is at the crossroads of our gifts and the world's need of them that true calling peaks. It is here that higher fulfillment sits at the very zenith of our workview continuum. It is here that one's personal path meets and merges with the common ground and collective experience of company and community. It is here that clear and central guiding purpose resides. It is here that we find our reason for being."

On Artenza's slate, Trutorio wrote:

Clarify your cause.

"Once we fully comprehend the specific nature of our contribution, we must then focus our energy on aligning purposeful action to our knowledge of self. To do that, we will need to learn to do two things well.

"At one level, we must learn to take an active role in consciously moving ourselves – and those within in our sphere of influence – beyond excessive individualism and disproportionate self-interest. Rest assured that while this may be easier for some than others, it is inherently counterintuitive and difficult. We are by nature selfish creatures. The goal, however, is not to eliminate self-interest, for it cannot be done. Even the most seemingly selfless deed has in it some measure of benefit for the purveyor. We need only surpass the ego with higher purpose, recognizing that not only do we seldom fully tap the deep well of our selfless capacity, but that we serve ourselves as we serve others.

"The key, of course, is to expand the base view and narrow approach of improving our own lot solely through competitive unilateral acquisition – that is, *taking* at the expense of others, rather than *giving* – and adopt an enlightened perspective that seeks to include and improve the interests of others as well. If we care for the orchard instead of simply picking the fruit, we shall have more fruit to eat!"

On Artenza's slate, Trutorio wrote:

Exceed the ego.

"At a higher level, we must consciously commit ourselves to awakening the human spirit to serve that often lies hidden and dormant within us. We must learn to become better servitors and stewards – to match our unique strengths to support the very real needs of those to whom we are connected in life. This involves understanding what others need most from us, making it our first priority, and delivering on it with power and purpose to not only meet the requirement, but to go above and beyond the normal course of expectation or obligation.

"We must, therefore, become adept at recognizing and responding to the ever-changing expectations of those in our charge, and to shoulder whatever sacrifice such action might entail. This is a responsibility we cannot shirk and still expect to impact others as positively. There can be no other more important or sublime act than this, for it is here that our legacy will outlive us in a most significant fashion."

On Artenza's slate, Trutorio wrote:

Strive to serve.

"Once we have clarified our cause, connected to our contribution and executed strategies to engender most noble and purposeful action, we can turn our attention to maximizing the impact of such. We will need to learn to do two things concurrently, employing twin strategies centered on reciprocity and responsibility.

"First, we must learn how to engage in the fine art of optimistic appreciation, for no human soul can survive without it. As we all wish our abilities, achievements, and contributions to be appreciated, so must we appreciate those of others. This thirst for appreciation is universal, yet for the most part gone unheeded, perhaps because we simply do not have enough confidence in this rather miraculous principle of life.

"Moreover, while failure to appreciate – and to do so in a manner precisely befitting the situation – eventually yields a disastrous effect upon others, the crescendo of reciprocal positivity resulting from even the smallest act of appreciation can be a most powerful pathway to inspired outcomes. The inexpensive gift of appreciation sincerely intended – the kind praise, the unexpected compliment, the good gesture of gratitude – gives rise to the powerful emotions that can effectively embolden commitment and performance. By learning to see with appreciative eyes – by finding, noticing, and praising the very best in others – we create reinforcing reciprocal actions that lift the collective experience to new heights.

"We must make a conscience effort to spark this rising spiral at every opportunity, wherever we go, whatever we do, and with whomever we meet."

On Artenza's slate, Trutorio wrote:

Foster positive feelings.

"At the same time, we must take personal responsibility for building the deeper relationships with others that derive from trust. As we look for the good in others, we will find it, and indeed come to understand them – and they us.

"The task then becomes a concerted effort to build the togetherness and teamwork that can drive not only performance, but create an authentic harmony. If we fail to do so, a pattern of dishonesty, cynicism, and distrust constructed by those of a contrary mind may prevail. Our Court may then be in peril of survival – for as we face a new era fraught with increasing complexity, it is the grand net of the collaborative capital present in the sum of our strongest relationships that will enable us to move into the future with solidarity.

"To be quite certain, this is not a simple issue of civility, grace, or decorum. Rather, it is multifarious concern that mandates skill in the construction of trust, for it does not happen by chance or circumstance.

"Gentlemen, we will need our best thinking to arrive at a practicum on this most serious topic, for we must defeat the tendency to speak in platitudes on this matter. We must have a viable and actionable definition of trust!"

On Artenza's slate, Trutorio wrote:

Render trustful relationships.

The others sat still while Trutorio took his place at the roundtable. As before, slowly, then gathering great decibel and tempo, applause filled the great room.

"Eloquent as ever, Trutorio," remarked the Prince, proudly. "I expected no less! The sum and substance of your counsel is undeniable. Could we achieve as much impact in our attempt to share our strengths omitting even one of these strategies? Nay! Let us then drill down into each of these learning challenges in singular fashion, with a view toward arriving at a solid pentacle pathpoint."

And so it was that the Prince and the Courtiers plunged into their discussion of how Maximus might learn to focus outside himself and serve his higher purpose.

Share Your Strengths

Clarify Your Cause

Exceed the Ego

Strive to Serve

Foster Positive Feelings

Render Trustful Relationships

Clarify Your Cause

The Prince once more picked up a small stone. Holding it in his palm, he set forth a new challenge for the Courtiers.

"Fellows, a short debate," he began, raising the stone to eye level for all to see. "Agree or disagree: everything has a higher purpose. Take this stone, for instance."

The Courtiers sensed that the most obvious answer would be incorrect. They each thought hard, then answered in turn.

"Ground to a coarse powder with others like it to be used for the Pantheon's new floor, it would stand to support forever our many visitors," replied Artenza. "Agree!"

"Mortared with others like it to be used for the construction of a new rampart, it would stand to protect our Province for centuries to come," replied Dutamis. "Agree!"

"Polished to a sheen and given as a gift to symbolize a unique meaning, it would have special significance to the recipient in perpetuity," replied Trutorio. "Agree!"

"Excellent!" commended the Prince. "What then is the implication for discovery of purpose?"

"Therein lies some element of design," answered Artenza. "We craft a cause!"

"Therein lies some element of decision," added Trutorio. "We choose a contribution!"

"Therein lies some element of dedication," said Dutamis. "We commit our creativity!"

"And the inherent powers of such purpose?" probed the Prince, again holding up the stone for reference.

"Transformation!" cried Artenza.

"Motivation!" cried Dutamis.

"Inspiration!" cried Trutorio.

"Precisely," confirmed the Prince. "Our stone is no longer merely a stone, but now a mighty entity to remain in service of its greater purpose for all eternity. If such a sense of cause and contribution so applies to even the most fundamental of inanimate objects, what then might we project for the human condition?"

"Certainly our potential will never be fully realized until we search for and set ourselves to some causative principle, no matter the depth and breadth of our strengths," observed Artenza. "We all have talent – the test is what one does with it. The marshaling of talent and release of human potential through purpose is awesome indeed."

"Certainly we cannot wait for another to assign us our charge," noted Dutamis. "Unlike our most fortunate stone, the heavens will not grant us our intentionality – we must endeavor to take responsibility for designing, deciding and dedicating the best use of our gifts. The accompanying required commitment creates a sense of personal accountability. And in times of great change, confusion and complexity, our high purpose further guides us in pursuing our work."

"Certainly our significance in the world shall remain unfulfilled until and unless we have a deep sense of clarity around our contribution to some larger, external effort," concluded Trutorio. "Experiencing the accomplishment of becoming immersed in constructing something far exceeding individual capability is profoundly meaningful and moving – it stirs the heart!"

"This and more, Courtiers!" exclaimed the Prince, standing once more in the center of the Pantheon. "Look around us! The paradox and power of purpose abounds! The great use of life spent for something that will outlast it – the import and worth of the individual overflowing personal borders to survive one's passing! The relentless pursuit of work never done! Not a mission, goal, or objective, but a timeless initiative! A central source of human motivation – of gifts engaged to the highest advantage of others! An unchanging, unfaltering personal ideology standing solidly to set one's course, rouse progress, and stimulate growth!"

"Our reason for rising!" cried Trutorio.

"Our lilt for living!" cried Artenza.

"Our point of provenance!" cried Dutamis.

"The benefits of clarifying one's cause would seem compelling enough," said the Prince slyly, somewhat understating the Courtiers' energy and enthusiasm.

"From clear cause comes potent action!" argued Trutorio. "Our efforts flow with much greater focus and force. We become much more cognizant of — and thus able to avoid — distracting opportunities and potential tangents, enabling even greater impact!"

"From clear cause comes uncommon valor!" argued Dutamis. "Life is more of a courageous adventure under lucid aim! We are far more resilient and resourceful as purposeful individuals!"

"From clear cause comes newfound freedom!" argued Artenza. "The ability to change course on any journey is of considerable advantage, and constancy to one's grand intent breeds that license. Our purpose does not change, but our strategies in pursuit of it may. In fact, such a commitment mandates lifelong learning, for continual reinvention is required!"

The Prince then launched a new dialectic.

"It is here our journey into the *outer* world of work truly begins, is it not?" he asked. "Can we effectively build the highest levels of performance without understanding where to start, how to start, and what to do? Is this not our life focus and central organizing principle? Clear cause begets clear directive guidance in our odyssey, correct? To pose the question of cause and contribution is to search for the needs of the world — and of those closely connected to us — in want of our gifts, is it not?"

"It is!" agreed Trutorio. "And such a question must act to make that connection with all due respect to our natural gifts. Using myself as an example, I might appropriately ask: What can I teach others? How can I best bring people together? What worthy cause can I champion?"

"How can I help? What needs to be done? What duties can I shoulder?" added Dutamis, knowing his forte.

True purpose is an unchanging, unfaltering ideology standing solidly to set one's course, rouse progress, and stimulate growth

"How can I make a difference today? What results are required to make a difference? What immediate action can I take?" added Artenza, conscious of his strengths.

"Most excellent! If we fail to ask these questions, will we not then miss the mark?" furthered the Prince. "Might we not aim off center? Might we not focus in error? Might we not confine ourselves, and thus fall short of all we might be capable of?"

"We might!" cried the Courtiers.

"However," cautioned Dutamis, ever wary, "we must be careful to address these important questions in the proper manner."

All turned to look at Dutamis inquisitively.

"What is the concern?" asked Artenza.

"I fear many will attempt the quest in the context of whim and fancy," responded Dutamis. "The question of contribution must be asked as we have just done – aligning strengths with a creed of service to others. We must take care to frame the issue against what *should* be done and what *needs* to be done – with an eye for the highest positive effect possible."

"And to keep the query separate and apart from the issue of profession," added Trutorio. "The occupational position merely depicts the nature of our specific activity. That is to say, it is more important to decide what we are suited to contribute than to ask the means of livelihood. Again, the issue of calling arises."

"Agreed," nodded Artenza. "Let us make it simple, then, shall we? The question is quite simply: given my unique gifts, of what service can and should I be? Whatever the answer, whatever the domain of activity, this contribution is the wellspring of our purpose!"

Dutamis still looked perplexed.

"What troubles you, friend?" asked Trutorio, keen to pick up on such cues.

"That even if asked properly, the question may be

The question of contribution must be asked in the context of aligning strengths with a creed of service to others – given our unique gifts, of what service can and should we be?

answered insufficiently," replied Dutamis. "I am thinking both of Maximus and the everyman."

"Say more," urged the Prince.

"In the case of Maximus," began Dutamis, "might he not state his purpose as simply Court Prince and Ruler of the Province? And in the case of the everyman, might he not state his cause likewise with respect to his particular function?"

"Ah," said the Prince, his eyes twinkling. "Functions and titles are simply descriptions of position and task, not cause! It does not respond to the *reason why*. Is your purpose Minister of the Interior? Is Trutorio's cause Chancellor of Diplomatic Affairs? Artenza's General of the Provincial Army?"

"No," replied Dutamis, beginning to understand. "Trutorio has made explicit his cause – that of maintaining our unity and virtuosity. I know Artenza's to be that of ensuring our progress and strengthening our influence. I know mine to be one of keeping us secure and productive. Regardless of our titles, we would each seek roles to put our purpose in play – it has always been thus, and always shall be. Our respective causes have enabled us to evolve, reinvent, and renew while staying true to our course."

The Prince then embarked upon a brief thesis.

"He who mistakenly states his contribution as, for example, Stable Manager, or Landowner, or Esquire, or Census Taker, or Parent – has not clarified his cause. This is a downward view, one of authority and control, rather than an upward view of support and service – the focus is misplaced on effort, rather than correctly on effect. The Stable Manager who views his purpose as running the stable has missed the point entirely. When he can say with commitment that he provides healthy horses so that others may travel safely and securely, he has found his contribution. The Census Taker who views his purpose as gathering household information has likewise erred. When he can say with conviction that he provides our cabinet with critical knowledge needed to make important decisions for the welfare of all, he has found his cause. The Parent who views his purpose as raising a child to adulthood is similarly mistaken. When he can say with confidence that he provides lifelong guidance for his progeny to become all they are capable of in this life, he has found his charge."

The Prince paused to exact a moment of insight.

"Those who view their purpose in limited terms of activity and authority shall be deemed subordinate, no matter how eminent their echelon. Those who view their purpose in terms of contributing to the success of the greater whole shall be deemed true leaders, regardless of their rank."

The Prince then looked directly at his Courtiers, and said: "In my absence it will be upon you to guide Maximus to find his purpose within his role as Prince, just as the everyman must find his own."

The Courtiers nodded in full acknowledgement of this weighty challenge.

"It is here that I struggle most with the pragmatism," admitted Dutamis. "We have said that we should seek to bring more of who we are to bear on our present enterprise, correct? So, how can we practically help one struggling to find purpose in his present work? Might there not be a tangible means by which we can ensure personal cause is clarified?"

"I believe I have the solution," offered Artenza. "We can begin with the assumption that most will err in discovering and defining their true reason for existence, perhaps because they have not engaged in the proper inquiry. I think we are on safe ground to say that most are not practiced in this most critical area."

Artenza began to pace as he thought out loud.

"We can begin with a simple descriptive statement of position. To use a present example, let us utilize the Census Taker who has mistakenly defined his aim in descriptive terms of effort; to wit, *'I exist to fulfill my Provincial charter to accurately collect household information and compile thorough reports for the Court.'* An acceptable hypothetical?"

"Absolutely," approved Dutamis, while the Prince and Trutorio nodded their assent.

"Would not a simple serial inquest as regards the

Those who view their purpose in terms of activity and authority shall be deemed subordinate, no matter how eminent their echelon – those who view their purpose in terms of contributing to the success of the greater whole shall be deemed true leaders, regardless of their rank

A vocational position is merely a descriptive vessel for our voyage – a means through which we pursue our deeper cause, for we may have many careers and hold many occupations in a lifelong quest to serve our purpose

significance of such a description eventually lead us to real cause?" posed Artenza.

Dutamis looked unsure. "Play it out for me, if you will."

"Certainly!" rejoined Artenza. "Collecting household information and compiling reports – why might that matter?"

"Because it gives the Court the best and most current information available on our Provincial population," replied Dutamis, easily.

"And why is that important?" asked Artenza.

Dutamis took a bit longer this time before making his reply.

"Because we can use that knowledge to understand the dimensions of the human condition within our Province better than we could by any other means," answered Dutamis.

Artenza pressed on. "And the import of that?"

"Well, it helps the Court make informed decisions of critical importance, for one thing," replied Dutamis, taking even longer.

"And why is that so important?" challenged Artenza once more.

"Because it enables the Court to improve the social welfare of our land!" stated Dutamis triumphantly.

"Voilá!" cried Artenza. "And our Census Taker's true cause?"

"To help improve the social welfare of the Province by enabling the Court to understand the population!" exclaimed Dutamis. "Thank you!"

"An elegant technique, Artenza!" approved the Prince proudly. "The inspirational force and directional focus of this latter view transcends the former by an order of magnitude – it is the difference between commodity and calling!"

"A method universal in its utility!" said Trutorio. "The motivational power and resulting impact from a conviction in one's deeper cause is undeniable."

"And illustrative of the freedom and reinventive power of higher purpose," noted Artenza. "Our Census Taker may now take on a variety of new and different positions in pursuit of his purpose."

"I see what you mean!" exclaimed Dutamis. "An occupational position as actuarial, auditor or accountant would enable him to serve like purpose!"

"He remains true to his cause regardless of function!" cried Trutorio. "It is not one's cause that differentiates, but one's expression of it! "

"A mighty advantage, is it not?" observed the Prince. "In times of great change, one's steadfastness to cause paradoxically provides the very element of continuity necessary to fend off obsolescence at the hands of time. Our specific vocation is merely a descriptive vessel for our voyage – a means through which we pursue our deeper cause. We may have many careers and hold many occupations in the course of a lifelong quest to serve our purpose."

The Courtiers were silent for a moment, absorbing the power of constancy to cause.

Artenza then spoke quietly, urgently. "I believe it is time to move our discussion forward to aligning action with understanding!"

Exceed the Ego

Any man may easily do harm, but not every man can do good to another.

Plato

"On the matter of disproportionate individualism," asked the Prince, turning to Trutorio, "what shall be our course of attack?"

"This is the first of all obstacles to putting our purpose into play," replied Trutorio. "I believe we can do no better than to raise the specter of unbalanced self-interest, and consciously commit to match our mettle against it at every opportunity."

"Then let us proceed," encouraged the Prince. "What is the nature of the beast?"

"It is one of unnecessary comparison," explained Trutorio.

"And of undue competition," added Artenza.

"And of unwarranted criticism," added Dutamis.

"And of unjustifiable combativeness. How does it thrive?" queried the Prince.

"On ego," replied Trutorio.

"On excess," replied Artenza.

"On entitlement," replied Dutamis.

Unchecked self-interest is an ugly monster thriving on ego, excess, and entitlement — bent on action that cripples and inevitably destroys the very thing it seeks to acquire and affirm

"Let us be clear, then, that we are speaking of an over-indulgent involvement with self quite apart from the brand of individualism that both sparks self-reliance and piques progress," concluded the Prince. "We refer now to an animal of an all together different breed – an ugly monster bent on action that cripples and inevitably destroys the very thing it seeks to acquire and affirm."

"Yes!" agreed the Courtiers in unison.

"To my mind, we speak of a pervasive *me first, me only* attitude," expounded Dutamis. "It is wrong, gents! Such a base mentality places unearned rights above responsibility – diminishing obligation, accountability, and duty."

"It is at best a limited perspective, to be sure," added Trutorio, forcefully. "It is a view held by small-minded individuals and founded on a parasitic measure of self-worth by those who would seek to advance the quality of their lives at the expense of others – a mindset born out of a perverse and cowardly delusion that one's life has value only relative to some twisted comparative scale fashioned to purport measures of success that are, in reality, nothing more than false and fabricated terms of prestige, position and power over others."

Trutorio's vitriol startled the others.

"I've been saving that," he smiled, nodding to Artenza in acknowledgement of the passion brought to bear.

"A sad and illusory notion of advancement, indeed," agreed the Prince. "It is foolish to equate power or position over others with power over oneself. Rather, the incessant feeling that we must always win or outdo another in order to maintain self-respect effectively shrinks our power, our potential, our perspective – by comparing, competing, combating, and criticizing, we become petty and small."

"One does not rise from another's fall," agreed Artenza. "If we care only enough for a unilateral result, we will almost certainly attain it. But allowing, enabling, or even causing another's loss in pursuit of our own gain is tantamount to simplistic primordial survival. We cannot simply *take*. Prithee, have we not moved well beyond this point of civil evolution? What have we to realistically gain by feeding on the lives of others to sustain us? What is the most we can hope for in viewing others merely as the means to our own desired ends? What can we truly accomplish with our hands virtually about another's throat?"

"Little beyond self-destruction," answered Dutamis. "Preoccupation with our personal gratification can only weaken our capacity to advance and enhance our interests in the long term – paralyzing our ability to grow, change and develop. If we remain stuck in solely ego-driven modes of behaviors, we become irresponsible, taking short cuts and easy ways out, placing blame, ever playing the put-upon, and eventually harming ourselves as we inflict harm on others. I can easily envision a scenario in which obsession with one's selfish gain leads to loneliness, cynicism, and frustration – followed closely by isolation, rejection, and even ostracism."

"Carry your scenario one step further," said Trutorio.

One does not rise by causing another's fall – seeking to advance at the expense of others by comparing, competing, combating and criticizing, we become petty and small

"Imagine," he went on, "such widespread alienation across the land! Wouldn't the next likely scenario entail disinterest toward the sanctity of the larger community, leading to the wholesale abandonment of unity and solidarity, creating an opportunity for despots to emerge and exert totalitarian control over the population, thereby essentially removing the very individuality originally sought? More importantly and most frighteningly, hasn't our history seen its share of many such misleaders – bullies to be beaten back?"

Trutorio paused to drive home his point. "Colleagues, pursuit of purely selfish concern is ironically self-defeating!"

Obsession with one's selfish gain leads to loneliness, cynicism, and frustration – followed closely by isolation, rejection, and even ostracism

"Be that as it may," began the Prince, "I daresay we shall never see the last of those for whom there is no meaning in anything beyond self-centered behavior – those who see benefit to others as merely incidental and coincidental to their exploits. These few shall forever remain destined to a life of arrested development, evolving no further than primitive instinct."

"Refusing to assign any meaning to their existence," added Trutorio.

"Refusing to project any sentient purpose upon their acts," added Artenza.

"Refusing to accept responsibility for their conduct," added Dutamis.

"The perils of unchecked self-interest are clear," said the Prince. "The challenge thus centers on proactively safeguarding against such rampant individualism – on moving ourselves and others beyond the level of excessive ego involvement."

"By the same token," interjected Dutamis, "I urge caution in swinging too far to the other extreme."

"Please say more," urged the Prince, intrigued by the warning.

"Those who cannot take care of their own interests

likewise cannot be effective caretakers to those of others," Dutamis continued. "I of all people understand the need for affiliation and participation with the larger group; however, I see danger in forsaking self for others, in unbalanced sacrifice, in an intentional martyrdom. I fear the potential loss of self, a growing disproportionate dependence on others, and an overemphasis on conformity. I can envision a scenario whereby an inflexible, group-centered mentality destroys the confidence and conviction that one soul can make a difference. In the final analysis, the resulting widespread disenchantment with society yields the very same opportunity for autocratic dictate to seize control that does preponderance of self-indulgence."

"Balancing the interests of both self and others being the critical key," noted Trutorio.

"In my humble opinion, yes," affirmed Dutamis.

"Along this cautionary line and by way of a transition to our active antidote, I would like to reiterate a point made earlier," offered Artenza.

"By all means," said the Prince.

"My concern lies with how we approach achieving the balance to which we now refer," began Artenza.

"Conventional thinking at this point centers on a still-limited and separatist attitude – one of charity – an almost adversarial *service over self-interest* perspective which necessarily presumes the interests of individuals and others are in conflict. This is wrong, fellows! This traditional thinking is doomed to fail, and misses the power of self-interest rightly understood. Insistence on separating and positioning the two at odds with each other, or one above the other, inevitably forces a choice between them based on some subjective prioritization – a no-win situation fostering not mutual interest, but the very self-interest we wish to avoid. We are then between Scylla and Charyldis – two equally perilous alternatives, neither of which can be passed without

Conventional thinking suggesting a forced choice between self-interest and service presents a no-win situation that entirely misses the point and power of self-interest rightly understood – at the heart of which is a higher perspective acknowledging that interests of self and others are indeed inter-dependent

falling victim to the other. It then becomes a dismal game without gain."

"What do you suggest?" asked Dutamis.

"A more integrative and holistic approach that seeks to merge and integrate interests!" replied Artenza. "One recognizing that the interests of self and others are indeed interdependent – that although we are indeed individuals, our success is defined only within the context of the larger system and our interaction with it."

Trutorio joined in Artenza's train of thought, sensing the need to clarify the concept.

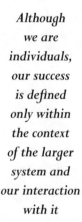

Although we are individuals, our success is defined only within the context of the larger system and our interaction with it

"Your concept is well-aligned to our overall aim of always moving from strength," he noted. "The pivotal notion here being that we *gain* strength from *sharing* our strength – by working with others for collective and mutual gain. In this view, by freely immersing one's self into that which exists *beyond* one's self in a truly integrative fashion, the essential interests of the individual are both protected and enhanced."

Trutorio looked to Artenza as if to hand him the floor to continue.

"Individual achievement and service to others are not mutually exclusive, as many would have us believe," furthered Artenza.

"Individuals and groups in fact require one another," he explained. "One simply cannot and does not exist without the other; they share the same center, the same foundation, the same path."

"A most metaphysical concept!" cried the Prince.

"Yes, but not so very ethereal," put in Trutorio. "In fact, examples abound in the everyday world around us."

"Such as?" queried Dutamis.

"We need look no further than our master guilds," replied Trutorio. "In each of these trade associations, members give of their time, energy, expertise, and monetary resource to advance a common interest. They can achieve much more together, capitalizing on each other's strengths. They become stronger by sharing their strengths!"

A look of recollection came over Artenza.

"It was not long ago that Valtel, the master of our ironworks fabrication and our largest employer, faced a crisis of dramatic proportion," he began. "Sales of his wares were dropping far too low to sustain his operation – few could afford his cast iron cookware, blacksmithing, and gates. Rather than take the short-term, selfish route of simply reducing his prices, he chose instead to use his cash assets to increase the wages of his workers – a move decried by peers and pundits alike. But the higher income enabled hundreds to purchase the products they made, which in turn sparked sales and profitability. His higher perspective enabled a reasonable sacrifice to benefit those in his charge, in turn engendering the realization of ultimate benefit to himself and his operation."

"Both excellent examples," commended the Prince. "The more inclusive view works well in both the individual and organizational domains – groups and communities included."

"If I understand this idea correctly, then," recapped Dutamis, "we must move toward adopting a more expansive view that does not simply juxtapose interests of self and others in parallel fashion, but that truly joins them as component parts of a cohesive whole. We must enlarge our definition of self-interest to include a sense of social obligation, with a feeling of responsibility regarding one's impact on others. Achieving more self-indulgent goals should be – and must be – equal and proportionate to our conscious effort to serve others."

"Yes!" Trutorio. "Isn't our self-interest in reality dependent upon others? Isn't it true that we can be

⚜

We must learn to adopt a more expansive view that truly joins interests of self and others as component parts of a cohesive whole – placing attainment of more self-indulgent aims necessarily equal and proportionate to our conscious efforts to serve others

⚜

fulfilled only by and through our relations with others?"

Trutorio continued on rhetorically, not so much seeking answers as setting an affirmative tone.

"And if so, is it not in our individual best interest to attend to the interests of any larger group to which we belong? Don't the needs of the community serve the needs of the individual? By protecting the interests of the whole, do we not in turn protect our own? Don't we by our sincere attempt to take care of others also take care of ourselves?"

Dutamis easily caught the point.

"Our outlook must recognize that responsibility to and for others is inexorably and inescapably linked to responsibility to and for self. Mutuality is the call!"

"Precisely!" exclaimed Trutorio.

"I believe we have effectively redefined self-interest – or at least detailed self-interest rightly understood," concluded the Prince. "This elevated perspective will become most critical to Maximus' success."

"And lest we think it some high and mighty principle or ethical ideal beyond the mental reach of the everyman," added Artenza, "let us remember these simple, yet relevant, illustrations to remind us of both how accessible and easy it is to incorporate the concept into almost every facet of our daily activities. As we have just seen, it does not require unreasonable or magnificent sacrifice. In fact, a simple and easily-recalled phrase serves to both capture the idea and offer a concrete guide."

Artenza paused for dramatic effect. "Give to get."

"Emphasis on the *give*," he continued.

"Wonderful!" cried the Prince. "This shall be our hue and cry! Giving engenders receiving, and vice versa – we get out of something that which we put into it…even more so!"

Both Trutorio and Dutamis joined the Prince in

Self-interest rightly understood is not a lofty concept – examples of giving engendering receiving are all around us embracing Artenza's mnemonic.

"A caution to all, however," warned Artenza. "It is the authenticity of intent and sincerity of motive with which we give that shall distinguish true contribution from manipulative technique."

"Hear, hear!" cried the others.

"In light of this discussion, I see at least two clear beneficial effects to Maximus and the Court accruing from encouraging and adopting this rather enlightened perspective," said Dutamis.

"To the first," he continued, "we prevent, or at least lessen, the likelihood of unbridled individualization of the harmful variety – overindulgence in selfish aims. To the second, the integration of self-interests with those of the larger system becomes a progressive self-perpetuating force – seeing our own desires more easily achieved through collective effort both increases the likelihood of our continuing to do so, as well as of convincing our fellows to follow suit. We effectively eliminate the harmful extremes – protecting private and public concerns while simultaneously limiting both egocentricity and martyrdom."

"Providing a practical system of checks and balances preventing take-all or lose-all states, thus helping to ensure our personal security as well as the stability of our Court and Province," concluded Artenza.

"Excellent observations!" approved the Prince. "If we are successful in splitting the polar states, we avoid the ills associated with both in a most artful and balanced manner."

"I believe this positions us well to advance to our next discussion," he continued. "Any final thoughts before we move on?"

"Only that Maximus shall always face the challenge of cynics," offered Dutamis, quietly, gravely. "There will forever be those who shall never abandon the

By integrating larger interests, we effectively eliminate the harmful extremes of both egotism and martyrdom

view that indulgent self-involvement is the only worthy motive; who shall never see that the interests of self and others inextricably converge; who shall never see that the life of one lends strength to and draws strength from the lives of others; who will never fully comprehend the network of mutuality that binds us all together; who shall never shed the dishonorable shade of selfishness that so consumes them; and, who shall never see the bleak boundaries between themselves and others dissolve to experience the profound fulfillment that comes not at the expense of others, but rather in the exaltation of them."

A solemn silence filled the Pantheon as the Prince and his Courtiers embraced this somber truth.

Strive to Serve

He who is not a good servant will not be a good master.

Plato

"We have completed our prologue," declared the Prince. "We are now to the heart of the practical matter – it is here our contributive cause becomes effectively manifest through our personal ethos of stewardship and service to those who both depend on us and upon whom we likewise depend."

"Our strengths demonstrably shared," added Trutorio.

"Our purpose evidently delivered," added Artenza.

"Our drive patently expressed," added Dutamis.

The Prince nodded in silent acknowledgement of the Courtiers' affirmations.

"What is the tenor of our territory?" queried the Prince, commencing the debate with the knowledge that each Courtier would represent a different perspective reflecting his respective intellect.

"It is one of consideration," replied Artenza. "Placing as our first priority the well-being of those in our charge."

"And of compassion," answered Trutorio. "Listening to understand what those in our charge require most from us and delivering upon it with the very best of our strength."

"And of commitment," added Dutamis. "Constancy to the duty owed in attending to the great needs of those in our charge."

"I would agree in sum," approved the Prince. "What of the action implications?"

"Exceeding all expectations," offered Artenza.

"Responding to requirements," offered Trutorio.

"Owning the obligation," offered Dutamis.

"Excellent!" praised the Prince. "And the underlying principles?"

"Responsiveness," said Artenza.

"Regard," said Trutorio.

"Responsibility," said Dutamis.

"Values that if not held high in some measure shall act to restrain our ability to serve well," affirmed the Prince. "What might be the ultimate outcomes we can expect to realize from successfully serving the needs of important others?"

"Admiration," replied Artenza.

"Appreciation," replied Trutorio.

"Allegiance," replied Dutamis.

"Yes!" cried the Prince. "A leader's legacy lit by these intangible, invaluable, immeasurable rewards – self-worth far exceeding net worth! Let us not forget the story of Croesus!"

"The richest king in the world," recalled Artenza.

"A ruler of great power and dominion who thought himself to be the happiest man in the world!" joined in Trutorio, smiling and remembering the fable.

"Vast riches beyond compare!" exclaimed Dutamis. "Castles, land and subjects – indeed the very finest of everything! Croesus could not think of anything that

True service to others involves constancy to the duty owed in attending to the great needs of those in our charge – placing as our first priority their well-being, listening to understand what they need from us, and delivering upon it with the very best of our strength

he needed to make himself more comfortable and contented. Still, he sought confirmation."

"It so happened that a great man was traveling through the land, the lawmaker Solon of Athens," said the Prince, taking a turn at the story. "He was known the world over for his wisdom, and centuries after his death, the highest praise that could be given to a learned man was to say *'He is as wise as Solon.'*"

"When he learned of Solon's proximity, Croesus invited him to his palace," retold Artenza. "Croesus was now happier and prouder than ever before, for the wisest man in the world was his guest. He led Solon through his estate and showed him the grandeur in all its glory – the grounds, the slaves, the magnificent rooms."

Artenza took to his feet to continue.

"As they dined together, the richest and wisest of men, Croesus asked Solon who he deemed to be the happiest of all men – expecting, of course, to hear his own name."

"But instead Solon told of a poor man by the name of Tellus," recounted Trutorio.

"Not quite the answer that Croesus wanted, obviously!" commented the Prince.

"But he hid his disappointment and challenged Solon for his reasoning," replied Trutorio.

Dutamis took his turn at the story.

"And Solon responded by saying that Tellus was an honest man who had labored hard for many years to bring up his children and to give them a good education. And when they were grown and able to do for themselves, he joined the army and gave his life bravely in the defense of his country. Solon then challenged Croesus to think of anyone more deserving of happiness!"

"Croesus almost choked!" recalled Artenza, chuckling.

"He was livid!" said the Prince, gleefully. "Croesus challenged the wise man angrily, accusing Solon of placing poor working people above the richest king and of disregarding wealth and power. Courtiers, do you recall the wisdom of Solon?"

Dutamis delivered the insight, employing his own interpretation and adding his own poetic embellishment.

"The true wealth of the world lies in people, and the only ones among us who shall know true happiness are those who have sought to serve our brethren. No man can say what misery may visit upon you and your splendor as the sun rises tomorrow – your wealth may wane, your castles may crumble, and your riches may recede; but the rousings in the hearts of those for whom one has sacrificed and soldiered are invaluable and invincible, and shall endure the test of time and tragedy."

"Indeed, Croesus eventually lost his entire empire to a marauding and murderous king," concluded Trutorio. "His life was spared only by passing on the wisdom of Solon to his attacker."

"The lesson is a compelling one," advised the Prince. "When we serve others well, we shall not escape life's highest compensation – to be regarded in perpetuity as one who has touched our hearts and minds. This, my friends, is the mark of a true leader. In every sincere attempt to hold others high and lighten their load, we lift ourselves to new levels – it is the most magnificent reward of our existence, is it not?"

The Courtiers murmured their agreement.

"Yet herein lies the gauntlet," cautioned the Prince. "Is it not this purely humanistic philosophy of people as the end and not the means that is so in need of development in most who would purport to wave the banner of leader?"

This thought gave the Courtiers pause. Then, one by one, each responded in turn to the Prince.

"Many are those who would seek to create order by command and compliance," agreed Dutamis. "Quite few are those so committed, as you are, to move and motivate their followers to obtain and own the grand vision and higher mission."

Our wealth may wane, our castles may crumble, and our riches may recede – but the rousings in the hearts of those for whom we have sacrificed and soldiered are invaluable and invincible, and shall endure the test of time and tragedy

"We cannot legislate emotional investment," replied the Prince.

"Many are those who would seek to achieve results by influence and incentive," agreed Artenza. "Quite few are those so competent, as you are, to include and imbue their followers with the power and passion to creatively engage and fully participate."

"We cannot purchase inspired performance," replied the Prince.

"Many are those who would seek to gain primacy by solicitation and sermon," agreed Trutorio. "Quite few are those so confident, as you are, to aid and abet their followers to reach and realize their individual aspirations and unique excellence."

"We cannot shepherd free choice," replied the Prince.

"I do believe you have single-handedly demolished the divine right of sovereign kings everywhere!" chuckled Artenza.

"A revolution for the ruling class!" smiled Dutamis.

"The legacy of your righteous reign shall be marked by partnership, not patriarchy or paternalism!" exclaimed Trutorio.

Then, and somewhat unexpectedly, the Prince took on a grave tone.

"In truth I have been tested and tempted in times of turmoil and turbulence to try these tyrannical tactics. But each of the means you mention carries with it injustice for someone, somewhere. Trusted Courtiers, I could not, and cannot, betray the simple yet defining belief in respect for others, that I hold to be so core – to *do no harm* – for it is this that lies at the very heart of the spirit to serve."

The Prince looked into the eyes of the Courtiers deeply and profoundly as he further revealed his thought.

"And, simple though it seems, this most critical issue is of central concern to me as it relates to Maximus. Without it, commitment to the Court, and to Maximus in his capacity as a governing leader, will fade. Let there be no confusion on this point, Courtiers! We cannot usurp a leader's power, it must be granted to us by those we serve, and a failure to serve is a failure to lead. I offer this as a universally moral absolute transcending the intrinsic personal values we spoke of earlier. No reason or rationalization exists for the unacceptable alternative – disrespect of any kind, evil in the extreme. There can be no compromise or equivocation – he must unerringly act at all times in the best interests of those who would follow him, no matter the predicament, situation, or circumstance. To do otherwise would only brand him a morally myopic misleader destined to shine only under a certain state of affairs."

The Prince raised his challenge even higher in a most serious tone.

"Only impact in this righteous vein – impact void of injustice of any kind – can qualify as truly absolute. Courtiers, can Maximus learn to become actively involved in the needs of those in his charge while maintaining the necessary progress and performance? Can he articulate, accept, and answer the call to serve?"

"I am confident that he can," answered Dutamis.

"I am confident that he can," answered Artenza.

"I am confident that he can," answered Trutorio.

"This gives me great comfort," said the Prince, calmed. "However, I am anxious to know the course of counsel by which you intend to advise him – for we can neither script his behavior nor style his leadership, as in truth that is an inherent injustice to his individuality. Seemingly helpful as it might seem to do so, it is cosmetic at best."

The Courtiers grew silent for a time. Dutamis was the first to speak.

"I believe I have a possible solution. It occurs to me that each Courtier here shall forthwith have the opportunity to revisit our own service ethic in a most relevant and challenging way. I refer, of course, to our ability to serve Maximus in the near future. Might we not take this time to explore the practical application of this large and lofty theorem to which we all subscribe, in the context of how we as Courtiers shall realistically respond to our own pending challenge of service?"

"And by doing so, design and develop a workable template for personal leadership tempered by a true spirit to serve," finished Trutorio. "Acknowledging and demonstrating that as we serve Maximus, so he serves

Only impact void of injustice may qualify as truly absolute, for at the heart of the service spirit lies a simple yet defining belief in respect for others – a universally moral absolute requiring us to unerringly act at all times in the best interests of those in our charge, to do no harm, no matter the circumstance; failing this, we fail to lead

us. I concur wholeheartedly!"

"Let us get to it!" urged Artenza. "Proceed!"

The Prince settled back to adopt a more observatory role, for he knew that the Courtiers must struggle to learn their way through this challenge on their own.

And so the Courtiers began their lively discourse on the practical path of service to others.

"While it is, of course, a given for our merry band," began Dutamis, "we must begin with the *belief* that service to Maximus and the Court is the highest of our priorities. I would reiterate and reinforce a point made earlier – the notion that such commitment can only come from alignment to contributive purpose."

⚜

Serving Others

✧ *Commit*

✧ *Comprehend*

✧ *Convey*

⚜

"A mindset that surely must be supported by a clear and full comprehension of what Maximus requires of us," added Trutorio. "This with full knowledge that as he depends upon us, so do we depend upon him."

"This followed by best efforts expended on attending to and faithfully delivering upon those needs as they support the Court's high purpose," concluded Artenza. "And, of course, do so in such an exemplary manner so as to exceed his expectations."

"*Commit, comprehend, convey* – an elegant and easy structure!" commented the Prince.

"Let us then expound upon each to determine our best approach," suggested Dutamis.

"Agreed!" said Trutorio.

"Avanté!" said Artenza.

"We begin by realizing the importance of service as we have outlined it thus far, from the recipient's point of view," began Dutamis. "I would propose that a primary differentiator of true service is that of creating value for those we are connected to."

"Define value," countered Artenza.

"In truth, I cannot," replied Dutamis. "It must be

defined by those we serve. However, in a most general way, it is the extent which our actions benefit them beyond any associated burden."

"So, in a tangible way, I – as Courtier – provide value to the extent I perform my duties to the satisfaction of Maximus and the Court?" clarified Artenza.

"Correct," replied Dutamis.

"My only objection would be that this seems to be a minimum standard focused merely on a simple fee for service transaction – a price of entry and no more," noted Trutorio.

"True, yet imperative nonetheless," replied Dutamis. "At this level, committing to serve is a commitment to dutifully and effectively perform our work. Failing this, we undermine ourselves, shortchange those we serve, and deprive the larger concern – relegating ourselves to become nothing more than an also-ran."

"But we are to travel beyond this simple dimension, correct?" challenged Artenza. "I fail to see this aspect as a true differentiator. Where is the real impact, the distinction as leader?"

Dutamis smiled knowingly, confident in his reply. "I would propose that it lies in the more intangible transfers – invisible aspects of our service that indeed move beyond the stated requirement to become a more prized principle of value to those with whom we are inexorably linked."

"Meaning?" asked Trutorio.

"Meaning – to use the present case – our ability to counsel and advise the Prince on matters beyond our descriptive charter or title. I refer to the collaborative partnership we engage in – exchanging ideas, sharing information and knowledge, participating in decisions, solving problems, improving each other's life in some way. Our present project stands as proof!"

"Artenza's counsel beyond the military, Trutorio's

A primary differentiator of true service to others is that of creating value for those we are connected to – bettering their lives through tangible and intangible transfers conducted in the course of our interactions

advice beyond the affairs of state, Dutamis' guidance beyond matters of homeland security," confirmed the Prince.

"Yes!" cried Dutamis. "These are the transformational dimensions of service, are they not?"

"Practically speaking," offered Artenza, "by helping those we serve to be more impactful in their life and work, we realize more impact in ours."

"Yes," agreed Trutorio. "And the path is one lit by humility and respect. Once we have proven that we can provide service reliably and dependably, we can rise to the level of valued steward, and thus a true leader."

"The measure of our leadership being not the number of our servants but in the value we provide to those *we* serve," remarked the Prince. "Superiors, subordinates, friends, family members, peers, partners, customers – all those whose needs we mean to meet."

"Precisely," concluded Dutamis.

"Check my understanding, if you will," said Trutorio. "The spirit to serve finds its source in a personal commitment requiring a fundamental belief that we collectively exist to create benefit for others through our interactions and connections – that some invisible web of value exists consisting of both tangible and intangible transfers – the ultimate goal of which is to move beyond arms-length transactions and processes to create collaborative partnerships with those with whom we are significantly linked."

"That is the proposition, yes, in much more elegant terms," confirmed Dutamis, smiling.

"That would lead us, then, to our first task in acting on this commitment – that of *comprehension* – to understand fully the wants, needs, and expectations of those we work with and provide services to," suggested Artenza. "We cannot hope to exceed the need if we have not attained such clarity."

By helping others to be more impactful in their work and life, we realize more impact in our own

"This requires taking an active role in discovering the interests of others we interact with, and what they expect or need from us in all daily interactions and activities," furthered Trutorio.

"We cannot diminish the critical nature of this rather difficult challenge," the Prince interjected. "Most fail the test of true service. They have little understanding of its depth, of what it demands."

"An ailment easily remedied if we are aware of how true value is created," replied Dutamis. "Perhaps one defining aspect to our understanding entails expanding our view beyond our immediate work function to discover how both our individual and group activities combine and interact to produce something of value."

"I concur," agreed Trutorio. "Relating our narrow area to the larger effort in this way breeds the realization that in order for us to add value – to ensure that others can indeed benefit from our strengths – we must endeavor to learn the full spectrum of views, aims, beliefs, demands, interests, expectations, principles, strengths and limitations of those with whom we interact."

"We must see the value of our thoughts, words, actions, and deeds through the eyes of our fellows," concluded Artenza. "In sum, we must understand our impact on others."

"Well put!" said the Prince.

"It occurs to me that the easiest, most practical path in this matter is to simply ask those we serve what they need from us," stated Dutamis.

"Agreed," said Trutorio. "And I believe we are safe in assuming most simply proceed blindly on a track of trial and error. In fact, I would go as far as to say that even the preliminary steps of clearly and correctly identifying all those within one's sphere of service go forsaken by most."

"Reliance being a key criterion," furthered Dutamis.

To add value and ensure that others can benefit from our gifts, we must endeavor to learn the full spectrum of views, aims, beliefs, demands, interests, expectations, principles, strengths and limitations of those with whom we interact – in sum, we must understand our impact on others

"Who depends upon us? Upon whom do we depend? Who is in receipt of the benefit we provide? From whom do we derive a benefit?"

"Knowing that Maximus falls easily within our charge, then," suggested Artenza, "our course must be to approach him directly in an effort to delineate the parameters of value as *he* defines it."

"Your counsel?" prompted the Prince.

"To Dutamis' point," replied Artenza, "I propose a simple open dialogue conducted in a frank query fashion with an intent to discover, to learn, and to see ourselves – our work – through the eyes of those with whom we exchange value."

"If I understand you correctly, and to use Maximus as our example, I shall interview him in the context of my present capacity and strengths," said Dutamis. "What do I owe him? What does he need most from me? What is the form most palatable? What is the time requirement?"

"Likewise," continued Trutorio, "what is it he values most from me? How does he view that which I have to offer?"

"Precisely," confirmed Artenza. "What are his goals? What is he trying to accomplish? What does he consider success? What results does he expect? How can I contribute most to his aims?"

"Powerful questions, which, when combined with your understanding of his gifts and cause, shall release the energy latent in the emerging relationships with him," commended the Prince. "This approach shows respect for the person – it captures the realization that others are unique individuals and may work quite differently from us. Most excellent."

"We shall know if we are successful in modeling service if Maximus in turn asks the same from us," noted Trutorio. *"What are the contributions for which the Court and I, Maximus, should hold you accountable? What should I expect from your Courtiership? What is the best utilization of your gifts? What are your priorities and powers?"*

"Indeed," replied the Prince. "And so begins a neverending dialogue centered on discovering, gauging, and truly serving each other's interests, serving the higher purpose."

"It seems like so much common sense!" cried Dutamis. "To understand how we can be of most impact is to find out how others work and what they need, to discover how those we serve can be most impactful."

"Yet quite rare in practice," counseled the Prince. "Not only for all of the conceptual reasons we debated earlier surrounding the issues of self-interest, but for those of execution as well."

The Prince continued his train of thought, delivering a short treatise on the practical difficulty of providing true service to others.

"For example, it is no easy feat to keep an open mind to the views of others – observing closely, listening actively and asking attentively to discover their dynamic and intangible requirements. It seems counterinstinctive to assume ever-shifting viewpoints, unique perceptions, and variable behaviors. It is as well difficult to completely avoid the assumption that others share our pattern of thought, feeling, behavior, or belief. It is likewise hard to eliminate the corresponding tendency to forecast the reaction of others in favor of a specifically tailored answer to an express request."

"As it applies to Maximus, then," concluded Trutorio, "we must collectively understand that predicting his reaction based on our own mindset and pattern of personal behavior can be costly, inaccurate, and thus wasteful – certainly the antithesis of adding value effectively and efficiently!"

"You have just touched upon our third value element – that of *conveyance*," noted Artenza. "We must focus our efforts on those activities that result in the most positive impact and greatest benefit delivered."

"It is here that our spirit to serve manifests itself in tangible ways to those we serve," observed Dutamis.

"Yes," replied Trutorio. "Our practices and processes – personally and collectively – must be centered on Maximus, and tailored to add the greatest value."

"It occurs to me some measure of our progress, our success in serving, may be in order," stated Artenza.

"Seek not the quantitative in this regard," advised Trutorio. "I submit that the continuous dialogue with

It is no easy feat to keep an open mind to the views of others, or to completely avoid the assumption that others share our pattern of thought, feeling, behavior, or belief

those we strive to serve is the best monitor – the most vital source of information we know of. Placing our trust in the value created in our personal connection to those we serve is the most powerful brand of accountability. And, let us not forget our self-dialogue – our constancy to our purpose, our commitment to cause."

"And to be quite concrete," offered Dutamis, "we must act on that conversation, routinely checking our actions and adapting our behaviors to eliminate anything that may burden our interactions, or that do not produce a clear benefit."

"Again, no easy feat," cautioned the Prince. "Yet if we fail to adapt as you suggest – through either inability or unwillingness – we shall fail to add value, and thus fail to serve. The outcome is easily projected in such a case. If unchanging in its form and delivery to meet the demand, that which we have to offer is quite simply rendered irrelevant. With the rise of either such obtuse obsolescence or impudent ignorance falls our excellence, our effectiveness, our efficiency – our impact! We shall be branded with the curse of mediocrity, regardless of past success."

"All things change, and we must change with them!" cried Artenza.

"And we confront once more the challenge of continuous learning and improvement," noted Trutorio, "only now in the external context of serving others, presently and in the future."

Artenza leapt to his feet.

"Courtiers! In our work we must replicate the river! Like the water, we must remain flexible in our methods, ever adjusting our work activities to maintain and maximize the optimal flow in responding to and surpassing the expectations of those whose needs we mean to meet!"

"Ever taking the required shape and form, as our strengths permit, to stream around barriers and obstacles in pursuit of our purpose, and of the common purpose!" cried Artenza.

"Ever improving our value in the eyes of those we seek to serve!" cried Dutamis.

The Prince stood beaming.

"Say no more, Courtiers. I now believe Maximus shall know what it means to seek service as a personal path to leading with impact."

The roundtable discussion turned now toward the issue of maximizing the impact of sharing one's strengths.

Foster Positive Feelings

Twice and thrice over, as they say, good is it to repeat and review what is good.

Plato

The Prince stood to take the floor, and turned to address the Courtiers.

"If you will permit me," he began, deferring to Trutorio, "I should like to usher us through a brief exercise by way of transition to our current theme – that of engendering a prevailing sense of positivity."

"By all means," replied Trutorio, confident that whatever the Prince had in store for them, it would epitomize experiential wisdom.

The Prince submitted his challenge succinctly.

"Courtiers, what is the point of pride?"

The Courtiers were momentarily baffled, addled by the Prince's seeming non sequitur.

The Prince smiled empathetically. "Bear with me, gentlemen, as the objective shall unfold in due course."

And with that, the Prince strode to the center of the Pantheon. He spread his arms wide as if to embrace the entirety of the space. He closed his eyes, lifted his face toward the rafters, and began again.

"Do you feel it?" he asked, beckoning them to accompany him.

Bewildered, the Courtiers looked to each other for direction, not knowing exactly what to do. Then, one by one, they joined the Prince in the heart of the hall.

"Behold once more our heroes of yesteryear," said the Prince, his eyes still closed. "Dive again below the pomp and pageantry. What do you see personified?"

"Cause," replied Trutorio.

"Conviction," replied Dutamis.

"Courage," replied Artenza.

"Deeper still," coaxed the Prince. "Of what purpose is our Pantheon – it's real value?"

"Homage," said Trutorio.

"Heritage," said Dutamis.

"Honor," said Artenza.

"Better," said the Prince, "but what lies beneath even these? What stirs your heart as you gaze upon our forebears? Close your eyes – can you hear their legacy to us? Can you feel it?"

And as they did, the Courtiers felt a swell of emotion deep within them rise up to lend the flush of strength.

"Gratitude!" whispered Dutamis.

"Hope!" whispered Trutorio.

"Joy!" whispered Artenza.

"Pride!" whispered the Prince.

The Prince and the Courtiers opened their eyes, each lifted by the experience, each feeling the fortitude to follow in the footsteps of their forefathers.

The Prince spoke quietly, forcefully.

"Throughout my life, in the darkest of hours, I have reaped the benefits of the elevated experience engendered by the simple act of standing on this august mark, grateful for, and drawing upon, the strength and virtue surrounding me – each time acquiring and adopting a more positive and optimistic outlook. In so doing, I have learned the art of appreciation as the path to pride, joy, gratitude, and hope. I believe Maximus can learn to do the same – for himself, and, most importantly, for others."

The Courtiers now realized the thrust and direction of the Prince's prompt.

"Positive emotions such as these are perhaps the most potent source of energy, effort and efficacy I know of," continued the Prince. "They like nothing else are capable of boosting our reserve, buoying our resilience, and bolstering our resolve in the face of challenge and adversity."

And, as if to prove the point, the Prince turned to Artenza to test his theory.

"Imagine the most desperate hours of a battle. Do you call forth honor or reason to summon a valiant charge?"

"Honor, easily," replied Artenza. "No tactic or stratagem can replace the motivational momentum of the heart inflamed!"

"And thus it is eminently worthwhile to explore this path as a means by which we can further share our strengths – for it takes enormous amounts of positive energy to create momentum for purposeful action," stated the Prince. "If we are successful in identifying the relevant sources of such a boundless force, might there not be cogent ways in which we can enliven these emotions in ourselves and others, with potentially far-reaching reciprocal and reverberating effects that may work to transform the Court, the Province, and ultimately advance the entire human element therein?"

"Cultivating positive sentiment is indeed the ground upon which we must tread," agreed Trutorio. "However, I do believe there exist certain precepts to this most human magic, and we must embrace them to ensure our success."

"We must decipher the code of such a positive approach," agreed Dutamis. "However, I do believe there exist certain barriers to this most complex dynamic, and we must address them to ply our application."

"Certainly this avenue is well aligned to our notion of moving from strength," added Artenza. "However, I do believe that certain actions are integral to this most dramatic course, and we must capitalize on them to maximize our impact."

"All true," agreed the Prince.

Turning once more back to Trutorio, the Prince asked: "What is your recommendation concerning how we should address these issues?"

"To properly frame the subject, I would like to first define the realm of positivity, and in so doing reiterate my original thesis on this point," replied Trutorio. "We can then proceed to debate the immediate concerns of my cohorts – those of potential restraints and tangible actions."

"Excellent," affirmed the Prince. "Carry on!"

"As I see it," began Trutorio, "positivity of the brand relevant to our project transcends a simple cheerfulness and sunny disposition to become more about consciously valuing and recognizing the best in others, in the world around us."

"From my vantage point," added Dutamis, "this approach moves from a purposeful affirmation and appreciation of past and present strengths and successes toward a concerted effort to realize and release the potential in people."

"To this I would add an openness to exploration, opportunity, and new possibility," offered Artenza. "This idea revolves around perceiving

Appreciation offers a path to engendering positive emotions – such as pride, hope, and joy – that provide a potent source of energy, effort, and efficacy

⚜

Taking an appreciative approach to sharing our strengths entails an active search for the very best in others, in life, and in the world around us

– actively searching for and finding – those things that garner the good life, such as vitality, passion and excellence."

"A comprehensive view," agreed the Prince. "But to further our understanding, what do you deem to be the spark and spur of such acquired optimism?"

"I submit that significant and personally meaningful events act as the stimulus," responded Trutorio.

"To be distinguished from whimsy, personal mood or preferred states of mind – all of which float free of any direction or objective," added Dutamis.

"Different still from a trait of personality, such as sanguinity – which is more of a natural predisposition and intrinsic characteristic," added Artenza.

"Good," affirmed the Prince. "And what then do you see as the tangible elements of impact in this domain?"

"To your earlier mention in this regard, I believe such good feelings effectively elevate our perspective," offered Trutorio. "We are incapable of processing two thoughts in our head simultaneously, certainly not conflicting ones. Therefore, if we are successful in perishing negative thought, which by both definition and necessity narrows one's perspective, and filling the void with positive thought, we open new routes of thinking and acting."

"When we're positive, our thinking is much more expansive, much more resourceful," said Dutamis, translating. "We open ourselves up to a wider range of possibilities and consider many more alternatives – unhindered are we by depressive and confusing thoughts that dumb us down and render us ineffective. Positivity of this sort effectively expands our potency!"

"From personal experience, I can say with confidence that my performance is enhanced when I'm feeling positive," said Artenza. "Greater is my urge to play, create, learn, relate, help, grow and achieve!"

"Our thoughts and actions are indeed reciprocally influential in cause and effect, as you all have rightly put it," said the Prince. "The power of thought, positive or negative, cannot be ignored. The dynamics are worth exploring further. Trutorio?"

Trutorio thought for a moment, then replied with a rhetorical question.

"To the positive interplay, who here has not witnessed a good deed and experienced the palpable tingle in the chest – lifting our spirits for a measurable span – and felt the urge to pay it forward in kind to others, resulting in an almost viral reverberation throughout the community?"

The others murmured their recognition. Trutorio continued his Socratic query.

"And who here has not been the actual recipient of even the smallest act of kindness and experienced the elation and gratitude – and felt the urge to repay the gesture in equal or greater scale, either directly or again, imparting it in kind to others?"

The others nodded in understanding.

Dutamis was smiling to himself. The Prince noticed.

"Dutamis?"

Dutamis looked up. "Oh, I was thinking of a lame boy, unable to walk, the crippled son of a washerwoman, who lives above the grocer I frequent daily on my way home. He is no more than a lad of eight, yet he is the very incarnation of your case."

The others were curious. "Yes?" they asked, eager to hear more.

"He waits all day at the window for his mother to come down the street laden with wash to be taken in. Pity for his plight, sad for his state? Not he! Instead, he waves and calls encouragement down to her: *'I would help you if I could, mother!'* And each time she cries, *'Oh, but you do! Your eager wave helps me, and your bright smile*

When we're positive, we elevate our experience and perspective – unhindered are we by depressive and confusing thoughts that dumb us down and render us ineffective

makes my very day!' Each time, he beams with pride, for she has given his life meaning. And that is not the end of it, friends."

"Go on!" they urged.

"Over time, the entire homebound crowd has become his minions. It began with one laborer, walking close to the mother, returning the boy's wave as well. Receiving the man's gesture, the boy returned it with great vigor, adding a cheery *'Good day, sir!'* On the following eve, it became two men. Then four, then eight, then many. Now, not a day goes by without the boy's familiar smile and wave to lift the lives of weary workers, including yours truly. Colleagues, people now go out of their way to receive and return his brave little wave, for it makes us all feel a bit braver! I'm told he receives small gifts – a card, an apple, a toy. Even children cease their bicker and banter in the street below when they see him, and perform tricks to make him laugh. It's as if we can't complete our day without him! He gives his gift of goodwill selflessly – his purpose is clear and compelling, and at such a tender age. By encouraging others, he encourages himself – by strengthening others, he strengthens himself. We can all learn from him; I count him as a leader of the first order!"

All were warmed by Dutamis' touching story.

"And so it goes," concluded Trutorio. "Grand accomplishments are all well and good, but it is these small and nameless acts of kindness that flow between people, spreading through humanity like so many tiny trickles of water which, if given time, will constitute the better portion of a good life. Such positivity is contagious – we see the world with new eyes, newfound spirit and open minds. Our hopes for the future and faith in humanity are restored, our mental barriers broken down. As Dutamis' story illustrates, this ascending spiral of increasing reciprocity has the potential to raise the personal and collective experience to new heights – and one soul *can* make the difference, ever more so if it commences with the established leader. Such is the case before us all, and certainly before Maximus."

Trutorio paused before levying a caution.

"By the very same token, and to the Prince's earlier point, witnessing or experiencing a bad event can be potentially devastating – equally as powerful in creating a descending spin of negative and narrow thought, eventually working to depress the personal and collective experience to the depths of dysfunction."

It took some time for the others to process Trutorio's treatise.

"This undeniably begs the questions and concerns posed earlier by Dutamis and Artenza," said the Prince.

"Identifying and recognizing the potential restraints," recapped Dutamis.

"Acquiring the skills required to create and maintain a positive posture," reiterated Artenza.

"To the former, what say you?" asked the Prince, turning to Dutamis.

Dutamis took a breath, and began.

"By way of illustration only, you must permit me to temporarily adopt the mind and manner of that which I am about to decry – for it shall be the antithesis of positivity. I have touched lightly upon this theme before, and in sum it is this: condemnation is the mortal enemy of appreciation – it can crush confidence and extinguish esteem.

"We have so much working against us, associates – and we live in a most cynical and critical age! The town crier speaks only the bad news; we find fault in others all too readily; we eagerly place blame and point fingers; we more often than not jump to a doomsday view of bad events and all too easily consider good events freakish occurrences; we gainfully employ critics whose detractive thinking screams out from behind a bitter ink, unable to see the forest for the trees; we abound with naysayers whose mindless prattle does little more than subtract from the grand sum of all human knowledge; credit where credit is due is in disturbingly low supply; censors abound to limit our creativity and stifle our imagination; the vast majority of people look for, and delight in, failures of others as a false means of validating their own carriage; most would more easily tear another down to fraudulently lift themselves up; most in fact die a little death of envy in full view of another's success;

One person __can__ make a difference – a simple act of kindness can spark an ascending spiral of increasing reciprocity that has the potential to raise the personal and collective experience to new heights

our systems all focus on weakness; our society plays to the lowest common denominator; few actively look for the good in others, impotent are they to move beyond their petty self-interest. Such comprehensive condescension does our heart no credit – in it we become monumentally little. Our unwitting pursuit of the nadir has unilaterally all but destroyed our confidence in things gone right – in short, my friends, we have lost our endowed and singularly human ability to appreciate through an inadvertent lack of attention and practice! Shame on us!!"

The others sat wide-eyed at Dutamis' vituperation.

"I've been saving that," he smiled, winking to all.

"And the antidote?" asked the Prince, solemnly, after a time.

"Appreciative acts, by two counts," replied Dutamis, matter-of-factly. "First, learn to appreciate what we have, rather than what we have not. Second, learn to appreciate others, and they will pass it on."

"This is the heart of it," stated Trutorio. "To achieve the acme of impact in sharing our strengths, we must understand that we cannot fail in learning to recognize the best in others, to see and honor others for what they are – pure potential."

"I concur," remarked Artenza. "Appreciation is undeniably a universal need – none can thrive without it. While the realization of our true work well done brings great satisfaction, I know of no one who cares not for their personal esteem to be recognized – to have their abilities, achievements, and contributions be appreciated, especially by those they look up to, those they deem leaders."

"Truer wisdom does not exist," said the Prince. "How then shall we put this appreciative principle into play?"

"It seems reasonable to break the broad concept of

Appreciation is an undeniably universal need – therefore to achieve the acme of impact in sharing our strengths, we cannot fail in learning to recognize and acknowledge the best in others

appreciation down into more accessible actions," replied Artenza.

"Your thoughts?" furthered the Prince.

"I see three essential elements to appreciation," replied Artenza. "The first being that of *acceptance*."

"And by acceptance I assume you mean honoring the differences in others?" queried Trutorio.

"In principle, yes," replied Artenza. "To openly embrace, include, and value those whose identities have evolved in ways fundamentally different from our own – welcoming their contributions and recognizing that our differences both distinguish us and connect us to others, and that real power lies in diversity of thought. In practice, it is the demonstration of respect for, and ability to fully leverage, the whole of the uniqueness in the individual – to draw upon and openly include those whose gifts, experiences, and behaviors may be different from our own."

"Viewing differences as strengths to be capitalized upon, not limitations to exclude or repair," added Dutamis. "This goes for ourselves as well, I would think – to accept what we have been given as gifts is always a challenge, as we discussed earlier."

"Absolutely," confirmed Artenza.

"As a most practical matter," interjected the Prince, "this ability to successfully leverage diversity and build inclusion shall become ever more important to the future of the Court. Our Province is growing increasingly eclectic and expansive, requiring a regime whose cabinet reflects the diversity of its constituency and is thus more likely to understand and serve the wide and varied needs of the population."

"I certainly see the link to creating a pathway to positivity," noted Trutorio. "If we can effect a safe haven in which all people are valued and able to bring their full selves to their work, we increase the available pool of skills, ideas, perspectives, and experiences. The benefits are many! People are more approachable; communication is improved and increased; the environment is more open to sharing; voices are heard and a greater sense of meaning prevails – all positives!"

"Which brings us to the second element as I see it," said Artenza. "That of *affirmation*."

"And by affirmation I assume you mean discovering, creating, and instilling a sense of efficacy in others?" asked Trutorio.

"In principle, yes," replied Artenza. "I refer now to the power of positive expectation. I have personally experienced this rather miraculous effect with the development of my officers and troops alike – when I treat people as if they were all of what I perceive they can become, they in fact grow into what they are capable of being. I have witnessed not only higher performance, but also profoundly changed conceptions of self – the course of a life transformed! A positive expectation engendered by an appreciative eye tends to act as a self-fulfilling prophecy."

"How so?" asked Dutamis.

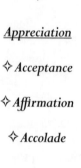

Appreciation

✧ *Acceptance*

✧ *Affirmation*

✧ *Accolade*

"We tend to act in response to an expectation, be it positive or negative," replied Artenza. "Expectation influences behavior, and thus increases the likelihood of results in kind."

"Never forget that we are products of intellect and imagination," offered Trutorio. "We are fundamentally adaptive to the mental projections of those who impact us – our humanness gives us a tremendous capacity to grow, change, and develop."

"As a practical matter, then," continued Dutamis, "if I have a positive image of someone, I look for the good within them, I perceive the best in them, and they in turn respond and live up to the positive image I project of them?"

"Precisely," replied Artenza. "And as we become more attuned to the past triumphs and present successes of the individual, we in turn develop an affirmative capacity to recognize and respond to the positive."

Dutamis looked unsure.

"If I repeatedly tell a talented soldier that I expect he will rise to the rank of commander, that he is made of the stuff of generals, he will prove me right one day," explained Artenza.

"Now I understand," smiled Dutamis. "And what of

the final element?"

"It is that of *accolade*," replied Artenza.

"And by accolade I assume you mean recognizing and rewarding the positive contributions of others?" asked Trutorio.

"Exactly," replied Artenza. "I am convinced that it is incumbent upon us as good people to openly express our appreciation, for it is a prime motivational force. Further, I would submit that great achievement requires great appreciation – the greater the achievement, the greater the thirst for appreciation. To wit, my best lieutenants require more of my attention than do my worst soldiers – counterinstinctive as that seems, and much to the consternation of many a would-be leader. Any failure on my part to rightfully recognize key members of my team – and to do so in a manner precisely befitting the individual and proportional to the scope and scale of the accomplishment – has yielded only adverse effects in performance, commitment, and engagement."

"Yet we cannot limit the practice to special efforts," joined Trutorio. "The real power of one's virtue resides in their ordinary and obligatory doings – for which simple and constant expressions of gratitude suffice to work wonders."

"Still, few are those of a mind to remember a *thank you* above and beyond monetary compensation to those in their charge," said Dutamis. "I must admit that I must constantly remind myself to do so."

"A point well worth examining, Dutamis," noted the Prince. "Extolling others does not come quite so easily for Philosophers and Guardians as it does for the more naturally optimistic intellects of Artisans and Diplomats, as I am sure our colleagues will confirm."

"Speaking for myself, my difficulty stems from my inherent reluctance to state what seems – albeit only to me – quite obvious. My natural instinct would be to

Acceptance is defined as honoring the differences of others

⚜

Affirmation is defined as instilling a sense of efficacy in others

⚜

Accolade is defined as recognizing and rewarding the positive contributions of others

rationalize along the line of reasoning that if a task is well done, it is clear to everyone – and expressing the obvious would seem manipulative. This, however, is merely a faulty projection of my own mindset onto others – in fact it is *not* as apparent to others – and I have learned the importance of rewarding and recognizing, and have become practiced at doing so both publicly and privately, in accordance to the wishes of the individual."

"And because I, on the other hand, operate from a sense of obligation and ethic of hard work," admitted Dutamis, "I tend to unconsciously limit praise to only those I believe to be the most earnest and responsible, unwitting am I in the belief that credit undue demoralizes. In fact, we know the opposite to be true. In my defense, I do have an easier time of it when I perceive another to have gone above and beyond the call of duty. Again, it is the natural tendency to view the world through our own lens without considering the differences of others!"

"I must admit I find it easy to give high praise," said Artenza. "Perhaps because it is in my nature, I have more easily and effortlessly employed the art of accolade, and thus have had more opportunity to see and experience the tangible payoff. In truth, my challenge is in the other extreme – too *much* appreciation, when such has not been earned. In fact, I've been known to offer accolade before accomplishment, in my haste to spur greater effort!"

"I also find little trouble in placing high value on communicating appreciation, as we know," commented Trutorio. "I naturally empathize and encourage in abundance. I would add a bit of insight here to say that our previously discussed element of acceptance plays a critical role in the art of proper accolade. In general we tend to more easily appreciate those we perceive to be like us in thought and deed, and thus praise them more if we are not careful – hence the importance in learning to recognize and honor differences."

Trutorio paused as if to have a second thought, then continued.

"I am happy to share with Maximus my best practice in this regard: on balance, appreciate more often than not, and be as specific to the individual as possible. This will require him to become an avid listener and observer of people, even if he is not predisposed to do so. What are their strengths? What matters most to them? What is their specific preference as regards recognition? The Prince is a master at this – and all three elements of appreciation – in spite of his declinations. Do you recall how he greeted us this evening upon our arrival? A compliment to each, and to each a specific compliment. Did this not spark our energy and effort? Do you recall how he expressed his confidence in our ability to deliver this very project? And so we shall, regardless of difficulty, complexity, and utter inexperience in ever executing one like it! Do you recall how he deftly facilitated the discussion of our own talents? We were quite detailed in our panegyrics of each other's gifts. All in the name of appreciation, friends – acceptance, affirmation, and accolade!"

"Excellent advice," commended the Prince, smiling, delighting in his Courtiers' collective effort.

"And," he added, "this is an equally excellent point at which to transition to our fifth and final stratagem in learning to share our strengths."

Render Trustful Relationships

Whenever, therefore, people are deceived and form opinions wide of the truth, it is clear that the error has slid into their minds through the medium of certain resemblances to that truth.

Plato

Trutorio launched the new topic without further ado by voicing a concern.

"As I warned in my preamble, we must summon every iota of our best thinking in tackling the challenge of constructing enduring trust in our connections with those we strive to serve. If Maximus is viewed as untrustworthy, the Court shall fail in the future. While our previously detailed approaches – commitment to values, clarity of cause, balanced self interest, service to others, and demonstration of appreciation – all work in great measure to establish trust, we must go yet one step further to delineate focused personal action targeted to indemnify that foundation, for mistrust to any degree shall work to undermine our efforts."

"I share your concern," commented the Prince. "Without the highest levels of trust in our relationships, our impact will not be absolute – we shall swing wide of the cooperation and collaboration that drives both greater unity and higher performance, at the heart of which is

*We greatly
underestimate
the importance
of trustful
relationships
in our work;
yet without
trust, our
impact cannot
be absolute
– we are
rendered
ineffective and
powerless,
unable to
capitalize
on the
cooperation
and
collaboration
that drives
both greater
unity and
higher
performance*

some central working relationship. I am certain we underestimate the importance of trustful relationships in our efforts to advance. Trust is the lodestar of the leader, and mistrust the mark of the misleader!"

"Without trustful relationships," furthered Dutamis, "we are rendered ineffective – our productivity wanes, our creativity ebbs, and we simply cannot perform or complete our work efficiently. Our commitments become meaningless."

"Without trustful relationships," added Artenza, "we are rendered powerless – we retreat from the world, afraid of all. Apathy, suspicion, and fear rule the day. Our actions are viewed as designed to hurt, our motives deceitful – even our most sincere and helpful behavior becomes circumspect."

"Where would our Court and cabinet be now without trust between us?" asked the Prince. "Where would *I* be? I would have no use for Courtiers, for seeking advice would be foolish in such circumstances! Short of trusting each other, we would cooperate only under legislative edict – laboring under some system of rigid policies and procedures mandating constant vigil, engendering compromise and evoking enforcement. What an enormous loss in energy earmarked for truly impactful work!"

The Courtiers shook their heads sadly in solemn recognition that much of the world over toiled under the very conditions the Prince had described.

"Our greatest personal capital lies not in our physical chattel," observed Trutorio, "but rather in the aggregate value of our most important relationships – connective interpersonal assets for which the truest measure can only be trust. It is through this vital plexus of social dynamics and cooperative interplays that we perform our work. And so it is that trust shall have a great hand in determining the final calibre of our triumph."

"High trust, high performance," noted Artenza.

"Great trust, great unity," concluded Dutamis.

"And the reasons would seem clear enough," said Trutorio. "When we trust and understand each other, information and knowledge is in open abundance – our communication flows freely, honestly, accurately, and purposefully."

"I must say that I am more than a little intrigued by your characterization of connectivity as capital," said the Prince. "To continue this simile, might we go so far as to say that such capital would – like any wealth-creating asset – require continuous personal investment to grow in value?"

"And require constant protection and preservation as well?" asked Dutamis.

"And require leverage to advance and accumulate more of the same?" asked Artenza.

"Indeed, one and all, and that is the work before us now – if trust is the measure of worth in our relationships, we must learn the skills needed to build it," said Trutorio.

And so Trutorio accelerated the discussion.

"I believe we all agree on the critical importance of trustful relationships. I propose that we advance our project by first defining with some specificity what we mean by trust, for I am certain even the most learned of our doctrinaires simply assume that the definition is clear to all. I respectfully disagree."

"This to be followed by exploring the key dynamics and critical dimensions of trust," added Dutamis.

"And concluding with clear steps to take in building and balancing these components," finished Artenza.

"A proven course well worth repeating!" agreed the Prince.

"We must reject the traditional tendency to speak in concept only on this topic," warned Artenza. "Eye-level action is the call."

Our greatest personal capital lies in the aggregate value of our most important relationships – connective interpersonal assets for which the truest measure is trust – it is through this vital plexus of social dynamics and cooperative interplays that we perform our work

"Too, we must reach well beyond the prevailing conventional approach centering on social skills in this matter," cautioned Dutamis. "Deeper relating founded on responsibility and accountability is the call."

"I agree, on both counts," said Trutorio, pausing, thinking.

"To begin with, then, I submit that trust in the relevant context is something short of pure faith," he continued.

"Such faith would imply a blind belief that flies in the face of credible evidence to the contrary," concurred Dutamis.

"And is thus a brand of conviction largely beyond reason," added the Prince. "The devoutly faithful easily rationalize inconsistency and justify discrepancy."

"Fanatics need neither rhyme nor reason – nothing can shake or shatter their adamancy," agreed Artenza. "I see trust as something more delicate, more easily withdrawn – and thus more complex."

"To your point," noted Trutorio, "it is as well more complex than, say, confidence."

"The latter being that brand of conviction based purely on logic, experience, or fact," noted the Prince. "Trust lies somewhere between the two."

"Part belief, part reason," said Dutamis, summing up. "Might we be safe in saying that trust finds its source in our belief that those upon whom we rely will realistically fulfill our positive expectations of them?" suggested Trutorio.

"Excellent!" commended the Prince. "This definition is well aligned to both our context and content, and provides the necessary transition upon which we can move our discussion forward to address the mechanics of trust."

The Prince then began to discuss the complicated workings of trust in relationships.

Trust finds it source in the belief that those upon whom we rely will realistically fulfill our positive expectations of them

"In a broader sense," he began, "a trustful relationship is one based on the assumption and assessment of the other's credibility and capability to advance the common purpose and greatest good. More specifically, we place trust in those we have come to believe will act in our best interest, who demonstratively share their strengths to our highest benefit. The essential requirement, then, in the creation of a trustful relationship is indeed territory we have already traveled well – that is, understanding both manifest and implicit needs, expectations, and interests of those we are connected to, and delivering upon them to the best of our ability."

"And because trust is in part based on such a positive belief," added Artenza, "we trust those who see the best in us, and in whom we in turn see the good – thus the exchange of trust becomes yet another self-fulfilling prophecy."

"As others place their trust in us, we behave in a manner consistent with becoming more worthy of that trust," clarified Dutamis. "As we place our trust in others, they become more trustworthy."

"I would tend to agree – certainly this is the ideal. But the need for trust is borne only out of our vulnerability, is it not?" asked the Prince. "We expose ourselves when we place our trust, thus we go on a heightened alert for behavior we deem trustworthy – signs that work to confirm our decision. I would urge that we examine the issues involved in the management of this hazard, for it will shape our approach."

"If there is no risk of harm, trust is of no matter," restated Trutorio. "Each of us determines on an individual basis how much trust we wish to grant another at any given time. For example, most tend to offer only limited trust on a trial basis in forming new relationships. As the affiliation develops, the amount of exposure we are willing to accept grows to the extent our expectations continue to be met. Disappointment leads us to reduce our risk, to limit our susceptibility."

Trutorio had a second thought.

"But as it concerns human behavior and interaction, zero risk can never be! We have said that we are all connected, that our interests merge, that our actions have cause and effect, that we cannot avoid impacting others, that we can only help or harm – we depend and rely on others, therefore we cannot avoid risk."

"Enter the need for trust!" exclaimed Dutamis. "Individuals are unique in their interests and abilities, and we can no more guarantee the actions of another than we can foretell the future with any degree of certainty. Trust shall always be a factor in our work and life – trust in self, trust in others – for without it, we cannot grow, change, and develop. We cannot effectively learn!"

"Hail the irony!" cried Artenza. "Once more into the puzzle of paradox, dear friends! Trust and risk give rise to one another – they do not exist apart. We have engaged a parallel concept in the context of governing our gifts. Recall our discussion concerning leaning into limits, the gist of which concerned placing trust in our own abilities to hazard intelligent challenges outside our zone of certainty in order to grow and build our strength. The same dynamic holds for our relationships – trust cannot grow unless we place ourselves in a position that puts our current level of trust at some peril!"

"How ever shall we gauge the degree of trust within a relationship if we have not put it to the test?" asked Trutorio. "How are we to ever determine whether we are right in trusting another unless we risk letdown? Likewise, how shall others determine whether we can be trusted unless they risk placing their trust in us? In short, how do we determine whether trust is warranted?"

"It is one of life's conundrums – and your questions frame the issues quite nicely," stated the Prince. "We all have a variable setpoint of trust more easily lowered than raised. It is simply in our nature. This then, is our challenge at hand – learning to manage the tier of tolerance, developing the level of trust others have in us, and in so doing realize the determinants of trust that enable us to place our trust in others."

"I am quite curious to know more about this setpoint of which you speak," said Dutamis.

"Certainly," replied the Prince. "It is not unlike our pain threshold. You see, we each perceive discomfort

Trust will always be a factor in our work and life – trust in self, trust in others – for without it, we cannot grow, change, and develop

differently, with varying degrees of tolerance for different kinds of distress, and pain becoming apparent when our discomfort reaches a point of zero tolerance. It is at this point that a threshold is established, and we take care to avoid it in the future. Trust, in concept, works much the same way. We each have a limit of trust that we are willing to risk, and once breached, we withdraw that trust, sometimes permanently."

The Prince allowed the metaphor to sink in.

"Now," he continued, "imagine a continuum with mistrust to one extreme, and high trust to the other. The degree to which we trust another floats in dynamic fashion along the scale, varying from situation to situation, relationship to relationship. The trust I place in each of you, my Courtiers, differs from the trust I place in my physician, my acquaintances, my family – because the nature of reliance and dependence in each relationship varies."

"This variance adds many layers of difficulty and complexity to our challenge," observed Dutamis. "In addition to our own natural tendency to trust – unique for each individual – we must consider the connection and circumstance."

"Yes," replied the Prince. "Hence Trutorio's concern. We can neither design trust nor demand it from others any more than we can declare ourselves trustworthy; in fact, we may engender skepticism and suspicion if we so much as attempt such tactics. But across the Rubicon lies a solution elegant in its simplicity, perhaps more difficult in execution."

The Courtiers awaited the Prince's sagacity.

"Our strategy is twofold," he continued. "First, give compelling reasons for others to trust us. Second, give no reasons for mistrust."

The Courtiers knew full well what was to follow.

"Now then," smiled the Prince. "In addition to the

We can neither design trust nor demand it from others any more than we can declare ourselves trustworthy – we must therefore model trust-worthiness while extending trust ourselves, at the same time extinguishing immediately any chance mistrust is given to prosper

admittedly comprehensive strategies presented heretofore – how might we provide the requisite surety?"

"We must model trustworthiness while simultaneously extending our own trust," replied Trutorio. "At the same time, we must extinguish immediately any chance mistrust is given to prosper – banish all instances of perfidy."

"Again, how?" parried the Prince.

Before the Courtiers could utter a reply, the Prince echoed the earlier warnings of Dutamis and Artenza.

"Beware the weary platitudes that in effect amount to no more than *Play nice!* – to be trusted we need neither to be liked nor agreed with. Take heed the obvious clichés perched high atop lofty aphorisms bespeaking the generalized precepts of probity! *Honesty* and *integrity* are all too easily voiced, all too eagerly demanded, all too rarely practiced. We need deeper specificity upon which to act!"

This gave the Courtiers great pause, and they were cautious in their reply.

"Given that the alchemy of trust is unique to the individual," began Trutorio slowly, "and given that an assessment based on a perception of one's personal timber is involved…might we not use our knowledge of the four intellectual patterns discussed earlier – and represented well within this very circle – to arrive at the intrinsic imperatives involved in trust at any level, leaving it to the individual to decipher and decode the rather nebulous factorial equation given their unique situation and connection?"

"Once we are clear in the components," added Artenza, "we are free to deploy them in an adaptive and responsive fashion in such a manner as to enable trust to blossom and flourish."

"This with full awareness that no two relationships or situations will be identical," added Dutamis, "and it becomes the responsibility of those involved to seek full knowledge and understanding of each other."

The Courtiers looked to the Prince, who was smiling and chuckling, marveling at their insightful approach with an affirmative nod.

"It remains only for one to begin," said the Prince. "Perhaps it would facilitate our discussion if we couch our commentary in terms of what most influences each of us in the exchange of trust. It is a simple matter then to derive and project enabling action."

Dutamis rose first.

"To my mind, *consistency* is the mandate," he began. "I place my trust in consistency, first and foremost. This is the primary path to the moral high ground of integrity, and I see it as a coherent and manifest alignment of thought, word, and deed. If one thinks one thing, says another, and acts to belie one or both, there can be no trust. Consistency is a matter of consciously avoiding contradictory and, in the extreme, hypocritical behavior – conduct that can give the impression that one's selfish interest is the primary concern. Protracted incongruence erodes trust, for it is not predictable, dependable, or reliable. Inconsistency creates doubt in my mind about someone's real motives, tells me they are either not truthful or not willing and able to meet their obligation to me – clear signals not to trust. Quite simply, it is a clear and repetitive demonstration of keeping one's sincere word – over time and across a myriad of situations – that shall act to gain and sustain my trust significantly."

"We certainly cannot trust those we cannot count on," agreed Trutorio. "Inconsistency drives me wary as well. For example, I become suspect of those who do not divulge appropriately the full extent of their knowledge of things that may have direct impact on or be of high importance to me. Such selective information sharing – whether outright lie, subtle manipulation, or obvious omission – is a form of deliberate deception and clear inconsistency of word and deed."

"Certainly we cannot trust those who disclose the same message differently to different audiences in different settings, especially if the information is in any way contradictory," agreed Artenza. "We must also note that while one's beliefs and principles may understandably evolve over time, erratic behavior, frequent sudden departures, and abrupt dramatic

Trust requires consistency – honoring commitments, facing reality, and revealing motives – for we cannot trust those we cannot count on

shifts in position will serve to destroy credibility, if unexpected and unexplained."

Artenza had a new thought.

"Consistency is indeed imperative," he noted. "But at the risk of reiterating, let us not forget the positive characteristic of trust. To wit, one who consistently disappoints us cannot be trusted. Too, when inconsistency exists, shouldn't we seek to understand the cause?"

"Good point," replied Dutamis. "It bears repeating that trust depends upon the situation and relationship. For example, a true confidante's simple mistake easily explained and prevented in the future may not warrant mistrust, for it is likely to be an anomaly. However, in a newly formed affiliation, such early inconsistency is reasonable grounds for doubt."

"Worthy counsel, one and all," commented the Prince. "What then shall be our suggested practices?"

"Honoring commitment," suggested Dutamis. "It is a matter of holding oneself responsible and accountable for following through on promises made – employing the entirety of our strength, if need be, to deliver upon the expectation to the extent it is within our control."

"Facing reality," suggested Artenza. "Openly confront difficult issues head-on with constant massive direct communication informing others of where we – and they – truly stand in relation to the common prevailing expectation and current situation."

"Revealing motive," suggested Trutorio. "Manage any tensions and conflicting interests by abandoning political posturing and manipulative protectorates in favor of transparent, open agendas that support the values and best interests of all connected to the situation."

"Eminently and elegantly practical!" praised the Prince. "As I listen to your discussion, though, it becomes apparent that while it is clearly a critical factor, consistency alone is not enough to maintain trust at every level."

"I concur, as I place my trust in *competence*, first and foremost," agreed Artenza. "We have already discussed the compulsory nature of competence from the perspective of mandatory knowledge and skills to be acquired on the path to mastery. While I shall not belabor the point, I should like to revisit the notion in the context of our present discussion as it pertains to the development of trust, for I see competence as the primary path to achieving the positive outcomes and results expected of us. If one does not have the capability to accomplish what is expected, there can be no trust. It is a matter of rendering a commitment based on a realistic assessment and communication of one's ability in relation to the need, priority, or objective. Incompetence – which I define as long on promise and short on delivery – erodes trust, for it undermines credibility. This is the most concrete aspect of trust, and perhaps the most unforgiving. Consequences cannot be argued or denied – no results, no trust!"

"We certainly cannot trust those who cannot get the job done," agreed Trutorio. "Character aside, we trust only those we believe to possess the capacity – meaning experience, effectiveness, and expertise – to produce the desired outcome or stated intent. Doubt in one's ability undermines trust to a significant degree."

"But to Artenza's point," commented Dutamis, "if we are successfully governing our gifts, incompetence is not an issue."

"True enough," stated the Prince. "However, as it concerns constructing the impression of confident credibility in the eyes of those from whom we seek trust, are there not some proactive measures we can exact in an effort to bolster that belief?"

"We can demonstrate confidence," offered Artenza. "Confidence in our own power to perform instills confidence in others. This might easily take the form of sharing appropriate information on our successes and failures, providing an accurate picture of our ability to meet the demands of the relationship and situation."

"Taking care, of course, to avoid overstatement," added Dutamis. "Being forthright in communicating our perceived limits, given the challenge at hand, enables another to gauge the amount of risk they might be willing to accept. When we are knowingly

Trust requires competence– demonstrating confidence, avoiding over- promising, and accurately assesing ourselves – for we cannot trust those who cannot get the job done

out of our depth, we must show a respectful deference to those whose strengths better serve the situation to avoid interfering with the work of others, and to facilitate higher performance."

"This requires accurate self-assessment," added Trutorio, "which in turn demands constant feedback. We have touched on this before, but finding out how others see us is especially vital to our efforts to render trustful relationships. When we learn to encourage and receive honest feedback on our performance, deeper learning is enabled, allowing us to make timely corrections and improve our work – higher competency realized, higher trust enabled!"

Trust requires caring – exhibiting sincere concern for others – for we cannot trust those we believe don't care

"Maximus will indeed face this very challenge from the start," noted the Prince. "Since he is untested and unknown, establishing his credibility will most likely begin in this very arena. As Dutamis has correctly made clear, his effectiveness in governing his gifts shall play the integral role in this endeavor."

The Prince looked to Trutorio with a nod, signaling him to move forward.

"I would like to add a third component to the equation – that of *caring* – for it is this that I trust first and foremost," said Trutorio. "This is perhaps the softer side to trust, yet perhaps the most difficult. Certainly we have touched upon a number of ideas implicit in this theme; however, the complexity enters the picture by way of demonstrating our sincere concern for others in the face of mounting daily pressures and accelerating intensity of forces beyond our control. Simply put, we cannot trust those we believe don't care about us."

"This is certainly the most immediate gauge of one's trustworthiness," noted Dutamis, "Consistency and competency require the test of time, but the behaviors demonstrated in but a single fleeting interaction can herald future expectations, and thus set initial levels of trust."

"Yes," replied Trutorio. "And as we are challenged by the Prince for further everyday action, I believe we can go a bit further in detailing the very behaviors that can significantly impact one's trust threshold."

"As I see it, we need only enact the polar opposites of any of a vast array of the most common self-defeating behaviors," remarked Artenza. "For example, confidentiality over rumoring, candor over deception, action over apathy, empathy over insensitivity, humility over arrogance, sincerity over sarcasm, cooperation over defiance."

The others registered their say.

"Objectivity over ambiguity," added Dutamis. "Collaboration over positioning, accuracy over hyperbole, balance over excess, sacrifice over selfishness, fairness over favoritism, encouragement over hazing, reserve over anger."

"Understanding over ignorance," put in Trutorio. "Self-disclosure over maneuvering, tolerance over prejudice, alliance over antagonizing, harmony over discord, listening over preoccupation, deference over ego, sympathy over revenge, esteem over envy, generosity over greed, détente over retaliation."

"And so the list goes on," interjected the Prince. "You of course realize that we have made an implicit assumption in all of this?"

The Courtiers looked to the Prince, awaiting his thought. Before he could continue, Dutamis spoke up.

"Community!" he cried. "As our Province expands and populates, are we not in danger of losing the close contact that trust demands? As our ranks multiply, do we not risk the togetherness that engenders and emboldens trust? Can we effectively trust those we don't know?"

"Exactly," affirmed the Prince. "If we are not careful to protect and preserve the proximity that maintains our interconnectedness, our entire collaborative capital is at risk. The very advancement we seek can deny us the trust required for absolute impact – the uncontrollable march of progress brings with it volatile forces of new technologies and the threat of depersonalization. We cannot succumb! Maximus must never lay to waste the high touch needed in his efforts to build trust and commitment to the Court!"

"Some things must never change!" cried the Courtiers.

"There is but a final note to consider before I believe we can close out the discussion of sharing our strengths," announced the Prince. "It concerns the composition of trust as we have outlined it. If consistency, competence, and caring are all required for the construction of trust, and for regaining trust when we have lost it, how do our identified elements balance when they are in conflict? It has been my experience that the facets of trust can, and often do, find themselves at odds with each other."

The Courtiers had not considered this angle, but now realized the truth revealed in the Prince's question.

"Consistency may come at the cost of competency, if reliability is the only focus," noted Dutamis. "I can easily envision a situation in which overemphasis on consistency may yield disappointment in results."

"Competence may come at the cost of caring, if results are the only focus," noted Artenza. "I can easily envision a situation in which overemphasis on outcomes may give the impression of not caring about others."

"Caring may come at the cost of consistency, if rectitude is the only focus," noted Trutorio. "I can easily envision a situation in which overemphasis on concern for others may appear to be inconsistent."

"And if the situation or relationship demands one element over the others, don't we by definition erode trust to some extent?" challenged the Prince.

The Courtiers remained silent for some time, considering the conundrum before them. Finally, Trutorio spoke up.

"This brings us full circle to our overarching theme of doing what we can to further the greatest good for all," he began. "In the difficult predicament presented, if we act to further the common purpose and larger interests, and communicate our actions as we outlined in our earlier discussion of values-driven decisions, some subordinate stakes may go unfulfilled, but the larger view will hold that a choice has been made in

Trust requires the careful and purposeful weighing and balancing of:

✧ *Consistency*

✧ *Competence*

✧ *Caring*

the best interests of all concerned."

"Hence the need for clarifying our cause and exceeding the ego," added Dutamis.

"Striving to serve and fostering positive feelings," concluded Artenza.

"Courtiers, you have mastered the challenge of focusing outside oneself," praised the Prince, displaying a knowing smile.

"That unreachable star that acts to guide us forever in our quest for impact should now be quite clear. From understanding our contribution to balancing self-interest and serving others, to engendering positivity and building trust in a purposeful manner — I believe we can safely put the topic of learning to share our strengths to rest. I am certain we have broken new ground in our discussion. Feel proud, Courtiers, for this matter was a weighty and intricate one, and your work has shown the light of truth and wisdom. Maximus is a lucky fellow to have your guidance. Gentlemen, it is high time we recharge."

The Courtiers stood to leave, knowing that while perhaps the hardest work was behind them, further effort lay ahead.

"A moment, Courtiers," said the Prince, with a twinkle in his eye.

"You need both rest and sustenance! In appreciation of your toil on my behalf, I have taken the liberty of providing the finest of epicurean experiences for us here in the Pantheon — it shall be a feast for the truly accomplished. A quick break to prepare, then return to repast!"

The Courtiers stood beaming and brimming with pride, speechless at the Prince's show of gratitude and appreciation.

"Thank you, Sire!" they cried, ever more eager now to engage in the final challenge.

Govern Your
Gifts
Source Your Strength
Play From Power
Manage What Matters
Lean Into Limits
Move Toward Mastery

Absolute
Impact !

Anchor Your
Ambition

Share Your
Strengths
Clarify Your Cause
Exceed the Ego
Strive to Serve
Foster Positive Feelings
Render Trustful Relationships

A hero is born among a hundred, a wise man is found among a thousand, but an accomplished one might not be found even among a hundred thousand men.

Plato

Anchor Your Ambition

In which the Prince and his Courtiers discuss the challenge of creating new reality

The long pendulum of the massive clock kept a steady beat to the bittersweet merriment underway in the Pantheon as the Prince and his Courtiers shared what they knew might be their final communion as an intact cabinet. As the dark of night fell over the Pantheon, they lit lanterns and regaled each other with a nostalgic review of their grandest strokes and strategies, their most magnificent foibles and follies. Finally, it was time to return to the work at hand.

"Dutamis?" beckoned the Prince, "the floor is yours – lead the way!"

Dutamis rose to begin his missive.

"We have accomplished much, colleagues," he began. "This is where we cohere our previous work – the point of the process in which we must consider the various approaches by which one can design a course of action to confidently advance the journey toward impact. Here is where we pose the question of conquest: *Given our calling and cause, what do we aspire most to accomplish?*"

"Do you recall my initial proposition?" he asked of all.

"That our journey's destination is not a fixed point in time or space," answered Trutorio. "That there is thus an art and science to making one's future."

"That we must separate fantasy from actionable dreams realistically achievable," answered Artenza. "That we must frame our destiny in light of our knowledge and understanding of our strength and contribution."

"That what we view as achievable must reside outside probability, yet firmly in the realm of true possibility," answered the Prince. "That we must commit fully to compelling goals set just beyond our immediate reach."

"And," finished Dutamis, "that if our aspirations are rooted in both our ability and aim – in that which we truly have to offer – we are then, and only then, free to proceed toward making the most of them, to enter the domain of belief, requiring us to stretch and overcome any obstacles that may block our path."

The roundtable participants were nodding, and Dutamis saw that all understood the gist of the ground to be covered.

"Good!" he exclaimed. "Let us then proceed with a deeper look at what we believe to be the overarching issues to be addressed, so that we might provide the proper context for this our final challenge."

"Your proffer?" queried the Prince.

"I believe we must begin with a rigorous treatment of ambition," replied Dutamis. "I wish to transcend the popular conventional notion – which tends to imply a predominantly acquisitive or competitive motive aimed at distinction, wealth, or influence – to embrace something more aspirational in nature, and move toward a more elevated concept aligned with our ideas of personal leadership that have flowed as a strong undercurrent throughout our exploration."

"I agree," stated Artenza. "Certainly we have alluded to leadership from a personal perspective on more than one occasion, and any forceful definition of ambition must be consistent with the principles we have discussed."

"Our impact will not be absolute without a more robust specification," furthered Trutorio. "Certainly we have touched upon a few moral absolutes, and a higher perspective of ambition centering on our most excellent and impactful work would indeed seem to be in order."

"Paradox! The truly anchored ambition reveals an elevated aspiration!" exclaimed the Prince.

"You obviously have some definite ideas on this matter," he continued, directing his remark back to Dutamis.

"Yes," replied Dutamis. "Bear with me, as I have neither Trutorio's eloquence nor Artenza's élan."

Pausing to take a breath, Dutamis launched into a brief proof.

"My thinking is thus: we have agreed that absolute impact in life is the ultimate personal triumph – to believe someday hence that we have made the most of what we have to offer the world. Now, we have loosely described personal leadership as the ability to lead oneself on the journey to this end by employing a self-driven process of governing our gifts, sharing our strengths, and anchoring our ambition."

"A fair summary?" he asked, looking around the table to the others for some confirmation.

The others vigorously nodded their affirmation.

"Well, then," continued Dutamis, "the subject of ambition necessarily entails a discussion of goals, for ambition by any definition concerns the direction of one's drive toward the achievement of an objective. A goal by definition is something yet to be attained, something we aim to accomplish at some point beyond the immediate present – therefore the issue of the future enters the mix. And, the execution of a plan of action in pursuit of the future in an attempt to bring into existence something heretofore nonexistent – the creative act of positively rendering a new reality – delivers us to the very doorstep of leadership, as such effort rather succinctly describes what I believe to be the central manifest activity of leadership at its foundation, regardless of condition or circumstance.

"Now contrast this with the prevailing limited concept of ambition relating more to acquisition, consumption, or even destruction. It is gaining by making, not gaining by getting or spending, that defines the creative act of leadership. This brings us full circle to the need to incorporate what we mean

Ironically, the truly anchored ambition reveals an elevated aspiration transcending the more conventional acquisitive notion

by ambition in a way consistent with our notions of personal leadership and absolute impact. Simply put, the nature of our ambition properly cast shall be the grand determinant of both."

Dutamis was adamant. "Colleagues, we must get this right!"

The others were quiet as they each contemplated Dutamis' charge. Not waiting for a response, Dutamis propounded his thesis.

"Significant ideas, responsible action," he said simply, once and again. "Significant ideas, responsible action."

Again, all was quiet. The Prince broke the silence.

"I stand in humble admiration," he said. "The precision with which your inimitable economic intellect moves unerringly to the core of an issue never ceases to amaze me. In four simple words, not only have you provided a compelling and transcendental definition of anchored ambition, but you have cut to the quick of our entire discussion!"

It was true, the others realized.

"You have taken us to the heart of absolute impact," praised Artenza.

"You have captured the soul of personal leadership," commended Trutorio.

"Thank you, one and all," beamed Dutamis. "I have listened to our elegant debate, considered our most powerful process, and arrived at a mnemonic that has implications on a number of levels. First, know that the number of words corresponds to the number of prevailing human mental patterns we have identified. Second, each word plays to – in fact represents – one of the four. Third, I believe that deep impact requires the whole of human capacity to be in fact absolute."

"Speaking for those of my genre, significance sums up quite nicely the spirit of the Diplomat's empathic advocacy," noted Trutorio.

An anchored ambition is defined by significant ideas and responsible action, requiring the whole of our human intellectual capacity

"On behalf of those like me, ideas indeed represent the essence of the Philosopher's theoretic strategy," noted the Prince.

"Responsibility is the auspice of the Guardian's economic propriety," continued Dutamis.

"And action embodies the Artisan's kinetic agency," concluded Artenza.

"Knowing this will enable Maximus to fully involve those who may share or be impacted by his ambition, as well as those who may aid him in his efforts," said the Prince.

"Yes," agreed Trutorio. "However, several questions arise. If these are the central themes in our respective lives, what role do they play in driving our aspirations? If we appreciate even more of who we each are, might that not free us to develop more of who we're not, as needed to further advance our ambition, contrary as that might seem? Might it not aid us in anchoring our ambition?"

"A closer look at each of the four is quite in order, so that we create the proper context for the remainder of our work," agreed Dutamis. "Perhaps if we each in turn offer our personal insights as regards Trutorio's questions from our own representative perspective?"

"This would better enable us to move into the deeper strata of the challenges inherent in this, our final pathpoint," added Artenza.

"I shall start, then," began Trutorio. "To be driven by the pursuit of *significance* is to wear my skin! Significance to me translates to something personally meaningful. Three elements come to mind: authenticity, contribution, and positivity. Authenticity is about being true to one's self, to one's gifts – one's talents and values. Contribution, as I put forth in our discussion of sharing our strengths, is the essence of our purpose, our cause. Positivity, which we also covered at some length, means making our world a better place to be – to focus on the good, the strength, and the excellence. I believe we are all meant to lead meaningful and purposeful lives, for that is where the deeper fulfillment lies. If our ambition is aligned to our gifts and causes, the criterion of significance is, in my mind, satisfied."

Trutorio turned to the Prince, signaling him to address *ideas*.

"Ideas are my lifeblood," began the Prince. "I cannot resist them, my world revolves around them! This entire discussion has me squarely in my element – hypothesizing and theorizing, testing ideas, concepts, and constructs – I feel in control of my learning, my mastery, my creativity. The more elegant, the better! Elegance drives progress and precision. I thrive on the discussion of new ideas – on the debate with others over my thoughts – for it simply confirms that you have understood my project. Where would we be without the idea? Anything real was once but an idea. Without the idea, there is no anchored ambition."

The Prince turned to Dutamis, signaling him to address *responsibility*.

"It is no secret that responsibility is first and foremost in my life," stated Dutamis. "To me, this means I hold myself ultimately accountable for everything I must do and that must get done on my watch by those in my charge. I see it only my duty and obligation to ensure the world runs smoothly. I fail to see the rationale of placing blame on anyone but myself – if I am not the answer, there is no solution! If something goes awry, it is because I did not plan and prepare properly. I need strong connections, strong allies, strong associates. True, I push them, but no harder than I push myself. I encourage and empower – while my mistakes and triumphs are my own, so do I own the mistakes and triumphs of those to whom I am connected. I revel in their victory and share in their failure. It is only those who do not accept responsibility that view the success of others as a form of threat. It is those who seek rights without responsibility who would falsely lead. There is no leadership, no absolute impact, no ultimate triumph, no truly anchored ambition without this facet of responsibility."

Dutamis turned to Artenza, signaling him to address *action*.

"Without action, nothing will be accomplished," stated Artenza. "Signposts without travel are quite irrelevant, and any castle built in the air must have a foundation beneath it. We can never sit still, never stop moving, never idle – to do so is to stagnate, the very antithesis of growth and vitality. From my perspective, it is the bias toward action that channels talents, values, and causes, and brings about profound change. Now, in truth, the perfect act requires the significance, ideas, and responsibility to which you refer, but it is nonetheless the *act* that creates the evolution in circumstance. Everything we know we want, wish to create, and have to do must ultimately be translated, tried and sustained through action. You see, regardless of our preferred orientation, we can only act in the present, perhaps with an eye toward what has been and what shall be, but nonetheless in the here and now. Action is the wellspring of impact."

"Dutamis is thus correct," concluded the Prince. "The whole of our human intellectual capacity must be employed, for without even one of these dimensions, our ambition shall suffer the ails of deficiency. If our ideas and actions derive from significance and responsibility, our ambition will be anchored, our impact absolute, our leadership unassailable."

"It seems quite clear" said Dutamis, most seriously, "that Maximus must learn to embrace and enact this entirely new philosophy of ambition – to see and pursue meaningful aspirations in a manner befitting a leader."

The Courtiers looked to the Prince expectantly.

"Need I ask?" smiled the Prince.

Without being asked, Artenza offered his tablet to Dutamis.

"Thank you," nodded Dutamis, smiling and accepting the slate.

"I shall list the component strategies summarily using our previous template – again with the understanding that each will require deeper examination to become useful," he began.

The others nodded their agreement.

"Very well," began Dutamis, launching his chapter.

"To refresh, the goal of anchoring our ambition is to lend discipline to our dreams in an effort to proactively commit and purposefully channel our energies toward actualizing a compelling picture of a new future that guides our crusade, in so doing realize the fulfilling sense of achievement that derives from effecting the changes we desire to see in ourselves and in our world. It is here that our calling and cause coalesce in a concerted course of action focused on the quest for what we view to be the ideal outcome of our engagement – all the while growing, changing, and developing into the leaders, achievers, and contributors

The goal of anchoring one's ambition is to lend discipline to dreams in an effort to actualize a compelling picture of a new future – in so doing realize the fulfilling sense of achievement that derives from effecting the change we desire to see in ourselves and in our world

we aspire to become.

"Our new definition of ambition allows us to move beyond acquisitive advancement to focus more on uncommon achievement and the challenge of continuously creating a new reality for ourselves – and for those we serve and with whom we connect – employing all of the power, purpose, and potential we possess. I see five critical self-directed elements inherent in the ability to do so, moving from knowledge and understanding of self, to aligned action, and on to maximal capitalization – resulting in progressively deeper impact. Like our previous work, they are best thought of as integral components of a cohesive whole – one without the others yields far less impact."

As his colleagues before him, Dutamis then began writing his points on Artenza's tablet as he outlined each.

"To begin, we must seek to add the final layer of understanding to the clarity we have achieved around governing our gifts and sharing our strengths by asking and answering the question: *to what end?*

"Thus, the challenge now centers more on exacting visible impact, requiring us to cull from our most majestic of designs the crowning creative canon to which we will commit ourselves fully – the projected body of work that shall stand *res ipsa* as testimony to our enterprise for time immemorial. Achieving our aspirations can only come from this unerring focus on a realistic rendering of that which we envisage, for it is the actions arising out of our past and taken today in the direction of tomorrow that will yield the impact we seek.

"We simply do not have the human capacity to chase down every random dream we conjure up, and we must learn to objectively assess our current reality, decide our destiny and direct our drive toward only the ideal endstates with real possibility – those which represent our worldview and are imbued with the power of our enduring talents, core values, and noble causes. Focusing on this figurative frame of our creative enterprise is far more critical than most realize, for it provides not only the necessary demarcation between imagination and reality, but the full endowment for a lasting visionary structure – enabling the picture eventually enveloped by its bounds to morph as needed without losing its integrity as an authentic masterpiece."

On Artenza's slate, Dutamis wrote:

Vest your vision.

"Once we have conceived and chosen the ultimate impact we see for ourselves, we must then focus our energy on pointed action to achieve those ends – for in truth, forging our future is predominantly a cyclical force of well-aligned action. To fuel this creative cycle of achievement and accomplishment, we will need to learn to do two things well.

"First, we must recognize that while seeing is believing, the reverse is likewise true – believing is seeing. However, because our vision is by definition trained on the horizon and momentarily beyond our immediate grasp, we may lose sight of the ultimate target, disengage, or succumb to distracting forces, unless we have some means to continuously affirm the belief in our ability to achieve our ambition. For, if we lose sight, we lose belief, and vice versa. We must devise a support system that works to effectively pull the possibilities of tomorrow ever closer through positive actions that bolster our belief and reaffirm our reach. Constant advancement and patent progress toward the endgame achieved through successful accomplishment of interim objectives is perhaps the most motivating such force.

"The challenge thus moves to the artful grounding of unambiguous, yet nonetheless audacious, goals with clear culminating peaks that provide the inspiration, impetus and inertia needed to perpetually catalyze commitment, endow engagement, and maintain momentum, in turn supporting and enhancing our confidence and efficacy. If our sights are set true, we can realistically expect to excel – and because we act according to our expectations, we shall."

On Artenza's slate, Dutamis wrote:

True the trajectory.

"The second half of the creative cycle of achievement involves the translation of our ideals and aims through some mechanism by which we manage our goal-oriented commitments, in so doing close the schism between the present and the future.

"To my mind, this naturally falls into the realm of logistics – marshaling our energy and resources toward completing the *magnum opus* we have conceived. Viewing our ideas and objectives as a series of mission-level projects with well-defined starts and stops almost automatically invokes the human machinery needed to direct our attention, mobilize our effort, increase our persistence, and motivate our search for optimal strategies. Employing a cohesive managerial approach addresses and circumnavigates many of the self-imposed barriers we are likely to face in our quest, including ambiguous and conflicting objectives, inferior solutions, and undisciplined learning.

"This perspective mandates pragmatic and rational action, and works to embed a regimen of continuous innovation and improvement that allows us to stay current with – and ahead of – the disruptive forces of rapid change, as each new project will require the *ad hoc* acquisition of new skills and knowledge, in turn helping to facilitate our move toward mastery. Much of underachievement and ineffectiveness can be traced to an inability to implement the appropriate logistics required to simply complete a project, a circumstance that can steal the very energy required to generate a new cycle of creative accomplishment – depletion easily replenished through proper orchestration."

On Artenza's slate, Dutamis wrote:

Orchestrate the opus.

"Once we have chosen our intended targets, and executed strategies to pursue them, we can turn our attention to ensuring maximum impact. We will need to learn to do two things concurrently, employing twin strategies centered on adaptability and adversity.

"On the one hand, we must be prepared for the sure and constant shifts in the landscape ahead – relevant external forces having potential effect on our best laid plans. There are those that constrain, and those that propel – to the extent that they are a given or that we can do so, we must make every effort to identify and prepare for their eventuality so that we are not taken completely off guard and miss key opportunities. As we generally see what we look for, if we can sketch the various scenarios likely to loom on the horizon, we will be in the enviable position of being able to capitalize on the uncertainty and ambiguity we can be reasonably assured will pervade our every tomorrow.

"It is here that our framework once again proves itself invaluable – for in the most turbulent of times, while our ambition may undergo radical redirection, we retain our continuity through the clarity around our power and purpose. We cannot predict the future, but we can easily take steps toward ensuring that we are not drastically mistaken about it – if we don't, we may find ourselves following the current, no longer able to effectively navigate the river's flow, no longer able to lead ourselves, or anyone else for that matter."

On Artenza's slate, Dutamis wrote:

Figure on flux.

"By the same token, we will never be able to anticipate every difficulty. So, we must simultaneously learn to capitalize on those unforeseeable and uncontrollable tests of character and courage that nonetheless carry with them hidden opportunities that can often harbor transformative experiences that serve to strengthen our resolve and deepen our resilience. It is a commonly quoted maxim that adversity does not create leaders, it reveals them – so whether in response to catastrophe or something perhaps less traumatic, it is our ability to stay our course while effectively responding to a multifarious crisis that shall unveil the depths of our tenacity and personal leadership. As we know from our discussion on leaning into limits, our greatest learning – about ourselves and about life – shall occur through the action we take when confronted with such crucibles. Most of our hardest battles in these types of situations are fought not against others but within ourselves as we struggle against the deeper, darker, often unseen and unknown enemy of our own resident fear. We must welcome these tests, for they often force us in directions we perhaps should have already discovered on our own."

On Artenza's slate, Dutamis wrote:

Capitalize on crucibles.

The Pantheon was silent as Dutamis took his place at the roundtable.

Once more, applause thundered through the great hall.

"Above and beyond, my friend, above and beyond," praised the Prince.

"You have indeed brought us home in your most pragmatic way!" he continued. "You have exceeded all expectations – but then, we should expect no less from the Guardian master! Your guidance provides not simply a new definition of ambition, but an original philosophy that completes our process for absolute impact and the pathway to ultimate personal triumph in a truly transformational way. The force and fury of your comprehensive argument cannot be denied. We will indeed need every bit of our collective wisdom to arrive at the application. In the spirit of significant ideas and responsible action, let us move forward with every celerity."

And so it was that the Prince and Courtiers launched their final debate – the challenge of learning to create a new reality.

Anchor Your Ambition

Vest Your Vision

True The Trajectory

Orchestrate The Opus

Figure On Flux

Capitalize On Crucibles

Vest Your Vision

The soul never thinks without a picture.

Plato

"Gentlemen, the topic up for current debate is that of visual acuity," began Dutamis. "My position is that one cannot advance in any direction confidently without sharp visibility."

"The forest through which we race by light of day is the same through which we move slowly and hesitantly by dark of night," affirmed the Prince.

"The cliff along which we are sure of foot in the bright of sun is the same along which we cautiously test each step in the murk of fog," agreed Trutorio.

"What then is the debate?" challenged Artenza. "No argument!"

Dutamis smiled. "It centers, of course, on the attainment of the figurative personal vision – learning to focus our foresight on crafting the compelling picture that will surely and steadfastly draw us forward into the future."

Dutamis raised the challenge further. "I submit that most are in need of vision correction."

"Meaning?" asked Trutorio.

"Meaning," replied Dutamis, "that the properly and fully endowed vision requires not simply a forward view of the desired or ideal future, but one that draws upon our knowledge of the past and the reality of the present."

"Why the past?" asked Artenza, never a fan of the historical. "It is so much water over the dam, isn't it? Isn't it the future we're chasing? Of what possible and practical use can the past be in designing our destiny?"

Before Dutamis could reply, the others leapt to his defense.

"To discover the points of inflection," replied the Prince, explaining. "To revisit milestones that may have marked subtle or substantial directional shifts in our path to the present, providing rich insight into that which has shaped our current circumstance – all in an effort to make and manage our course for the future."

"To capture moments of truth," added Trutorio. "To mark key points of reference that have influenced our character and provided meaningful experiences, and that identify recurring patterns of meaning and action – illuminating our talents, values, and causes."

"All valid arguments," acquiesced Artenza.

"You know me well, Artenza," said Dutamis quietly. "Which of the ancient deities do I repeatedly honor and identify with most?"

"Janus!" cried Artenza. "The guardian of doors and gates, the god of new beginnings, as powerful as Jupiter himself – the first month of the year is named for him!"

Trutorio picked up the story. "Janus was the custodian of the universe! He was seen as the originator and orchestrator of all things – the system of the years, the changing of the seasons, the ebbs and flows of fortune, and the civilization of the human race by means of agriculture, industry, money, and laws. Janus ensured a time of peace, honesty and abundance for his people – it was an era known as the Golden Age."

"He particularly presided over all that is double-edged in life," added the Prince.

"And what is most unique about Janus?" probed Dutamis.

"His two faces gazing in opposite directions, naturally," replied Artenza. "One regarding what is behind and the other looking toward what lies ahead. I see where you're going with this."

"And why would the god of new beginnings be artistically depicted in this distinctive fashion?" furthered Dutamis, undaunted.

"Presumably because doors and gates look both backward and forward, inward and outward, simultaneously," answered Artenza.

"The connection between Janus and new beginnings being the idea that one must emerge through a gate or door before entering a new place," added Trutorio.

"Don't we all adopt the manner of Janus when we are starting something new?" asked the Prince. "Certainly the January turn of the calendar marks a new beginning, yet do we not reflect on the previous annum even as we usher in the new? We look forward with anticipation toward the future while we look backward to the past that has led us so far and in fact has brought us to the new beginning."

Artenza turned to Dutamis. "I believe I see your point. Give full face to the future but do not ignore your past!"

"Precisely," confirmed Dutamis. "While we cannot walk backward into the future – for we will never get ahead by doing so – it is our past experiences that enable us to vivify our thoughts of tomorrow, to help us separate superficial daydreams from actionable aspirations. We cannot effectively envision that with which we have absolutely no experience, no hints of foundation, no clues to real possibilities – we can only fantasize. Thus it is our reflections on the past that give meaning to our successes and failures not so that our destiny mimics the past – but so that we may incorporate what we've learned in our effort to discipline our dreaming…"

"So that we do not misplay key opportunities by responding to current and future challenges with yesterday's solutions," added Trutorio.

"So that we can lengthen our outlook based on our path through life thus far," added the Prince.

"So that we can better understand what we must sacrifice today to move into tomorrow," concluded Artenza.

"Which brings us to the present," said Dutamis. "Many are those who simply do not, can not, or know not how to face the facts of their current reality in attempting to map their ambition."

"Failing this makes us vulnerable to misdirection," agreed Artenza.

"Governing our gifts and sharing our strengths propels us far over the transom," noted Trutorio. "What in your view is missing?"

"Simply a broader perspective based on our personal worldview," replied Dutamis.

"Beyond our gifts and purpose, our overall orientation

The properly and fully endowed vision requires not simply a forward view of the desired or ideal future, but one that draws upon our knowledge of the past and the reality of the present toward time and place," furthered the Prince.

"Exactly," confirmed Dutamis. "I would submit that each of us at this roundtable represents a different outlook on life in general – no doubt aligned to our respective intellectual motifs – which must be accounted for in any aspirational effort. Knowing our natural inclination enables us to identify what may be missing in our attempts to anchor our ambition – for as we know, the whole of human intellect is required."

The others were silent, as if to prompt Dutamis to continue.

"To use myself as an example," offered Dutamis, "the more economic Guardians of the world must understand that we are by nature more comfortable with the past, less so with the future. We tend to seek ways to indemnify ourselves from the future, which we do by calling upon history and tradition – the tried and true. We are obliged to work hard in the present, and if we do so based on what has worked for us in the past, we will accumulate the resources we need to withstand the future, come what may. Like Janus, our place is at the gateways and doorways of life – keeping a constant vigil and protecting ourselves – and those in our charge – from the probable mishaps."

Trutorio took his turn, using Dutamis' format.

"The more empathic Diplomats of the world must understand that we are by nature believers in good – in ourselves, in other people, in the future. We somehow know that tomorrow will be even better than today, and we instinctively look for the pathway to it, which must always lead through an authentic and altruistic motive. Will misfortune plague us? Certainly, but life is what it is, and there is more power to be gained through experience than over it. We will make it through the trials, and the point of confronting or assailing potential causes of pressure and pain eludes us. The human spirit will ultimately prevail, and we

The more economic Guardians of the world must understand that they are by nature more comfortable with the past, less so with the future

The more empathic Diplomats of the world must understand that they are by nature believers in good – in themselves, in others, and in the future

must quest after the potential and possibility of what is yet to come our way – for there must be more to life than what exists today."

Artenza was next.

"The more kinetic Artisans of the world must understand that we are by nature swept up in the here and now. What has come before and is yet to come tends to be of less interest, for our influence has most impact today. Today will be gone shortly enough, and to waste the moment on something we can't touch, feel, and enjoy seems tragic. Time is our most precious currency! Planning for the morrow seems an unnatural and unnecessary burden. Things will go our way, rest assured, and if they don't…well, there isn't anything that a bit of courageous prowess on our part won't remedy. Life is a gamble to win, a game to be played – it is the draw of clear and present opportunity to make a masterful stroke that entices us. Risks will be taken and mistakes will be made, but the march of constant movement shall carry us always."

Finally, the Prince took his turn.

"The more theoretic Philosophers of the world must understand that the future presents a problem for us to solve. As such, the present consists of construing the ways and means to the future – the considerations, alternatives, and strategies. Nothing is more practical, more effective and efficient, than a clear view of the future supported by a vivid concept, sound strategy, and plans for contingency. The past is helpful to the extent we have gleaned from it something of use to build into our concept, perhaps the elimination of future misstep. Even our finest stratagems must be debated, probed and tested for logical flaw – and, more eyes and brains on the project inevitably yield a better product. Only focused attention on the event itself, irrespective of time and place, seems relevant – for most incidents are relative to both in nature, and

The more kinetic Artisans of the world must understand that they are by nature swept up in the here and now

⚜

The more theoretic Philosophers of the world must understand that the future presents a problem for them to solve

within every circumstance, both good and bad can be found and learned from."

The Pantheon was still as the Prince and the Courtiers absorbed what they had heard from each other. For each, it felt as if a mirror had been held up to reflect parts of themselves they knew existed but were subordinate to their dominant worldview.

"We must remind ourselves that these perspectives lie within each of us to some extent," added Trutorio.

"It is easy to see the strength in each," noted Dutamis, after some time.

"We would do well to consider each in vesting our vision," commented Artenza.

"Shall we then move into the approach for doing so?" suggested the Prince.

"Yes!" exclaimed the Courtiers, unanimous in their alacrity.

"Might I recommend we continue in the same vein in offering that which we each believe to be critical properties of a fully-vested vision?" suggested the Prince.

"Agreed!" cried the Courtiers.

Dutamis began.

"I believe that to be most compelling, our ambition must be articulate, appealing, and attainable," he stated.

"Articulate in order to add texture and daily guidance," commented Trutorio. "To offer a view of another reality clearly better than today."

"Appealing in order to provide desire and motivation," added Artenza. "To create a sense of urgency and move us to action."

"Attainable in order to create the proper dissonance," affirmed the Prince. "To screen out the irrelevant."

"And should it not as well be artistic, adaptive, and audacious?" asked Artenza.

"Artistic to provide the canvas upon which our talents can render the masterpiece," furthered Trutorio. "To inspire full engagement."

"Adaptive to accommodate the unforeseen," added Dutamis. "To bridge the past, present, and future."

"Audacious to index achievement and catalyze learning," finished the

Prince. "To grab and focus attention."

"From my point of view, we must include authentic, affirmative and abundant," stated Trutorio.

"Authentic to crystallize commitment, embolden belief and ensure alignment with our strengths and purpose," added Dutamis. "To reflect our uniqueness."

"Affirmative to provide a strong and positive image of the ideal," added Artenza. "To create pride and excellence in what we expect of ourselves."

"Abundant to enable others to whom we are closely connected to both see and share our ambition," said the Prince. "To touch a universal chord of meaning, especially among those we may call upon for support."

"These nine shall then guide our efforts," concluded Dutamis.

"There is a tenth and final criterion I wish to add," interrupted the Prince. "It is something I shall term *afterimage*."

The Courtiers looked questioningly at the Prince.

"Our vision must outlast our mortality," he said, in a most serious tone. "The gravest indictment of my tenure shall be the Court's collapse upon my earthly departure. I believe that to ensure absolute impact, our vision must endure our demise."

The Courtiers understood.

"Obviously," continued the Prince, "I have given the future much thought of late – indeed it is the genesis of our current project. I wonder if now is the time for us to share our respective envisages? Perhaps the most practical way to cover the remaining territory is to voice our visions and then apply our thinking down the line."

As the Courtiers considered the Prince's suggestion, he offered further guidance.

"What has always helped me in this activity is to

Vested Vision

✧ *Articulate*

✧ *Appealing*

✧ *Attainable*

✧ *Artistic*

✧ *Adaptive*

✧ *Audacious*

✧ *Authentic*

✧ *Affirmative*

✧ *Abundant*

✧ *Afterimage*

approach it from the aspect of mapping the image I hold in my mind," said the Prince. "I begin with a vivid depiction evoking a clear mental image, then provide a detailed and descriptive picture that embellishes that image using statements that commence with *I see…*"

"An excellent tool!" cried Artenza, impressed.

"Easily enabling us to design-in each of our ten criteria," noted Trutorio.

Dutamis was hesitant.

"Inasmuch as we refrain from any set period of time in defining the future, I would agree," stated Dutamis. "We have just seen how the orientation to time differs individually. Our vision must remain vague on this issue, at this point in our discussion. One's view of the future may not expand beyond tomorrow, another's may be of a decade hence – each of us has a different horizon."

"Well put," concurred the Prince. "At this juncture, it is neither a critical nor decisive parameter."

"Let us image forth!" cried Artenza.

Dutamis began.

"The image in my mind is one of a chorus of guardian angels keeping a watchful eye over a safe refuge.

"I see the Court guiding the Province to a new and unparalleled level of economic and social stability, fostering a true sense of security and prosperity for our population and their generations to come as they raise their families, build new communities, and conduct their work. This is my dream.

"I see our Provincial levels of economic production in all industry sectors hitting new highs through new advancements in manufacturing, distribution, and retailing. I see our currency strengthening in value through sound fiscal and monetary policies. I see our lands fertile for crops and cattle, providing for a solid economic market system. I see a modern plexus of roadways to foster connectivity and transportation within and between the towns and cities. I see a network of waterways, aqueducts, and damns that nourish the land for irrigation and divert water into reservoirs to sustain the ever-increasing needs of the population. I see a viable and equitable system of jurisprudence that upholds the rights of all citizens by instituting democratic legislation and social policy, enforced by a vigilant and protective police force focused on both prevention and prosecution.

"Within the Court itself, I see standardized work processes, policies, procedures and tools supported by the diligent administration of quality control and management, enabling internal operations to function at efficiency levels approaching perfection. I see accountability for excellence and precision in that system adopted and accepted by everyone working within it.

"Personally, I see myself working hard to provide a safe home and financial security for my family – saving and investing wisely for the later years, taking care to insure that they never have to worry about economic survival in the event of my untimely death or disability. I see myself increasing my involvement at the community level to build stronger ties between and among families and social groups.

"Finally, I see myself at the side of Maximus to serve as I have served his father."

Dutamis turned to the others to exact their reaction.

"Clearly this vision fulfills your driving need for duty and sanctuary," commented the Prince, visibly moved by the image.

"It is well-aligned to your values centering on responsibility, regulation, and refuge," furthered Trutorio, impressed by the vivid picture.

"Fully leveraging your economic talents," added Artenza, nodding.

"And tied solidly to your purpose in keeping us secure, disciplined, and productive," noted Trutorio.

"While meeting each of our ten criteria," concluded Artenza.

"A fully-vested vision!" they cried in unison.

"Thank you, one and all," acknowledged Dutamis.

Artenza spoke next.

"The image in my mind is one of a society of warrior poets at play in the field of progress.

"I see the Court accelerating the expansion of our influence throughout and beyond the Province, breaking new ground to extend our reach and creating a sense of vitality and culture for young townships and cities as they grow to become energetic centers of commerce, art, and government. This is my dream.

"I see us meeting the challenge of each new day in new ways, seeking every opportunity to respond to and capitalize on the dynamic changes occurring in our population, in our society, in our civilization. I see us developing centers for the performing, literary, culinary and fine visual arts for all to enjoy and appreciate. I see the highest levels of competitive play through formalized athletic events and associations. I see us quickly applying new developments in science and technology to build new tools and methods, all in an effort to further our taste for all that life holds. I see a strong and highly-trained military able to be mobilized on a moment's notice.

"I see young people mastering a craft and moving toward levels of virtuosity that, when applied, yield the monuments of exquisite architecture rendering a truly *avant-garde* image of a society with style. I see pillared duomos of ornate detail that represent decades of human effort and artistry. I see a landscape of advancement too beautiful to behold at once, an aesthetic experience of full sensory proportion.

"Personally, I see myself seizing every moment of my time here and wringing it of taste and texture – traveling far and wide to experience the excitement and pulse of life beyond the known, boldly creating satellites of our Court in new territories, conquering the daily challenges of the new and different, all the while honing my art to the very peak of performance.

"I shall let Fate spin the wheel of fortune for me in going forward, taking in stride what comes my way in a manner only water might replicate.

"Finally, I see myself at the side of Maximus to serve as I have served his father."

Artenza turned to the others to exact their reaction.

"Clearly this vision fulfills your driving need for action and impulse," commented the Prince, once more touched by his Courtier's vision.

"It is well-aligned to your values centering on adventure, autonomy, and aesthetics," furthered Trutorio, awed by the detail.

"Fully leveraging your kinetic talents," added Dutamis, wondrously.

"And tied solidly to your purpose in keeping us dynamic, vital, and responsive," noted Trutorio.

"While meeting each of our ten criteria," concluded Dutamis.

"Another fully-vested vision!" they cried in unison.

"Thank you, one and all," acknowledged Artenza.

Trutorio spoke next.

"The image in my mind is one of a band of brothers setting course to sail upon a sea of tranquility.

"I see our Court as the benevolent peacekeepers in a land still adolescent in its evolution, the voice of mature humanity sounding a clear trumpet to call forth belief in the virtues of Man, in the manifest ability of all to find harmony and joy under the same sun – to find meaning in the nostalgia of yesterday and the romance of tomorrow. This is my dream.

"I see a unified Province standing strong in solidarity to eradicate those who would seek to aggress, undermine, and destroy. I see diplomatic alliances in and among the regimes that move beyond a simple system of checks and balances in power and authority to become relationships of true understanding. I see a population rejoicing in its diversity of peoples, searching for and securing their singular identities while constructing connections founded on respect and trust. I see people who help people, people who realize the interconnectedness of the universe, people who understand the deeper, more noble purpose of life.

"I see our Court setting the example for embracing and exhibiting ideals of the highest ethical echelon. I see a citizenship founded in a common and collective spirit, demonstrating concern for each other, sacrificing as needed to maintain the purity of purpose.

"Personally, I see myself championing coalitions of compassion in helping the underprivileged, managing missions of mercy in helping the underdeveloped, and enlisting envoys of empathy in helping the disenfranchised.

"I see myself enriching the lives of those I have been so very fortunate to be blessed with in my life. I see myself sharing the rich experiences of family, career, partnership, and friendship – deeply involved in helping my children to reach their true potential, using a strong family life to help all generations gain a sense of who they are.

"Finally, I see myself at the side of Maximus to serve as I have served his father."

Trutorio turned to the others to exact their reaction.

"Clearly this vision fulfills your driving need for significance and truth," whispered the Prince, again struck by the forceful aspiration.

"It is well-aligned to your values centering on inspiration, integrity, and involvement," furthered Dutamis.

"Fully leveraging your empathic talents," added Artenza.

"And tied solidly to your aim in keeping us righteous, unified, and authentic," noted Dutamis.

"While meeting each of our ten criteria," concluded Artenza.

"Yet another fully-vested vision!" they cried in unison.

"Thank you, one and all," acknowledged Trutorio.

The Courtiers then turned to the Prince expectantly. The Prince stood slowly, and turning to face the Courtiers, began in a measured tone.

"Gentlemen, I see only hope – hope for yet another generation of that which has brought us here. At this point in my life, I have seen it all. You three have been actively engaged in my vision for as long as I can remember.

"Personally, I have always seen myself as living the good life, the strong life – the life of wisdom, courage, temperance and justice – to make the very most of what I had to offer the world.

"As Prince, I have always seen our Court as being integral to the happiness of all those within our principality, indeed our Province – the driving image in my mind has always been that our constituents could not possibly imagine a better world without us!

"I have always seen us as a legion of leaders and learners sharing knowledge in the logical pursuits – at the forefront of scientific exploration and technological advancement in an effort to make life more practical, more convenient for everyone. I have envisioned scientists and scholars working together to better understand our world, our civilization – distributing that understanding through education and books. I have seen teachers and pupils discovering greater ways of educating and learning, investigating and exploring the wonders of Nature, revisiting the known and shining the light of knowledge into the dark of the unknown.

"I have personally expended my energies and talents to this end. We have underwritten much of the creative activity that has increased our knowledge one hundred fold in the past five decades. And we have only just begun!

"Most importantly, I have embraced your aspirations as you have embraced mine.

"Through the eyes of Trutorio, I have always seen us as being the epitome of honesty, fairness, and ethics in our statecraft in an effort to build diplomatic bridges of trust between us and our neighbors. I have envisioned us working in harmony with other establishments to advance the human condition – making democratic decisions in the best interests of humanity, exchanging in mutually beneficial trade.

"It has been Trutorio to whom we have turned to help us keep our virtues true, our intent unified. He has been instrumental in developing the key alliances that have propelled us to our current levels of political respect and joyful peace throughout the land.

"Through the eyes of Dutamis, I have always seen us as the benchmark of effectiveness and efficiency in our operations in an effort to promote the stability needed to realize the highest levels of productivity and profitability. I have envisioned every proprietor, every laborer, every person working to their full potential to achieve a continuous cycle of improvement in quality, quantity, and speed.

"It has been Dutamis to whom we have turned to build an infrastructure capable of weathering both economic downturns and external forces that might threaten our sense of security.

"Through the eyes of Artenza, I have always seen us as the most aggressive pioneers of unsettled lands in an effort to expand civilization. I have envisioned new towns and centers of growth and prosperity burgeoning on the ever-extending horizon, bringing new people, new perspectives, new passions to the land.

"It has been Artenza to whom we have turned to craft the strongest military among all the protectorates to both lead our progress and minimize our vulnerability to potential aggressors that might act to curtail our expansion."

The Prince spread his arms wide to encompass all three Courtiers together.

"And, we have achieved it all together, my friends!"

The Courtiers were silent for a time.

"It is no small footprint that Maximus must follow," whispered Dutamis.

And with that, the Prince and the Courtiers turned their attention to the task of actualizing visions through cycles of creative achievement.

True the Trajectory

As the builders say, the larger stones do not lay well without the lesser.

Plato

Dutamis picked up a small pebble and walked toward the large Pantheon clock, stopping twenty paces from it. He turned to others and motioned to Artenza.

"Artenza, may I borrow you for a moment?" he asked.

"Certainly," replied Artenza, eager to be on his feet.

Trutorio and the Prince looked on in fascination at the demonstration.

Dutamis handed the pebble to Artenza and turned to face the clock.

"Now," directed Dutamis, "hit the pendulum face with this pebble."

Artenza smiled at the impossible challenge, studying the arc of the pendulum swing before letting loose the pebble. On his first attempt, he missed – short and wide.

The others gave a disappointed "Oh!"

"Now take five paces forward and try again," said Dutamis, retrieving the pebble and giving it over to Artenza.

Taking his time to gauge the rhythm of the pendulum, Artenza took aim and hurled the pebble once more. Ever so much closer, his pebble glanced off the pendulum, just low.

"Almost!" cried the others.

"A final three paces forward, then," urged Dutamis, once again giving Artenza the pebble.

This time, Artenza's aim was true, and he easily hit the pendulum squarely on its face.

The others cheered wildly, for at such a distance, the feat was still quite a difficult one.

Dutamis and Artenza returned to the roundtable, and Dutamis took the opportunity to exact a moment of learning.

"Artenza," he began, "walk us through your thoughts and actions – your process for success."

Artenza warmed to the invitation. "The odds were against me – the great distance, the moving target, the tiny missile, my inability to practice first. On the plus side, the objective was clear, the challenge compelling."

"And the requirements of the challenge?" prompted Dutamis.

"First I determined the optimum impact zone – the height of the swing where a slight pause occurs. I had to then gauge the arc and timing of the pendulum, the heft and speed of the pebble, the effect of gravity on the pebble itself, and then launch along a trajectory high and forward of the projected position of the mobile objective," replied Artenza.

"How certain of succeeding were you?" probed Dutamis.

"On my first attempt, I had only the opportunity to rehearse mentally. Nothing new there – anyone who has thrown a stone or fired an arrow has engaged in this sort of cerebral gymnastic. The first shot gave me initial feedback and a small level of familiarity with the vectors at play. My second attempt of limited success provided deeper learning, allowing me to subsequently believe I could hit the target. I envisioned the trajectory needed by figuring desired speed and altitude at various interim points on the path. On the third try, I was quite confident – I truly expected to hit it, I had no doubt."

Dutamis turned to the others.

"Ballistic prowess," he stated, matter-of-factly.

"Come again?" pardoned Trutorio.

"Ballistic prowess," repeated Dutamis. "It is a distinctly human ability – to project forward mentally and then utilize kinetic energy to propel an object to intercept a moving target. Only we have the ability to think

❦

*Ballistic
prowess
– the ability
to mentally
rehearse
events and
intercept
a moving
target with a
projectile – is
a distinctly
human
aptitude and
the very basis
for our equally
unique ability
to mark and
meet goals
and objectives
set far in the
future*

❦

ahead, to project ourselves into the future, and to launch a plan of attack that hits the objective. It is one of the most distinguishing attributes of our core aptitude for complex corporal movement, as we discussed earlier."

"Most interesting!" the Prince smiled, watching as the others absorbed this new insight.

"Combined with our creativity and ingenuity, our marksmanship has everything to do with our ability to envision and effect a new reality!" the Prince continued. "We have the unique capacity to perform a strictly cerebral run-through before engaging our bodies in actually executing the exercises as we have seen them. It comes so naturally to us it has become in large part reflex. For example, we think before we speak, and we easily project ourselves into upcoming events and situations. We have the singular ability to see with our mind's eye both the historical and the eventual, enabling us to take action in the present."

"I see the connection," said Artenza. "Our vision is a lofty and dynamic target, so we must set intermediate goals at various levels to pull the vision closer to reality and allow us to true our trajectory. Like hitting the pendulum with the pebble, we must aim high and forward to hit our vision by seeing the arc of our ambition."

"The metaphor works quite well," praised Trutorio. "The closer the target is while still remaining a challenging stretch eases our ability to set an effective course. With interim goals and subordinate objectives set properly to intercept our carefully-crafted, fully-vested vision – which we now know must incorporate our past learning and success – we easily enter the domain of belief in our ability to achieve what we expect of ourselves."

"I too am of the mind that our simple demonstration covers our current ground – that of goal-setting – quite well, quite completely," counseled Dutamis. "Not to be contrary, but I find most of the grand ballyhoo around goals to be much more complicated, much more difficult than it is! Goals simply comprise the first step in the cycle of achievement."

Receiving no argument, Dutamis continued.

"To my mind, a goal is defined simply as any intended activity with a definitive outcome – visions, aspirations, ambitions, and objectives are all forms of goals."

"Most everything we to do is attached to some goal, then," affirmed Artenza.

"Exactly," replied Dutamis, shrugging. "I can think of no voluntary action that has not been thought out first to some extent. The brain commands the body."

"Then there is no such thing as having no goals!" challenged Trutorio.

"It is impossible," confirmed Dutamis. "Even those who profess to reject the notion of goals cannot escape this reality."

"The intent to have no goals is a goal!" cried Artenza.

"Albeit not a productive, progressive, or proactive one," replied Dutamis.

"The matter involves direction and dimension of our intentionality," offered Trutorio.

"Of course you are quite right," interjected the Prince, who had been listening closely. "As I look back on my life, I can see now that there are only two kinds of goals – which I shall stratify as terminal goals, and enabling goals. In the grand scheme of things, I know of only two terminal goals. The first is the very subject of our discussion – making the most of what we have to offer the world. Everything else is properly classed as enabling – empowering yet subordinate means to the end."

"What is the second terminal goal?" asked Artenza, ever curious.

Goals comprise the first half of the creative achievement cycle

A goal is defined simply as any intended activity with a definitive outcome

"It is a topic for another day, another discussion," replied the Prince. "It is, of course, the other great end in life – giving and receiving love."

The others nodded in affirmative understanding.

"The differences between terminal goals and enabling goals relate more to outcome," continued the Prince. "The differences within the subset of enabling goals are those relating to the intended activity itself."

"Terminal goals having more cumulative, subjective outcomes," noted Trutorio.

"Enabling goals having more immediate, objective outcomes," noted Artenza.

"It is these enabling goals, then, that require our present attention," stated Dutamis.

"It is these enabling goals – these intermediate objectives – that true our trajectory," added Trutorio.

"It is the enabling goals that focus our energy and affect our immediate performance – directing our attention and action…" started Artenza.

"…mobilizing our effort…" continued Dutamis.

"…increasing our resolve…" continued Trutorio.

"…and motivating the search for appropriate strategies," finished the Prince. "You are indeed correct in your estimation – almost automatically, properly set goals can catalyze these internal processes."

"Then I see only two issues we must now consider," stated Artenza. "Marking our goals, and meeting them."

"I believe the requirements can be drawn from our pendulum example," offered Dutamis.

"Your thoughts?" asked the Prince.

"The arc of our ambition rests on two things – ballistics and belief," shrugged Dutamis. "Nothing more, nothing less."

"And by ballistics you mean precision, propulsion, and projection," clarified Artenza. "It is the clarity of

The arc of our ambition rests on two things – ballistics and belief

the outcome, the alignment of our gifts to it, and the accuracy of our foresight."

"And by belief you mean desire, determination, and dedication," clarified Trutorio. "It is the passion we hold for the dream, the doggedness with which we pursue it, and the commitment to our engagement."

"Correct to both," replied Dutamis. "At one level, we must speak to the specifics of the goal itself, and at a higher level, we must speak to the efficacy of one's self. They are inexorably linked, and cannot be taken separately."

"It is ambiguity that strikes a death knell to even the grandest of designs," affirmed Artenza.

"It is the doubt of self that limits the realization of even the most vivid of dreams," affirmed Trutorio.

"Given our demonstration, all of this · discussion seems quite intuitive," commented the Prince. "I would urge us to refrain from prescribing any further procedural detail at this point. We have delineated the requirements in a fashion apropos. Beyond ballistics and belief as we have defined them, it is best if the individual employs whatever specific technique of making and meeting objectives has been successful in the past. If the goal is truly intermediate to the grand ambition, and the ambition anchored to one's governed gifts and shared strengths, we may rest assured the proper alignment exists to foster both ballistics and belief. We know enough about different intellects now to be reasonably assured each person will have a unique but representative method that fits with their mindset and worldview. We cannot script this activity for Maximus. Might I suggest that further elaboration seems superfluous?"

"We are then to the application," offered Dutamis.

"Which should illuminate this concept of ballistics," added Artenza.

There is no one best way to set a goal – whatever specific technique of making and meeting objectives has been successful in the past should be employed – if the goal is truly intermediate to the ambition, the proper alignment exists

"While instilling the importance of belief," said Trutorio.

"Right," confirmed Dutamis. "It occurs to me that if we have properly vested our vision – perhaps the most *meta* of our enabling goals – the matter of setting the subordinate enabling goals is the one before us."

"Let us then move immediately from our previously detailed visions to the tier of goals whose achievement will lead us there," suggested Artenza.

"In the interest of time, perhaps we should focus our attention on one such goal each," suggested Trutorio.

"Acknowledging that our exercise is merely illustrative of the longer-range goals that spell the vectors of our vision," cautioned Dutamis.

"And that we must mark all domains of our life in a like manner," added Trutorio.

"Agreed," replied Artenza.

The Prince and the Courtiers took their respective turns. Dutamis, who had been first to offer his vision, was first again.

"I wish to transform our present socioeconomic condition into a highly-regulated, transparent market-driven economy with a well-entrenched system of central fiduciary institutions that monitor and maintain our monetary stability at the Continental level."

"A daunting challenge!" cried Artenza.

"Beyond all probability!" cried Trutorio.

"A big idea to be sure," commended the Prince, "but masterfully set – your goal adds the necessary element to your equally masterful vision. Combined with your purpose and strengths, your vision and goal become ever so palpable, ever so achievable, ever so exciting! Your ambition remains a well-anchored one, and I have every confidence your objective will come to pass."

Dutamis looked pleased. Artenza took his turn.

"I wish to elevate the status of our sports competitions to become a form of cultural entertainment at the level of Continental pastime, in so doing bring the Provinces together through organized friendly combat, enable young athletes to showcase their talents, and provide a means for us to establish our Province as the most athletically superior in all the land."

"Razor sharp!" cried Dutamis.

"Inspiring!" cried Trutorio.

"And so like you, Artenza," praised the Prince. "The connection to your very being is clear. It is also quite accessible – one does not require further explanation to understand your intent. As it should, your goal mandates you to transcend strategy, tactics, logistics, and diplomacy – to become visionary in order to effect your vision. I have no doubt this well-anchored ambition will be actualized."

Artenza smiled his acknowledgement. Trutorio took his turn.

"It is my desire to secure interprovincial cooperation in promulgating a proclamation of human rights and fundamental freedoms by creating a centralized multipartisan forum for harmonizing the actions of the Provinces in order to make and keep peace throughout the land."

"A compelling summit!" exclaimed Artenza.

"Stirring!" exclaimed Dutamis.

"A bold mission," commended the Prince. "A goal well set on the foresight in your elegant vision of the ideal, capturing your unique gifts quite nicely. Appropriately beyond our current capabilities and culture, it is an engaging stretch for all, and shall provide a focal point of effort toward the end you envision. We can look forward with hope for the day it becomes reality!"

Trutorio looked pleased. The Courtiers looked to the Prince, for it was only he that remained to voice his objective.

"You know my primary goal by now," he began. "It is what we have been working on for these past hours. It requires no further explanation."

The Prince paused a moment, then resumed.

"However," he began, "there does exist a goal attached to my vision of our Court's future that I should wish to pass on, for I shall not be able to meet it. I shall leave it for Maximus or for whomsoever might be so inclined to share what I see and bring it to life. Perhaps you yourselves shall find it worthy of adoption, as you have so done with unerring fidelity these many years."

The Courtiers waited anxiously.

"In light of my cause – which I have always held as advancing the frontiers of knowledge in all the areas of scholarship that will best serve the Province in the future – I wish to reengineer our system of education

❧

*Goals
become most
compelling
when they
are openly
declared,
positively
stated, set
beyond
immmediate
reach, define
a clear
outcome, and
entail a level
of difficulty
never before
attempted
– requiring
extraordinary
effort and a
measure of
luck to achieve*

❧

to better institutionalize the generation, dissemination, and preservation of knowledge that can be brought to bear on the world's great challenges, and that will prepare individuals for life, work, and leadership."

The Courtiers were silent for a moment.

"I believe I am safe in speaking for my colleagues when I say that our current project, in fact, advances this very goal," stated Dutamis.

"In some small way, I would agree," replied the Prince. "Certainly our discussion is representative of all I stand for. However, it is the sweeping overhaul and comprehensive reformalization of structure and systems that is left for tomorrow."

The Prince shifted his attention back to the subject of goals.

"Listening to you all detail your targets, it becomes rather apparent that there are some commonalities in these missionary marks that are worth mentioning. All have been openly declared, and such publicity aids in creating accountability and commitment. All require extraordinary effort and belief – as well as some measure of luck – for they are by no means a given. None can be easily or quickly accomplished, and certainly not without significant support. They are stated in the affirmative, and will thus positively inform your actions without need for translation. Although they are not necessarily quantifiable – and they need not be in order to compel movement – each has a clear end-state, enabling you to gauge your success."

"Each is unique in its ability to inspire belief and catalyze action, yet aspects of each strike a universal note," noted Trutorio.

"Each is set appropriately out of reach yet artfully within the realm of possibility – they are not so difficult that our engagement is at risk," added Dutamis.

"And each will be of great utility as we move to

positioning supporting objectives and prioritizing key agendas," agreed Artenza.

"We are then down to the business of conjuring a macro process for planning and executing the achievement of these aspirations, for we have yet to take action," concluded the Prince.

"Our goal-setting yields little as an isolated activity," added Dutamis.

"A fine list of grand objectives has no intrinsic value," agreed Trutorio.

"It is the art of accomplishment we must now enact," finished Artenza.

And so it was that the Prince and his Courtiers advanced their discussion to the topic of translating significant ideas into responsible action.

Orchestrate the Opus

The beginning is the chiefest part of any work.

Plato

Dutamis rose to walk toward three carved statues of Provincial heroes. Stopping in front of the three, he turned to the others.

"By way of introducing our next challenge," he began, "look upon these three figures. Each has been masterfully carved by a different sculptor from the finest of materials – one of hardwood, one of granite, and one of marble. In the context of the anchored ambition, what might we infer about the artists?"

"Their visions were likely of similar endowment," offered the Prince.

"Their goals were quite similar in trajectory," added Artenza.

"Their gifts were likely of similar genre," suggested Trutorio.

"Correct, one and all – the salient differentiators being execution and outcome," concluded Dutamis.

The others murmured their agreement.

"And so we move below the level of visions and goals to arrive at the challenge of master projects – picking, planning, and performing the opus that captures and conveys our ideas," continued Dutamis.

"It is through our projects – our creative endeavors of well-defined starts and stops – that we pull the future into the present," affirmed the Prince.

"While our goals focus on the morrow, our projects demand our attention today," stated Artenza.

"Most of what we do is a project of some sort," noted Trutorio.

"Differing only in scale, scope, and spire," observed Dutamis.

"The completion of which generates the creative energy required to drive our ambition toward the envisioned end," said Artenza.

"The abandonment of which steals the very inertia required to maintain the circle of creativity around the axle of accomplishment," countered Trutorio.

"All true," agreed the Prince. "Dutamis, where do we go from here?"

"As a practical matter, I propose that we immediately apply our thoughts to the very goals we have just set," replied Dutamis.

"How?" challenged the Prince.

"By each of us selecting a master project that responds to our respective goal," responded Dutamis.

"Excellent!" cried the Prince. "How then shall we proceed?"

Dutamis looked thoughtful.

"We have all set goals and completed compelling projects," he answered. "I suggest we first pool our collective wisdom so as to shed light on the subject of project selection – perhaps a few criteria to guide our decision. Then, we might easily test our template by declaring our projects."

"A most practical approach!" exclaimed the Prince.

"One such criterion seems obvious, given our requirement of alignment with our gifts, purpose,

---

Completing well-aligned projects generates the creative energy required to drive our ambition toward the envisioned end

vision, and goals," offered Trutorio. "Nevertheless, certainly our masterwork must be a labor of love – a project of personal *passion*."

"To this I would add the measure of *visibility*," offered Artenza. "High profile, high stakes projects attract potential investment. If our project never sees the light of day, if we can't propel it into the limelight, we may never get the recognition and resources needed to have great impact."

"And to this I would add the element of *innovation*," suggested the Prince. "The truly creative act demands a revolutionary breakthrough – something new and different to be constructed that positively responds to an identified opportunity or need, now or in the future."

"The ingenuity of which adds value by offering a minimally burdened benefit exceeding the expectations of those who may be impacted by, or have some interest in, the outcome," added Dutamis. "We must add *value*."

"Passion, visibility, innovation, value – a fine template – shall we then declare?" prompted the Prince.

Dutamis stood first to proclaim his *magnum opus*.

"Given my previously stated goal – which as you recall revolves around a system of central fiduciary institutions – I declare my project as this: to establish a Continental Reserve Bank. This shall be a central fiduciary concern to provide the Provinces with a safer, more flexible, and more stable monetary and financial system. The Continental Reserve will act under the guidance of a Board of Governors to conduct monetary policy, supervise and regulate lesser Provincial financial institutions, create and standardize an interbank lending system, monitor and set rates for credit and loans, and provide selected financial services to the Provinces, Principalities, and Courts across the Continent."

The others were silent for a time. Only the Prince spoke, but voiced what all were thinking.

⚜

Opus Criteria

✧ *Passion*

✧ *Visibility*

✧ *Innovation*

✧ *Value*

⚜

"Your goal captured now as a project becomes ever so much more gripping, owing to the very tangible nature of the challenge."

Inspired by Dutamis' proposed canon, Artenza took up the charge.

"Given my goal of promoting athletic endeavor and blending sport with culture, I declare my project as this: to create what I shall call the Continental Games. This is to be the most prestigious sporting event in the land – a multidiscipline competition in the tradition of ancient Olympia, where the elite of the athletic elite not only battle every other year in a *tour de force* for the distinction of world class superiority, but, more importantly, have the opportunity to participate in a theater for their talents with a true spirit of sportsmanship. The essential thing is not to conquer but to fight well, and to glory in the effort."

"I stand in quiet admiration of your ambition," praised the Prince.

Trutorio eagerly took his turn.

"Given my goal of centralizing peacekeeping efforts, I declare my project as this: to charter a United Congress of the Provinces. This member assembly shall place diplomacy in service to the harmonious and humanitarian development of homelands everywhere, with a view to encouraging the establishment of a cooperative and peaceful society concerned with the preservation of human dignity and the protection of human rights. The Congress shall act in unity in a world tainted by conflict to promote friendly relations between the Provinces, and to both condemn and squelch any and all barbarous acts of aggression, tyranny, or oppression as they may arise to outrage the conscience of civilization."

"A challenge universal in impact," praised the Prince.

The Courtiers looked to the Prince, awaiting his declaration.

"I have long wanted to build an Academy. It shall be a progressive institution of higher academics focused on lifelong learning as we have defined it – expanding and elevating the definition of education while addressing and overcoming the many limitations of current institutional schooling practices. The Academy will provide a unique environment in which leading scholars and promising students strive together to expand fundamental knowledge of human nature, society, and the natural world with the express purpose of making substantial economic and social contributions. It shall be a haven of inquiry for students at all levels to experience with their mentors the processes of developing and testing new hypotheses and fresh interpretations of phenomena, while providing learners with the tools needed to continue intellectual development over a lifetime and meet the needs of our rapidly changing society."

The Pantheon was still.

"Rest assured the Academy will see its day," stated Dutamis, quietly, forcefully.

"These are all enormous undertakings," he continued. "To fully realize them is a massive endeavor. Given our limitations of time, it seems obvious that planning a project here and now is unrealistic, as is actual implementation."

"Agreed," said the Prince. "However, this domain most definitely plays to your strengths – what then is your counsel?"

"It seems most appropriate to discuss the process by which these masterworks might be accomplished," replied Dutamis. "By doing so, we can map the *macro* phases of project work in an effort to offer a common approach that will enable Maximus to manage his own schemes, and allow us to offer cohesive guidance should the need arise."

"Good!" cried the Prince. "Continue!"

"As I see it," Dutamis began, "there are four distinct acts to the successful completion of any project – first is to *define*, second is to *design*, third is to *deploy*, and the last is to *decode*."

Dutamis stopped to collect his thoughts, then launched into a primer.

"In the *define* phase, we initiate and take charge of our project by outlining the tangible materialization of our goal – the selection and declaration of our enterprise as we have just done. This naturally leads us to an information-gathering effort – recognizing that a comprehensive inquiry into the requirements of our venture is necessary in order to accurately identify project needs and adequately manage our work. Not knowing all parameters presents a potential danger – there is a risk to working blind, and it must be assessed up front.

"From there, we move to setting the direction and course of our work by enumerating and prioritizing the specific objectives that set the agenda. It is then a matter of deciding upon a clear and concise specification of scope and scale – what is and isn't within the bounds of the project. This allows us to determine the various points of impact on others.

"Finally, we must date our project – doing so creates both the requisite intentionality that grants us control over circumstance as well as a constructive constraint that fosters urgency and creativity in completing the project."

Dutamis paused to allow the others time to absorb his treatise.

"And the phase of *design*?" queried the Prince.

"It is one of planning and preparation for execution," replied Dutamis. "This entails first detailing the tenor and timing of the steps, tasks and milestones that must be accomplished to achieve our desired outcome. This allows appropriate estimates of time and effort to be made, in turn enabling the identification of the shortest timeframe within which our project can be accomplished.

"If new knowledge and skill is required, it shall be revealed here, and provisions for acquiring those must be incorporated into our plans. If cost is an issue, budget estimates must be developed as well. From here, we move to structuring our approach, scheduling and sequencing our workflow, and if needed, securing a sponsor – in short, marshaling the resources, tools, material, and support required for project completion. In so doing, we must establish the assumptions under which we labor and assess the risks involved, additionally mapping contingencies to address both areas in an effort to prevent interference."

"Your process seems so lengthy and drawn out," argued Artenza. "Isn't it easier to simply try something, see if it works, assess the impact, learn from the effort, and execute once more with new-found intelligence? That way, we have tested our idea, gained valuable feedback, and minimized our investment."

"There is an art and science to managing possibility," said Dutamis. "Time and analysis must be weighed against the pressing needs to which our project responds. And you are quite right – the unpracticed may overindulge in planning and preparation. However, what you are really talking about amounts to an accelerated cycle, not an abbreviated one. The phases remain the same."

"True enough," agreed Artenza. "We must then *deploy!*"

"Indeed," affirmed Dutamis. "The third phase is quite simply the full implementation of the plan – the total engagement of our talents focused on a worthy challenge centered optimally in our zone of virtuosity! Skill in managing to our plan is the critical component here, for we are beyond commitment."

"Tools to track our progress help direct the effort," noted Artenza. "From my own experience, anything visual in nature which can be used to indicate current progress as well as any remaining milestones keeps the objectives fresh in my mind, while helping to maintain both the impetus to stay focused on task and the inertia to move forward on schedule."

"*Completion* is the key," noted the Prince. "Successful projects do not simply end on their own – the finish must be proclaimed! No matter what adjustments must be made to the plan, regardless of whether the outcome is of a different breed than the intent, and irrespective of any shortcoming in results, we simply *must* declare victory. We must be willing to pronounce even the most disappointing projects concluded. It is the proactivity in doing so that charges the next cycle of goals and projects."

"An important point to embrace," agreed Artenza. "We may never be completely satisfied, for perfection is indeed elusive. But to get mired down in the bog of veritable flawlessness is to realize perhaps only diminishing returns of impact. The pursuit of perfection must be balanced with the mandate to advance."

"Precisely," replied the Prince. "We need simply to appreciate our best efforts given the parameters of the project as envisioned."

"I am curious now about the last phase," commented Trutorio, addressing Dutamis. "Whatever do you mean by *decode?*"

"Artenza has already alluded to it, and we have broached the subject before in our discussion of mastery," answered Dutamis.

"It is the issue of sense-making – assessing our results against our plan, capturing the lessons learned from things gone wrong, documenting and standardizing the best of new and successful techniques acquired through

Orchestration

✧ *Define*

✧ *Design*

✧ *Deploy*

✧ *Decode*

the course of action, and incorporating all new knowledge into our repertoire before beginning a new cycle of achievement. The feedback from our attempts to accomplish our goals through focused project work is both necessary and desired. How might we determine our success otherwise? We know that if we manage our learning in this way, we move toward mastery and advance our ambition with ever-expanding wisdom, in turn availing ourselves of increasing impact."

"A strong and solid process," praised Trutorio. "We are then poised to cycle back to setting further goals to sustain our forward momentum. You are indeed a logistical wizard!"

"Thank you," said Dutamis, acknowledging the accolade.

Dutamis then issued a characteristic word of caution.

"We must realize, however, that all of this is done in full recognition that things will change – and somewhat to the points of both Artenza and the Prince, our projects will only very rarely implement and result as planned, but the planning process is invaluable simply because it requires us to think through our idea!"

The others nodded in a knowing acknowledgement, each having experienced the disruptive forces of change. Sensing a point of transition, Dutamis moved the discussion forward.

"Perhaps it is wise at this point to explore the uncontrollable forces of change," he suggested.

And so it was that the Prince and Courtiers turned their attention to their penultimate challenge.

Figure On Flux

So as this only point among the rest remaineth sure and certain, namely, that nothing is certain.

Plato

"Dutamis," voiced the Prince, "might I be so bold as to suggest that we return briefly to your notion of ballistic prowess as a means of broaching our next topic?"

"Please do!" encouraged Dutamis. "Our immediate subject transverses the complex territory of strategy, of which you are the grand master."

"And not to add complexity, but there is one issue we overlooked in our pendulum analogy," replied the Prince. "We made an inherent assumption which we must now reconsider."

The others looked at once intrigued and perplexed.

"Our experiment was performed in a controlled environment," he explained. "Had we conducted the same exercise in the open air, what then might we have needed to accommodate?"

"The wind!" cried Artenza. "My trajectory might have been vastly different if I had been at the mercy of uncontrollable gusts! I would have had to attempt to gauge the breeze, adjust my aim accordingly, envision the probable trajectory appropriately, and launch with an entirely different specification – all with decreased certainty. "

"You see my point, naturally," stated the Prince. "We have done a commendable job of pulling the future nearer so that we might act upon it – but in matters strategic, it is important to not only see distant objects as if they were close, but also to take a distanced view of close things. Understandably, we have subconsciously, and quite naturally, made an unvoiced assumption that the future will reveal itself in a slow evolution from the present, thinking that things will progress much as they have to this point – for that is most probable. But as we prepare to launch our projects, how should we best think about the impact of our actions? How can we learn whether our goals will be viable in the future? Will our projects lead to impact as envisioned? What might prevent such impact? These are the questions that we must look into, for if we simply assume or guess, we place our potential impact at some risk."

Seeing the looks of concern on the faces of his

Unless we attempt to map the various emerging forces and trends that may play and prey upon our aspirations, we place our potential impact at risk

Courtiers, the Prince offered further explanation.

"The issue before us is whether or not our prodigious projects represent good choices for a better future. The thought is not to paint an accurate picture of tomorrow, but to make a qualified decision regarding it. Are we not the grand net of the decisions we've made to this point – the substance of which empowers us to change the world? Insight and learning form the heart of such an effort, and we will do no harm, and a great measure of good, to ponder how our work will fit with – or run counter to – the various emerging forces and trends that may play and prey upon our aspirations, and to consider the myriad of inevitabilities and uncertainties that are perhaps unforeseeable unless we are actively attuned to them. Gentlemen, while we have anticipated change – and proffered significant ideas to create change ourselves – we have yet to adequately gauge the prevailing winds and scan the horizon for potential storms. In the name of responsible action, we have a clear mandate to do so."

"The point being to raise important questions and acknowledge that which has the means to bend our dreams," furthered Trutorio.

"Not so much to predict what will strike, but to avoid disruptive surprise," added Dutamis.

"And to create an awareness that will facilitate our ability to respond and stay the course," said Artenza.

"Quite right," confirmed the Prince. "Using the very same approach we have employed so far – looking ahead through the lens of our individual intellects and personal urgencies, and applying our ballistic prowess to widen our view."

"Of what manner are these winds?" asked Trutorio, after a time.

"There are those in our face, and those at our back," replied the Prince. "With us or against us – forces driving or restraining our visions, goals, and projects.

The most important and uncertain of the forces at play become the most pressing and influential variables in framing our decisions regarding the future

The question being, of course, from whence do they hail?"

"And what is their fury?" asked Trutorio.

"And have they the power to veer our course?" asked Dutamis.

"And how shall we tack ahead?" asked Artenza.

"These are the issues as I see them," finished the Prince.

"Then let us engage them!" suggested Artenza.

"Very well," agreed the Prince. "Let us first review the various fields of force currently at play around us that we have undoubtedly built into our current trajectories. If nothing else, we shall confirm our purposeful ideation. To the most casual observer, our goals and projects might seem to have been made rather fancifully, but we know that is not the case. What are such forces, and what is their genesis?"

"The state of society for one," answered Trutorio. "The political landscape for another."

"Economic currents," added Dutamis. "Environmental conditions."

"Technological trends," added Artenza. "Cultural shifts."

"Excellent!" cried the Prince. "All would seem to be capable of influence, correct? Let us examine them closer. As we look to each, what are the certitudes? What seems inevitable?"

Trutorio addressed the political and societal forces.

"Our population is growing – in number and diversity – and will continue to do so," replied Trutorio. "Our political system is growing in complexity and involvement. That Maximus will ascend the throne is a foregone conclusion."

"The implications?" challenged the Prince.

"We shall face a younger constituency varying widely in perspective," responded Trutorio. "There will be more laws and restrictions, more pressure between vested interests founded in political leanings across the land within and among the Courts, Principalities, and Provinces; and, we shall have a Court with a new perspective on all of it."

Dutamis addressed the economic and environmental forces.

"Our economy is growing larger in breadth and more segmented by industry," he began. "Our need for fuel increases exponentially, to support our industry and population."

"The implications?" queried the Prince.

"Costs will increase as diversified goods proliferate, the need for free flow of trade will overflow borders, and wealth will stratify," replied Dutamis. "At the same time, the earth will take a mighty toll from the environmental disruption of construction, resource deprivation, and waste."

Artenza addressed the technological and cultural forces.

"Our systems, tools and technologies advance daily," replied Artenza. "Our appetites for entertainment grow ever larger, our tastes more refined, our identities more eclectic, our desires more migratory."

"Implications?" parried the Prince.

"Education and learning will become more important as manual labor declines in the face of new tools and technologies requiring greater thinking skills to apply," replied Artenza. "The demand for new and more specialized art forms will grow in all sectors. Eventually, even the most basic of commodities may become specialty markets."

"If these are the givens, what then are the uncertainties?" challenged the Prince.

"The pace and direction of change, for one," replied Artenza. "We know science and technology are advancing, but we don't how quickly they will be accepted, or how fleetly they can be applied. We know the economy is expanding, but we don't know how the tiers of affluence will layer."

"Potential power conflicts, for another," replied Dutamis. "The growth of the economy beyond borders may be at odds with protective political interests and persuasions."

"Human attitudes and performance must also be considered," replied Trutorio. "We are by and large at the mercy of individuals with a wide range of variance in ability and aim."

"Most excellent!" cried the Prince. "It is this last item that I deemed most influential and relevant in driving our current project, this evening's entire discussion as it regards my son Maximus."

The Prince stood to tell his story.

"You see, when my earthly demise became a foregone conclusion, I asked myself what the future might hold for the Court with Maximus as Prince. It is a given he shall reign. What remained uncertain was the impact he'd exact. Would it be absolute in nature? What would happen if he were unable to make the most of what he had to offer the world? I too saw the trends that pointed to a crisis of meaning among the people of the Province. The most pressing and influential variables became his ability and aim, for they were the most important and uncertain of the forces at play in framing the decision to launch this very project."

"How then did you proceed?" asked Dutamis.

"I sketched the various scenarios as I saw them, plotting along one axis of ability, and along the other axis of aim," replied the Prince.

"What were these scenarios?" queried Trutorio.

"The first was one of high ability and low aim," explained the Prince.

"The result was something short of absolute impact – a search for continuity. I saw Maximus somewhat engaged in his work, but without an understanding of what it meant to be a leader as we have defined it – without a higher purpose, without sharing his strengths, without an anchored ambition. Thus, I saw him squandering his talent. In the end, the loss of performance and potential had powerful implications for his life and the future of the Court. It was a call to action."

"And the second?" asked Artenza.

"The second was one of high aim and low ability," answered the Prince. "The result again fell shy of absolute impact – a search for opportunity. I saw Maximus as having good intentions to serve well as Prince, but disengaged and unable to effectively implement strategy, leaving the Court in a weakened and vulnerable state. Unsure of his gifts, unsure of his deeper drive, unsure of his true calling, unable to govern his gifts, he could not begin to share his strengths nor anchor his ambition, for he knew not who he was or what he had to uniquely offer. Thus, I saw him chasing the wrong things. In the end, the potential loss of impact was unacceptable. It was a call for reflection.

"The final two scenarios are easy enough to imagine," continued the Prince. "Low ability and low aim left him utterly lost and the Court without viable leadership. High ability and high aim led to absolute impact and personal leadership, enabling a new generation of success in our Court. This scenario revealed the ultimate personal triumph!"

"And thus the decision to engage in our immediate project!" cried the Courtiers.

"Yes, to identify the pathway to absolute impact," confirmed the Prince.

The Prince paused to make his point.

"It is this process of plotting alternative images in the wake of potential disruption and ambiguity that we must employ to make sound choices regarding our life's work – our visions, goals, and projects."

"Focusing first on the discovery of all such potential influences," began Dutamis.

"Addressing both those most nebulous, and those most germane to our enterprise," added Trutorio.

"Examining various pitfalls and prospects offered by each," added Artenza.

"Thus rendering a spectrum of conceivable scenarios enabling us to then pick the strategic path that places our ambition under the very best of lights," finished the Prince.

"Each of us must do the same in relation to our own projects," noted Trutorio. "To wit, what is the future of politics? What are the scenarios under which a United Congress might flourish? Perish?"

"What is the future of economics?" added Dutamis. "Under what conditions is a Continental Reserve most successful? Disastrous?"

"What is the future of culture?" furthered Artenza. "What various circumstances render the Continental Games feasible? Vulnerable?"

"What is the future of technology?" joined the Prince. "Should we in fact build an Academy? Is it the most effective manifestation of the goal given the sea of change?"

"We must engage in a most strategic dialogue with ourselves," commented Trutorio. "We must keep in our minds that a settled view might only be a fatal illusion."

"We must keep our senses attuned to the signs of the

It is a process of plotting alternative images in the wake of potential disruption and ambiguity that we must employ to make sound choices regarding our life's work – our visions, goals, and projects

times and the harbingers of the morrow," said Dutamis. "We must listen carefully and observe acutely."

"And we must then adjust accordingly," said Artenza. "If we can't change our minds, we can't create a new reality!"

"Yet do so only within the framework of that which must not change," counseled the Prince. "While we will find continuity through change, it is our authenticity – our talents, values and causes – that stands firmly in the face of all turmoil and turbulence to ease the redirection of our ambition as required, and as the future reveals itself to us."

"Hear, hear!" cried the Courtiers.

"And," advised the Prince, "while we need not answer all of these questions right now – for we do not have the time to explore each goal and project as we have declared them – our ambition remains at risk until such time as we do. It is not so much that we must wait with dread for an imagined impending storm – for we shall miss the sunlight in doing so – but if we are properly primed, we shall more easily see and recognize the approaching signs of that which we have anticipated."

The Prince then issued a solemn warning.

"Words of caution, Courtiers. First, while we all have an inherent ability to engage in such prescience, this strategic application of our prowess must be developed and practiced, for it does not come easily for most."

"If Maximus is not so inclined, he must develop his foresight," averred Trutorio.

"It will fall to us to guide him," concluded Dutamis.

"Once we have become practiced ourselves!" cried Artenza.

"Second," continued the Prince, "we must abide by our own forecast. Courtiers, we cannot suffer the fate of the Cassandra Curse. Do you recall the myth?"

"Cassandra was the beautiful daughter of the King of

⚜

Although we will find continuity through change, it is our authenticity that stands firmly in the face of all turmoil and turbulence to ease the redirection of our ambition as required and as the future reveals itself

⚜

Troy!" recalled Artenza.

"She was given the gift of infallible foresight by Apollo!" cried Trutorio.

"But later cursed by Apollo with a terrible fate – never to be believed by anyone," remembered Dutamis.

"Terrible indeed, to always be right, but never believed!" agreed Trutorio, shaking his head.

"And in the Trojan War," retold the Prince, "Cassandra foretold of the an armed force hidden inside the wooden horse that the Achaeans had abandoned in the plain, feigning retreat."

"But no one listened!" exclaimed Trutorio.

"Her caution was spurned and rejected!" cried Dutamis.

"And Troy was destroyed at hands of the very forces Cassandra predicted," finished Artenza.

"The lesson is clear, gentlemen," whispered the Prince. "We must avoid finding ourselves saying: *Had I only known.*"

"*Had I only believed,*" added Trutorio.

"*Had I only heeded,*" added Dutamis.

"*Had I only responded,*" added Artenza.

And with that, the Prince and the Courtiers headed toward the conclusion of their debate.

Capitalize on Crucibles

We can easily forgive a child who is afraid of the dark; the real tragedy
of life is when men are afraid of the light.

Plato

The Prince rose to once more call attention to the heroic leaders of the Pantheon.

"Courtiers, has there been a single contributor decorating this hall to have risen without a struggle of considerable proportion – a test extraordinaire – a seemingly impossible ordeal with insurmountable odds?"

"No," stated Dutamis. "The hero's path is never easy."

"No," answered Artenza. "The obstacle defines the achievement."

"No," replied Trutorio. "The undaunted rise above."

"All true," confirmed the Prince. "We have discussed the nature of self-set obstacles and certainly explored the issues of courage, commitment and challenge, but we have yet to come to terms with the unplanned circumstances that try even the bravest of hearts."

"You speak of the crucibles, of course," confirmed Dutamis. "No matter how well we have focused our foresight, we will not escape the unforeseeable difficulties that test us – the trials that reveal the depths of our strength."

"The travails that demand reflection and mindfulness to inform us when we know not what to do," added Trutorio.

"The tribulations that force us to reexamine the roots of our very being," added Artenza.

"Yes," confirmed the Prince. "These are the points of inflection that have the paradoxical power to lay bare new avenues of accomplishment."

"By way of introduction," offered Dutamis, "I am reminded of a story my father once told me in my youth, of a simple farmer who came across an immense boulder when clearing his fields. No matter how hard he tried, the farmer could not budge or blast the massive stone. Repeated attempts to remove the rock only stole his energy and enthusiasm. The obstruction remained, however, and he could not plant his crops with the boulder in the way."

"What did he do?" asked Artenza.

"At first, nothing," replied Dutamis. "The farmer was at a loss, and he mourned his predicament, paralyzed by

No matter how sharp our foresight, we will not escape the unforeseeable trials that reveal the depths of our strength and from which we may learn far more than from our triumphs

⚜

These are the crucibles – the points of inflection that have the paradoxical power to lay bare new avenues of achievement

the thought of his pending misfortune. Finally, after some time of fretting, he became desperate. His fields could not go another day without sowing. That is when inspiration hit. The farmer dug a hole more than twice the size of the boulder. Then he dug away the lip below the stone and used a lever to tip the rock into the hole, and covered it with dirt."

"Ingenious!" exclaimed Artenza.

"But that is not all," said Dutamis. "From that day on, the farmer stood each day on the spot where he'd buried the boulder, right until the time he took his dying breath. You see, what had been his biggest barrier had now become part of his very foundation."

"An interesting and intriguing allegory," commented the Prince. "The boulder, of course, represents the questions we have about ourselves, the obstacles we face, and the doubts that creep into our minds as we pursue our course. The fable's lesson is clear – we may learn far more from our trials than from our triumphs."

The Prince grew silent, lost in distant thought.

"If only all of our problems were so easily solved," he mused. "Your story illustrates well the nature of the true tests in life – the outer and inner struggles we encounter. It brings to mind the story of Beowulf."

"A saga centuries old!" recalled Dutamis, fondly.

"A true warrior's tale!" recalled Artenza, fondly.

"A celebration of spirit!" recalled Trutorio, fondly.

"Yes," agreed the Prince. "But more than this, the story stands to illuminate the very ground upon which we must tread in this our final chapter by way of offering us a metaphor for the nature of the invisible war we all wage within. I am certain the wisdom in the fable of Beowulf will bring us full circle and enable us to conclude our project. I know of no other better means to share this final learning challenge. I am certain that a figurative approach to this theme is the only course of treatment that makes sense for such a nebulous and personal domain. There is no practical application as far as I can see, no clear process."

"Artenza, will you tell our story?" asked the Prince.

"Gladly!" replied Artenza, always eager to perform.

"Trutorio, will you guide our discovery?" asked the Prince.

"Gladly!" replied Trutorio, always eager to interpret.

"Dutamis, will you facilitate our inquiry?" asked the Prince.

"Gladly!" replied Dutamis, always eager to help.

"Very well, then, let us proceed!" cried the Prince, turning to Artenza.

And so it was that the Prince and his Courtiers explored the ancient and anonymously authored epic of Beowulf.

"The story of Beowulf is set in the troubled Dark Ages, when there was constant warfare," began Artenza, settling into the story.

"In those days, there were many small kingdoms fighting to save themselves from larger enemies. One such king, knowing that brave and skilled warriors were the only hope, gathered a fine band of fighting men around him. For some time there was peace in his kingdom. No one dared attack. To reward his men, the King built a great hall – not unlike our own Pantheon – set among the fens and moors, where they could meet and feast, talk of battles past, and plan strategies to defend the kingdom against possible attacks."

Artenza paused for dramatic effect.

"Then a great danger came which none had foreseen."

"And this danger?" asked Dutamis.

"A horrible monster – an incubus from the swamp named Grendel that had come to live in a dark cave below the icy black waters of the loch," answered Artenza, warming to his dramatic delivery.

"Grendel heard the sound of laughter and music coming from the great hall. He saw the King and his men laughing together, and became jealous of their merriment. Covered in swamp slime, Grendel arose from the bog, crept unseen and unheard into the hall in the small hours of the morning while the men slept and killed thirty of the King's best men, rending their flesh and stealing away their corpses. The next night, another thirty! The bravest of the King's men tried to defend against the great beast, but Grendel was nearly invisible and impossibly elusive. Swords and knives were useless against him. Soon no warriors would come to the hall, and the King sat alone."

"Trutorio?" prompted Dutamis, turning and inviting Trutorio's insight.

"The story touches upon the very thing that lies at the heart of any crisis – the ultimate crucible, the trial to end all trials," cited Trutorio.

"The monster Grendel represents all that keeps us awake at night. It is the sum of our nightmares, doubts and anxieties of self that in our sleep – when we are alone and most vulnerable – present themselves as a fearful nemesis to plague us. It is the embittered revenge of our authentic voice denied its song and refusing to be ignored – an uncontrollable spirit that if we have not been genuine in pursuing our life's work, if we have become like the bitter merchant ensnared in the trappings of success and mendacity of glamour, will rise up from the darkness of its own accord to elude our best defenses, prey upon our subconscious and threaten to destroy the mansions of glory we have so carefully constructed."

"And yet our conventional weapons – the external strategies, tools and techniques that work so effectively in extinguishing the exigencies of the day – will be useless against this adversary," added the Prince.

"Tell us of Beowulf," urged Dutamis.

"Ah, yes, Beowulf," continued Artenza.

"News of the dreaded Grendel reached Beowulf, the King's young nephew who lived across the sea. He was strong and courageous and highly trained as a warrior, having slain many monsters and giants. Beowulf assembled his comrades, sailed across the sea and stood before the king. *'I am here to rid your grand hall of this monster Grendel who comes in stealth by night,'* he proclaimed. In spite of the King's warnings, Beowulf vowed to slay Grendel that very night."

"He felt no fear?" asked Dutamis.

"None," replied Artenza. " In fact, that night he and his men feasted in the great hall. When the meal was over, Beowulf laid aside his sword and took off his coat of mail, saying to his men, *'If weapons are of no use on Grendel, I shall not need them.'*"

"Trutorio, your analysis?" asked Dutamis.

"The story would seem to imply that Beowulf has had some previous experience with such a nightmare," noted Trutorio, speculating.

"He is courageous enough to be confident in his own ability, and wise enough to know that he must let go, lay down his ordinary weapons, and shed his everyday defenses against this foe. He must allow himself the exposure that even modern day warriors come by so hard. It is through a surrender of our finest emotional armor that we will achieve the necessary vulnerability required to confront what haunts us."

"And it worked!" confirmed Artenza.

"In the darkness before dawn, Grendel easily passed through the locked iron bars. Red eyes aglow at the sight of so many to destroy, Grendel seized one young man and effortlessly stole his life away. But when he reached for Beowulf, his arm came under the strongest grip the ogre had ever felt. Try as he might, Grendel could not free himself from Beowulf. Screaming in anguish, Grendel wrenched his body away and ran back to the mere, leaving behind his severed arm."

"What is the meaning of the severed arm?" asked Dutamis, turning once more toward Trutorio.

"Quite possibly that some residual of the nightmare will forever remain with us," offered Trutorio. "Beowulf has employed valiant vigilance to eradicate what was undermining an already diminished stability, but it is worth noting that, up to this point, he has *reacted* and *responded*, but nothing beyond."

"What happened next?" asked Dutamis.

"Beowulf found Grendel's dead body the following day," continued Artenza. "Needless to say, there was much rejoicing in the kingdom. The King showered Beowulf and his men with many fine gifts, and the King's warriors returned to feast and sleep in their great hall. Beowulf and his men slept in nearby quarters, and prepared to leave for home the next day."

"But that was not the end of it," observed Dutamis, ominously.

"Oh no," affirmed Artenza.

"That very night, an even more terrifying and hideous demon entered the hall – Grendel's mother! Having found and retrieved her son's carcass to their den, she wreaked havoc on the hall, killing the warrior dearest to the King for revenge before returning to the mere."

"Trutorio?" asked Dutamis.

Trutorio delivered his interpretation with a quiet force.

It is through surrender our finest emotional armor that we will achieve the necessary vulnerability required to confront what haunts us

"In the most trying of times, that which appears to be the problem, usually isn't; therefore, that which appears to be the solution, cannot be. It isn't simply what haunts us with which we must be concerned; it is the thing that created the nightmare in the first place – the very mother of our fear! The story tells us that in the darkest hour of our most dire of straits, a much different kind of problem-solving must be employed, for the usual approach will only treat the symptom. We must seek a far deeper understanding to discover the true cause and grapple with the real problem."

"Beowulf must now struggle with the mother of the beast!" cried Dutamis.

"Quite so," nodded Artenza, continuing the tale.

"The story is clear that while no one knew where Grendel and his mother came from, they knew of the monsters' lair below the blackened icy loch. Beowulf tracks her to the lake, which burns on fire at night and is fed from a dark stream trickling down from the rocks above. Frightful sea monsters swim about in the cold pitch of the freezing water, and even a most magnificent stag fleeing from some unseen hunter won't step into it to save its own life."

"Trutorio, translation?" asked Dutamis.

"We intuitively know where to look for the source of our fear, for it resides within us," interpreted Trutorio.

"You see, Grendel's mother is the ghost of our true identity, exiled by our adaptive powers to reside in the wintery desolation of our unconscious discontent, sending forth her offspring to terrorize us. And we are to blame for the darkness below, for we not only create it but perpetuate it from above by conforming to the pressures tainted with deceptions of self – by surrendering our identity to the various competing claims upon it.

"The lake is but a facade, it's surface on fire, it's depths icy and black, not unlike the gameface we wear

In the darkest hour of our most dire of straits, a different kind of problem-solving must be employed – the usual approach is rendered useless

when we have denied our authenticity – aglow on the outside, yet dark and cold within.

"Beowulf – *we* – must now move beyond reactionary response to the deeper tier of pointed reflection and purposeful introspection to navigate these waters. The shoreline marks the periphery of our fear – in the most difficult of circumstances we often freeze, stopped cold in our tracks and unable to know exactly what to do. We have no choice but to breach the water's edge – but to do so is so frightening, so daunting that even the strongest among us quake at the thought, shying away from the depths to cling to the sanctuary of solid ground. A truly brave heart is required, but not enough. We fear the dark depths, to the point of disavowing any knowledge of it, much less that it's by our own design."

"And why might we not want to know?" probed Dutamis.

"Because with that deeper self-knowledge comes the clear responsibility for action," interjected the Prince. "In the simplest of terms, we fool ourselves into thinking that if we don't know, we can't be blamed. In the context of our overall project, if we know what our true work is, how can we possibly justify not pursuing it, to ourselves and to those we are connected to? In the end, if we have found our truest drive and denied it, we have no explanation for not making the most of what we have to offer the world. Claiming ignorance provides the feeble and fleeting escape from the truth – albeit one resulting in a lifelong nightmare Grendelesque in proportion. And in the end, if we have so claimed, we shall not gain an affirmative answer to the central question we have pursued this evening."

"What then is Beowulf's course?" asked Dutamis, looking back to Artenza.

"He braves the water, swearing that it shall not stop him from slaying the gruesome creature," continued

With a deeper knowledge of self comes the clear responsibility for action – if we have found our truest drive and denied it, we have no explanation for not making the most of what we have to offer the world, and we will not escape the nightmare such denial brings with it

Artenza. "This time, he is afraid, but he knows not why. This time, he knows that while his sword and armor will do no good against Grendel's mother, he dons them anyway to bolster his nerve as he acknowledges and accepts his senseless fear."

"Fear is nothing more than the anticipation of loss," explained Trutorio. "It is simply the imminent loss of control the immediate unknown of the lake itself presents that he anticipates at this point. The sea monsters and serpents in plain view give him no pause. And it is not Grendel's mother that strikes dread. It is the deep and dark waters of our true spirit heretofore uncharted – navigation of which we cannot rely on others."

"He is not exempt from the unspoken fear that grips us all sometimes," added the Prince. "He has no more special qualities than any other. What he possesses is judgment good enough to know that the alternative is impossible to accept – to lie awake each night in fear, to forever hide from ourselves, to live a life unfulfilled. For Beowulf, the choice is clear. And so it must be for all."

"What happened next?" urged Dutamis.

"Beowulf stepped into the lake and for days groped beneath the frozen black water – his men above all but gave up hope," continued Artenza. "Suddenly, a most powerful unseen force took him over. Grendel's mother had found him! With amazing strength and ease, the creature dragged Beowulf into her cave at the very bottom of the lake."

"All of which means what?" prompted Dutamis.

"That it is only at the very bottom that the problem will reveal itself," clarified Trutorio. "Our foresight is of no use in this situation, and we must feel our way – intuition over intelligence is required in this case. Too, the process is a lengthy one – there is no known shortcut to protracted reflection, and most will abandon the effort well before the required duration."

Artenza then retold the story's climax.

"The cave was lit by a strange beam of white light. Now able to see his rival, Beowulf wrenched himself free and struck out at her with his sword. But Grendel's mother could not be harmed by a sword made by mortal hands any more than could Grendel. Flinging Beowulf to the ground, she pulled a dagger and was poised to kill him when Beowulf saw a magnificent sword hanging on the wall, its blade emitting the white glow that lit the cave. He recognized it as the work of the giants of old, and seizing the opportunity with the last of his strength, he reached up, snatched the sword from its place and used it to decapitate Grendel's mother. Seeing the dead body of Grendel on the floor of the cave, Beowulf took his head as well."

"The defining struggle," recapped Dutamis. "But what does it mean?"

"That we shall find a saving light even in the darkest of dens," replied Trutorio. "The answer to our trouble has been there all along in the very domain of our fear, and now presents itself as the very means to eradicate our anxiety. There is nothing to prepare us; we can only seize the moment. It requires us to be fully present – mindful, if you will."

"And the conclusion of the story?" asked Dutamis.

"Beowulf was out of danger at last, but…" retold Artenza, mysteriously, "a strange thing happened. The poisoned blood of Grendel melted all but the jeweled hilt of the sword, which remained in Beowulf's hand. Carrying the heads of the two demons and the jeweled hilt of the ancient sword, Beowulf rose to the surface. There he was hailed by his anxious men waiting on the shore. The heads of Grendel and his mother were taken back to the great hall for all to see."

"Why did the blade disappear?" inquired Dutamis.

"It no longer holds value for Beowulf," answered Trutorio. "The enemies have been eliminated, they shall not reappear, and the means of destruction cannot be replicated, repurposed, or revealed to others. Each of us must deal with our demons in our own unique way. There is no clear process, tool or technique to employ. And whatever works for us, it is useless to fight the outer battles of daily life. The hilt remains merely to indicate the struggle, and while it is of no further use, it calls to our attention a newfound mode of engaging differently in our daily doings."

"And so ends the saga of Beowulf's journey," concluded Dutamis.

"A heroic warrior triumphant over the most powerful of enemies," concluded Artenza.

"An accomplished leader of true significance," concluded Trutorio.

The Courtiers turned to the Prince, awaiting his word.

"None can escape the crucibles, friends," began the Prince. "Yet we should never want to! Our crucibles harbor transformative experiences that serve to strengthen our resolve and deepen our resilience. Our

Only the consummate irrationality of our internal fear can stymie our efforts to capitalize on the crucibles and, for that matter, realize absolute impact in our work and life

crucibles reveal our leadership character by forcing us to re-examine, re-evaluate, and reclaim our most important values. Our crucibles provide our greatest learning about ourselves and about life. Our crucibles of greatest import lie within ourselves as we struggle against the deeper, darker, often unseen and unknown enemy of our own resident fear."

The Prince stood to make his final argument.

"It is only the fear of self that can stymie one's efforts. Whatever the internal fear — of pain, commitment, failure, or rejection — it is consummate irrationality! If we are in command of our energy, of what sense is the investment of it in that which will only serve to shrink our potential? If we judge ourselves in the end by our own authenticity, of what sense is it to value so highly the approval of others? If we know the pursuit of our life's work to be vital and dynamic, of what sense is the pursuit of ranks and titles that are in truth nothing more than static indicators? If we know our true work will effectively expand our freedom, of what sense is it to shy from the commitment and discipline needed to pursue it? If we remain steadfast to our talents and values, of what sense is it to fear critical choice? If we understand the reasons for past failures, of what sense is it to doubt tomorrow's successes?"

"None!" cried the Courtiers in unison.

The Prince concluded his thesis.

"As presaged, we have indeed come full circle to purposefully diving below the exigencies of our day and careers to make the very most of who we are and what we have to offer. Most will never make the journey until they are faced with the crucibles, for they are unable to engage in the brand of purposeful reflection needed. Thus, for many, the crucibles must be embraced as the very opportunity to establish the pathway to absolute impact."

The Prince looked into the faces of his Courtiers.

For a time, he said nothing. With a look of utter calm, the Prince finally spoke.

"Gentlemen, I am sad to think we are done. I can never thank you enough for the time we have just shared. I know Maximus to be in the best of care with you three to guide him as he pursues his life's work. It is the journey of a lifetime to make the most of what we have to offer the world, to quest after impact so absolute in nature that none can deny us the mark of a true leader. I am at once honored and humbled to have served with you. My mind is settled, my heart warmed, my soul satisfied. The hour is late, and we all must rest. The future awaits!"

The Courtiers stood and bowed to their great Prince.

Without another word, all four walked out from the Pantheon into the cool darkness of the evening.

The moon above shone down to light their path, while the stars gave witness to the clarity of the night.

As they parted company, each Courtier embraced the Prince in turn.

"We shall always remember this," whispered Trutorio.

"We shall serve no other like you," whispered Dutamis.

"We shall not disappoint you," whispered Artenza.

The Prince smiled and bowed to each.

⚜   ⚜   ⚜

And so it was that the Prince and his Courtiers, having concluded their business, went their separate ways.

Trutorio went home to reflect on the deeper meaning of the debate.

Dutamis went home to begin planning for the work ahead.

Artenza went home to start building the discovery tools to be developed.

The Prince retired to his chamber, and taking parchment and quill in hand composed a letter to Maximus.

Maximus,

In my absence, carry on. The Court is your birth right, yours to take into the future, yours to make the work of a lifetime.

I have lived an extraordinary life, and my solitary regret is that I will not be here to see you complete yours. I have no secrets to bestow upon you, no answers with which to endow you.

I leave you with but a single and simple parting gift — a pathway by which you may chase your own urgencies and guide your life's work.

This evening, the Courtiers and I discussed and debated a most important issue, one arising from a question that has consumed my remaining time; namely, have I made the most of what I had to offer the world? I am fortunate enough to be able to answer in the affirmative, for it is this that I consider to be the ultimate personal triumph in life.

You see, the true leaders in life are those who through their work, and regardless of lot, fully utilize their gifts to positively impact the lives of others, and who in so doing create a new and better world. This is what the ancient philosophers called the good life — the life beyond fleeting material success. It is a mode of being that cannot be taught, but that can paradoxically be learned. It is a life of impact absolute in nature. It is a life of uncommon excellence. It is a life of leadership defined in a most personal way.

Our discovery has identified a means by which you may chart your own course toward accomplishing your life's work as you define it. At its heart, it is a pathway of constant learning, a process of forever discovering, deepening, and directing your Self and all that drives you truly. It is a pathway lit by calling, cause, and conquest.

The pathway centers on you: your gifts, your contribution, your aspirations. At any time, you may call upon the Courtiers to explain the key learning challenges, which are three in number. The first concerns governing your gifts, which presents the challenge of releasing your personal energy by understanding and maximizing your native strengths. The second concerns sharing those strengths, which presents the challenge of focusing outside

*yourself by using your gifts to the highest benefit of others. The
third concerns anchoring your ambition, which presents the
challenge of creating new reality through aspirations borne of and
aligned to your strengths and purpose.*

*You must be of two minds to embark upon the rather heroic
journey along this pathway: one of curiosity, the other of
challenge, for there are two lanes to travel, reflection and action.*

*Know that it shall not be easy. You will need to learn the way
as you make your way. Your travel will not be without peril, and
forces beyond your control will test your mastery and mettle. Be
prepared for disappointment, but do not abandon the quest.*

In the end, it shall always be your choice whether or not to prevail.

*Be patient toward all that is unsettled in your soul and love
the questions themselves, for it is in the questions that you will
discover meaning.*

*I have the highest of hopes that you will realize as much from your
life as I have from mine.*

Life is truly extraordinary, if we so choose it to be.

My heart and soul will be with you always,

Father

The Prince closed his eyes, content in the knowledge that he had
made the most of one man's life and cleared the path for others to do the
same.

Absolute impact would be his legacy of leadership.

Exeunt.

Govern Your
Gifts
Source Your Strength
Play From Power
Manage What Matters
Lean Into Limits
Move Toward Mastery

Absolute
Impact !

Anchor Your
Ambition
Vest Your Vision
True The Trajectory
Orchestrate The Opus
Figure On Flux
Capitalize On Crucibles

Share Your
Strengths
Clarify Your Cause
Exceed The Ego
Strive To Serve
Foster Positive Feelings
Render Trustful Relationships

Artenzas' Tools

Note to Reader

In **Absolute Impact**, the character of Artenza (our resident Artisan) promised to devise certain evaluative tools to enable proper examination and discovery of one's gifts, purpose, and ambition.

These are they.

The exercises included here provide but a starting point in defining your pathway to absolute impact and personal leadership. Each is aligned to one of the key learning challenges.

PLEASE DO NOT ATTEMPT THEM ALL AT ONCE.

While the number of activities may seem low (27 to be exact), proper reflection and treatment of each is easily a year's worth of effort. Don't forget, the quest is lifelong!

My recommendations:

1. Attempt one or two a month. Devote enough time to give the exercise your full attention and energy. Taken lightly, your effort won't yield the deepest impact.
2. You need not start at the beginning. Depending upon where you are on the journey to impact, some parts will draw your eye more than others. It is, however, worthwhile to complete all the activities — if only to confirm what you already know.
3. Reread the relevant parts of Absolute Impact to refresh your memory and apply the insight revealed in the discussion.
4. Enlist those closest to you in your discovery (or rediscovery). They have a vested interest (remember, we cannot NOT have impact) in your endeavor, and may have a different take on a given issue that you haven't thought of.
5. Finally, please have some fun with the activities!

Here's to your realization of absolute impact!

Chapter 1: Questions

PATHTRACING

• *Are you making the most of what you have to offer the world?*

• *What is the single most important question you're here to answer?*

• *Are you chasing the right things in your work, and thus in your life?*

Here's a quick check to see if your current path is authentic in design:

Mendacity	Authenticity
Check those you may have pursued:	*Check those you'd like to answer:*
How can I achieve status & prestige?	What is my single greatest talent?
How can I gain wealth & power?	What is it that matters most to me?
What will bring me fame & notoriety?	What do I yearn to do more of?
How can I gain approval of others?	What do I feel mysteriously drawn to?
What is the easiest thing to do?	What activities engage me the most?
How can I get rich quickly & easily?	When do I most feel a sense of purpose?
How can I get by with the least effort?	Where are my abilities needed most?
What parts of me should I hide?	What is it that I find most fulfilling?
What is least risky for me?	What are my proudest achievements?
What would allow me to just get by?	What would I like my life to represent?

Look at the **Authenticity** questions you may have checked.

Develop short answers to those questions.

Then answer:

What are the common themes and elements?

Which of these qualities exist in your current activities?

In what ways can you bring more of those qualities to your work and life?

Chapter 2: Guidance

PATHCHARTING

Charting the path to absolute impact: where to start?

Place an X in the appropriate column.	Yes	No
Govern Your Gifts I am creatively engaged in truly meaningful work that I consider my calling.		
Source Your Strength I fully understand the qualities that make me unique and give me strength.		
Play from Power I consistently play to my strengths and work around my weaknesses.		
Manage What Matters I make consistent choices based on a clear understanding of my values.		
Lean Into Limits I take intelligent risks that frequently take me out of my comfort zone.		
Move Toward Mastery I apply my creativity to innovate breakthroughs in my key strength areas.		
Share Your Strengths I apply my gifts to make a positive difference in the lives of others.		
Clarify Your Cause I have a deep sense of clarity surrounding my purpose and contribution.		
Exceed the Ego I take an active role in moving myself and others beyond self-interest.		
Strive to Serve I seek to understand and serve the great needs of those I'm connected to.		
Foster Positive Feelings I take the most positive approach possible in all interactions and situations.		
Render Trustful Relationships I build trust through consistency, competence and caring in my relationships.		
Anchor Your Ambition I am actively working toward aspirations tied to my strengths and purpose.		
Vest Your Vision I have a clear and compelling picture of my future that guides my pursuits.		
True the Trajectory I have clear and compelling goals that drive my major accomplishments.		
Orchestrate the Opus I manage my progress through successful completion of key projects.		
Figure on Flux I stay alert to the emerging trends potentially affecting my work and life.		
Capitalize on Crucibles I leverage times of adversity to reflect, reassess, and redirect my energy.		

Chapter 3: Govern Your Gifts

CURRENT WORKVIEW

How do you view your current work?

Indicate your answer by marking a position on the continuum below.

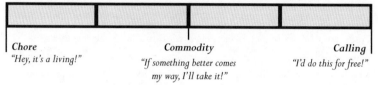

Chore	Commodity	Calling
"Hey, it's a living!"	*"If something better comes my way, I'll take it!"*	*"I'd do this for free!"*

• *How satisfied with this position are you?*

• *What actions can you take to move toward a view of your work as a calling?*

FITTING TALENT TO TASK

Are you cast properly in your current work role?

Check all those that apply:	Yes	No
My talents are fully utilized in my present work		
I am fully challenged in my present job		
I am energized by what I do		
It is easy for me to see improvement and innovation opportunities in my present work		
I find myself continually wanting to know more about my field of endeavor		
I find myself constantly setting goals related to my work		
I feel connected to something bigger than myself through my work		
My work is a way of expressing who I am		
I feel proud when describing my work to others		

Source Your Strengths

PERFORMANCE JOURNAL

Begin a Performance Journal to track your actions and outcomes. With every new challenge or endeavor, note the objective in your journal. Project your anticipated results. At the conclusion of the activity, make note of the actual outcomes. How do they compare to your projections?

Track your performance over several months. Note the instances where you've met or exceeded your expectations, as well as those in which your results fell short of expectation. Identify the key themes of performance – the roles and skills leading to excellent outcomes, and those that were a struggle and/or resulted in mediocre results.

Finally, review your conclusions with others who know your work. This should help confirm your assessment. Identify strategies to leverage your strengths and work around weakness.

GIFT TRACKER

Talents

Your unique talents will be revealed in the activities at which you naturally excel, that are naturally easy for you, and that you most enjoy.

All three criteria must be met to be considered a talent:

Excel – *You believe you display true virtuosity in this area, others have told you so, and your achievements have called on this talent repeatedly*

Easy – *This comes naturally and easily to you, and at times seems almost effortless; you don't have to struggle in any way to perform this activity*

Enjoy – *You always look forward to engaging in this activity, and it brings you great satisfaction; you're always doing this, and it's a favorite activity*

Most people don't have more than a handful that consistently meet all three. On the following pages you will find 40 major talents in the four intellects. Try to honestly assess yourself using the above criteria. Then, confirm your assessment by having someone close to you assess you, preferably someone who knows you and your work well. (Remember, others often have an easier time identifying our talents than we do!)

Philosophers (theoretic talents – naturals at analytics and strategy)

Talent (Role)	Description	Excel	Easy	Enjoy
Optimizer	*Creating excellence in all endeavors; maximizing competence; achieving the highest levels of performance*			
Marshal	*Strategically establishing a chain of command; arranging structural hierarchies to provide direction and mobilize people and plans*			
Strategist	*Comprehensively considering all contingencies and alternatives to chart the best course of action*			
Analyst	*Focusing on thorough analysis; relying on cold logic and sound reasoning; identifying causes and influences*			
Visionary	*Envisioning the future; painting compelling pictures of the future to guide action; very long range planning*			
Inventor	*Engineering and prototyping; devising and constructing working models of new solutions and technologies*			
Theorist	*Hypothesizing, imagining, and conceptualizing new frameworks of thought; experimenting with new ideas*			
Investigator	*Perpetually increasing knowledge; continually acquiring, creating, new information; constantly researching, questioning and learning*			
Designer	*Architecting and blueprinting ideas and concepts into structural models and working systems*			
Synthesizer	*Combining and piecing together seemingly unrelated components into a clear, cohesive, well-aligned system*			

My Talents in this area (those meeting all three criteria):

1.

2.

3.

4.

5.

Diplomats (empathic talents — naturals at ethics and advocacy)

Talent (Role)	Description	Excel	Easy	Enjoy
Facilitator	Creating cooperative action to achieve goals; drawing out issues that need to be addressed			
Empathizer	Connecting with others by sensing their emotions; demonstrating caring and understanding; sharing what others may be feeling in any given situation			
Mediator	Dealing with difficult people and situations; building bridges between people; resolving deep issues behind conflict; making and keeping the peace			
Perceiver	Reading the individual nuances and subtle behavioral clues of others to accurately interpret true motivation			
Confidante	Creating deep and meaningful relationships — both work and personal — built on trust and intimacy			
Coach	Fostering growth and development of others (and self); seeing the potential in people; mentoring, advising, educating; drawing out and building strength			
Counselor	Diagnosing weakness; "healing" and "fixing" people, ideas, and situations; consoling; restoring to wholeness			
Idealist	Maintaining strong belief in ideals; honoring and living the highest ethics and principles; encouraging integrity			
Integrator	Including and integrating disparate views to achieve solidarity and unity; finding common ground among many different perspectives; fostering togetherness			
Crusader	Passionately supporting an issue; spreading the word; advocating and championing worthy causes; creating inspiration and spirit around a meaningful aim			

<u>My Talents in this area</u> (those meeting all three criteria, if any):

1.

2.

3.

4.

5.

Guardians (economic talents – naturals at logistics and propriety)

Talent (Role)	Description	Excel	Easy	Enjoy
Steward	*Taking full responsibility; making and keeping all commitments; being dependable, reliable, and trustworthy*			
Legislator	*Creating, establishing and institutionalizing structure and routine (procedures, order, regimen, rules, discipline, norms, standards, measurement)*			
Enforcer	*Monitoring, inspecting, overseeing, certifying and ensuring adherence to established rules and regulations*			
Deliberator	*Being methodical, cautious and careful in creating plans and charting action; creating predictability and constancy through diligence*			
Equalizer	*Maintaining stability, balance and equilibrium; leveling, apportioning and delegating workload fairly; favoring proven conventional methods over newer techniques*			
Affiliator	*Fully participating in groups; joining and supporting organizations (companies, teams and communities)*			
Sentry	*Caretaking and providing for others; standing guard to protect and ensure safety and security; gate-keeping*			
Proprietor	*Procuring, preserving and conserving economic assets and material resources; managing and administering capital and collateral*			
Organizer	*Sequencing steps and scheduling tasks; coordinating and arranging; juggling people, plans and resources*			
Detailer	*Accumulating, inputting, archiving, categorizing and managing data, information, and objects; meticulously attending to details*			

<u>My Talents in this area</u> (those meeting all three criteria, if any):

1.

2.

3.

4.

5.

Artisans (kinetic talents – naturals at tactics and agency)

Talent (Role)	Description	Excel	Easy	Enjoy
Charger	Aggressively pursuing goals and objectives; constantly striving for results and achieving positive outcomes			
Expeditor	Accelerating the processing and handling of transactions; autonomous, quick, effective and efficient multi-tasking			
Catalyst	Initiating, activating, and setting plans in motion; implementing and executing strategies			
Stylizer	Masterfully managing the aesthetic elements of style; rendering variations on a theme; using artistic visual flair to create a distinctive image			
Persuader	Influencing others; proposing and promoting ideas; winning others over to achieve a desired end			
Troubleshooter	Actively confronting difficult situations; adjusting, reacting and responding; skillfully managing crisis to turnaround through immediate action			
Pioneer	Boldly exploring and adventuring; testing boundaries; creating excitement and stimulation			
Negotiator	Capitalizing on all available opportunities to advance; artfully reading situations and openings to make the right tactical move			
Player	Competing to better current position; entertaining, performing, acting, demonstrating; actively engaging in "the game"			
Fabricator	Crafting and skillfully working with tools, instruments, and materials			

My Talents in this area (those meeting all three criteria, if any):

1.

2.

3.

4.

5.

Dominant Intellect (pattern with most talents): _____

Personal Values

Your personal values (the ones that are more or less "hardwired" in you) give you strength and guide your work – they are principles you find inherently important, and are part of the "natural you".

Using the table of 40 values in the four intellects below, answer these questions to help you identify the values that are core to who you are:

- *When you make an important decision, what is that you rely on most?*
- *When you're performing your work, what is it you strive for most?*
- *If you were no longer in your current role, what values would be missing in your life?*
- *What values are present in the principles will you absolutely never compromise on?*

Now circle the top five values (in the table below) that guide your work.

PHILOSOPHER (think "*head*")	DIPLOMAT (think "*heart*")	GUARDIAN (think "*home*")	ARTISAN (think "*hands*")
Competence	Cooperation	Responsibility	Results
Direction	Understanding	Regulation	Autonomy
Challenge	Harmony	Authority	Initiative
Logic	Intuition	Diligence	Aesthetics
Foresight	Involvement	Stability	Influence
Progress	Growth	Refuge	Flexibility
Concepts	Compassion	Security	Adventure
Intelligence	Integrity	Economy	Advancement
Ingenuity	Unity	Order	Competition
Alignment	Inspiration	Precision	Artistry

Now list both your Top 5 talents and Top 5 values. Draw solid lines to denote direct connections. Draw dotted lines to indicate indirect connections. Your solid line pairs are your key strengths!

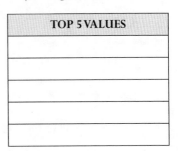

TOP 5 TALENTS

TOP 5 VALUES

Your Gifts At a Glance

Here are the four archetypical intellects at a glance. These are indications only – tendencies, patterns, and themes – not prescriptions!

DIPLOMATS		GUARDIANS	
(Empathic Gifts: Think "Heart")		*(Economic Gifts: Think "Home")*	
Drivers		**Drivers**	
Significance Truth		Duty Sanctuary	
Talents	**Values**	**Talents**	**Values**
Facilitator	Cooperation	Steward	Responsibility
Empathizer	Understanding	Legislator	Regulation
Mediator	Harmony	Enforcer	Authority
Perceiver	Intuition	Deliberator	Diligence
Confidante	Involvement	Equalizer	Stability
Coach	Growth	Affiliator	Refuge
Counselor	Compassion	Sentry	Security
Idealist	Integrity	Proprietor	Economy
Integrator	Unity	Organizer	Order
Crusader	Inspiration	Detailer	Precision
PHILOSOPHERS		**ARTISANS**	
(Analytic Gifts: Think "Head")		*(Kinetic Gifts: Think "Hands")*	
Drivers		**Drivers**	
Knowledge Reason		Action Impulse	
Talents	**Values**	**Talents**	**Values**
Optimizer	Competence	Charger	Results
Marshal	Direction	Expeditor	Autonomy
Strategist	Challenge	Catalyst	Initiative
Analyst	Logic	Stylizer	Aesthetics
Visionary	Foresight	Persuader	Influence
Inventor	Progress	Troubleshooter	Flexibility
Theorist	Concepts	Pioneer	Adventure
Investigator	Intelligence	Negotiator	Advancement
Designer	Ingenuity	Player	Competition
Synthesizer	Alignment	Fabricator	Artistry

What parts of each of the four patterns do you identify with most?

Play From Power

HONING TALENT

To truly govern your gifts, you will need to consistently develop your leading talents into working strengths – and begin to play from power. Your talents are your most important raw materials for driving the inspired performance that leads to uncommon excellence.

To fully develop virtuosity in just one talent would test your resourcefulness. To master all of your talents will take a lifetime, and you will never fully complete the process of honing them!

Exercise
Focus on your Top 5 talents. Take each talent one at a time, and list one to three key strategies, actions or ideas that will help you to more fully utilize that talent in your present work. Carefully consider what parts of the brief description connect with you, then develop strategies that make sense for you and your role.

Example
If Charger is a talent of yours, create a personal scorecard of key work outcomes. Chargers value results – so a scorecard provides important feedback on progress. Decide on some important leading indicators and start making them visible, first to yourself and then to important others.

WEAKNESS WORKAROUND

Playing from Power is a two-fold strategy – emphasizing strength and de-emphasizing weakness. Having a better understanding of your gifts in turn illuminates areas in which you're not so gifted – areas to render irrelevant in your work.

What activities in your current role play to your short suit? How can you work around them? How can you leverage others' gifts in doing so?

Example
If Idealist is a talent of yours, find ways to avoid politically charged situations that require maneuvering and compromise on ethics.

Manage What Matters

CLARIFYING VALUES

Dig into each of your values and get clear about what you really mean. How do they play out in reality – in your work and in your personal life? In your relationships? In your many and various roles?

Write a few phrases that illuminate your values.

Example

If one of your values is security, what exactly does security mean to you? Does it mean: A $2 million 401(K)? Guaranteed lifelong employment? Universal life insurance? Home security system? Living in a guard-gated community?

ALIGNING VALUES & RESOURCES

Once you've clarified your values, the next step is to ensure you're living your values. How you spend your resources gives you great insight into whether you're living a values-based life.

Exercise

Pull out a recent bank statement *(credit card statement, checkbook, etc.)* **and your calendar. Go through each of your examples from "Clarifying Values" above.**

• *Where are you spending your time, money, and effort?*
• *Which of your values, if any, can you put more resources toward furthering in your work and in your personal life?*

If you're making choices and spending resources in ways that are in fact anti to what you hold to be most important, you will suffer stress and anxiety. Realign your resources to your values, and watch the difference it makes on a daily basis!

Exercise

Review in your mind a recent stressful decision or choice.

• *Which of your values was ignored or subordinated?*
• *How can you prevent it from happening again in the future?*
(reread the section on values-based decisions in *Manage What Matters*)

Lean Into Limits

BREAKING BOUNDS

If you are not willing to take intelligent risks, if you don't push your talents beyond the certain, if you forever indulge in your fear of failure, you will never experience the highest levels of impact and performance. Your greatest growth occurs when you chance to raise the bar and seek new limits. You will surprise yourself when you step outside your comfort zone and rise to a new challenge!

Assess your threshold for uncertainty and ambiguity, giving yourself 10 points for every 'yes' (0 for 'no').

	Yes	No
I take greater risks and make more mistakes than my peers		
I view all mistakes as learning opportunities, and avoid repeats		
I keep an open mind to views which may differ from my own		
I embrace tension and conflict as sparks for creativity		
I am constantly asking questions to learn more		
I continuously challenge old ideas and assumptions		
I can easily argue two different views on the same subject		
I am constantly trying new things and developing new interests		
I enjoy change and welcome it as a part of every day		
I often order custom "off menu" dishes when dining out		

TOTAL _____

90–100: Maverick!
70–80: Push a little harder!
50–60: Break some boundaries, today!
 <50: Your comfort zone is holding you back!

What would you do if you were twice as BOLD?

_____

_____

_____

Move Toward Mastery

THE BIG IDEA

True mastery transcends the conventional notion (competence) to become more about ingenuity – creatively applying your talents to effectively change the game. At the heart every breakthrough achievement is the question *"What is possible?"*

Exercise:
In this activity, you will employ a form of individual brainstorming called Brainwriting. The idea is to write on an idea for 5 minutes without stopping – no pauses to analyze or edit your thinking!

1. Pick an area of talent or interest. Write down five sentences beginning with "What if?" *(Example: What if there was a new way to measure brand image?)*

2. Pick one sentence that appeals to you. Invent a new idea, product, service, or strategy around your "What if?" by writing continuously for at least 5 minutes. DON'T LIFT YOUR PEN OFF THE PAGE IF YOU CAN POSSIBLY HELP IT!

3. Now develop your idea!

    *   *Summarize your entire idea or strategy from a highline, "concept at a glance" perspective in no more than four sentences.*

    *   *Summarize the goal or intended outcome of your idea or strategy in no more than four sentences.*

    *   *Summarize the opportunity identified by your idea or strategy in no more than four sentences.*

    *   *Summarize the target audience/stakeholder need met by your idea or strategy in no more than four sentences.*

    *   *Summarize the benefit offered to the target audience/key stakeholder groups by your idea or strategy in no more than four sentences.*

SCIENTIFIC PROBLEM SOLVING

Mastery demands discipline in the pursuit of the ideal. Continuous improvement, innovation, and the search for optimal solutions to complex problems involves experimenting, exploring, and searching for (and testing) new knowledge – requiring the systems thinking of the Philosopher, the sequential thinking of the Guardian, the integrative thinking of the Diplomat, and the applicative thinking of the Artisan.

Masterful Problem Solving: The Diamond Model

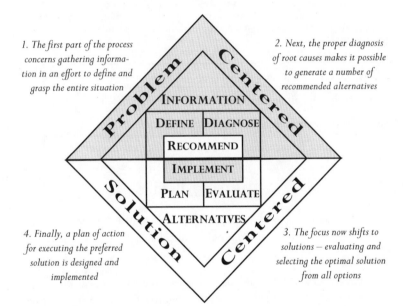

1. The first part of the process concerns gathering information in an effort to define and grasp the entire situation

2. Next, the proper diagnosis of root causes makes it possible to generate a number of recommended alternatives

4. Finally, a plan of action for executing the preferred solution is designed and implemented

3. The focus now shifts to solutions – evaluating and selecting the optimal solution from all options

PHASE	QUESTIONS
Define	Grasp the situation: *What? Where? When? How? Who?*
Diagnose	Discover the cause: *Why? Why? Why? Why? Why?*
Recommend	Generate solutions: *What can potentially be done to solve the issue?*
Evaluate	Select the optimum: *Which course of action best addresses the issue?*
Plan	Chart the course: *What gets done when, by whom, and HOW?*
Implement	Execute the solution: *Was it successful? What must be adjusted?*

Chapter 4: Share Your Strengths

STRENGTH SHARING

How clear is your purpose?	Yes	No
I understand the unique contribution I'm able to offer the world		
I have defined the role service plays in my work and life		
I understand the impact of my actions and abilities on others		
I am clear in how I am best able to serve the needs of others		
I see how my interests merge with those of the larger group's		
I feel connected to something larger through my work		
I have a compelling picture of the change I wish to see in the world		
I accept the commitment and sacrifice required to serve others		
I look for the very best in those with whom I interact		
I have a number of important relationships in which trust exists		

PARTS WE PLAY

You wear many hats in life: as a professional, teammate, friend, partner, parent, employer, community member, family member, etc.

Exercise:

1. *Make a list of all the roles you play in your life. Describe each role, noting who is impacted by your role, what you do, offer, or provide (and to whom) in each role. How do you meet the needs of those in your life?*

2. *Develop answers to the question: "In each of my roles in life, what has been most meaningful to me?" (Hint: be specific.)*

3. *For each role, describe what your purpose is. How will you make a positive contribution or difference to others in each role?*

   (Example: As a professional, I want to educate and develop people's minds and character — to help them grow their unique talents, expand their areas of knowledge, and hone their skills. I want to help them broaden their horizons, deepen their understanding of themselves, and maximize their true potential.

   Example: As an artist, I want to inspire, entertain, and emotionally uplift people all over the world through song. I want to use my musical gifts as a means of expressing myself, and as a means to touch others by portraying universal truths.)

Clarify Your Cause

YOUR ROOT CAUSE

Sometimes our ability to share our strengths – to clarify and commit to our unique contribution – gets obscured by job titles and descriptions, in turn preventing us from connecting to our purpose.

The age-old quality technique of "The 5 Why's" used to identify the root cause of an issue can be useful.

(Reread "Clarify Your Cause" to see an example of the application.)

<u>*Exercise:*</u>

- *Describe your position or function. (e.g. "I am a sales manager for XYZ Company.")*
- *Focusing on the impact on others, now answer: "Why is that an important function?"*
- *Based on the answer, now ask: "Why is that important?"*
- *Continue in this manner until you've asked the question five times or until you have a clear sense of purpose in your work.*

(NOTE: You can use this technique in any domain of your life, for any role. It works equally well for identifying team, group, and organizational purpose.)

DESCRIPTION OF ROLE/FUNCTION:
Why is that important for (the company, others, etc.)?
Why is it important to (previous answer)?
Why is that important? (for others)
Why is that important? (for others)
Why is that important? (for others)

Exceed The Ego

MERGING TOWARD MUTUALITY

Pitting self-interest against service to others is a no-win, zero-sum game. The key is to adopt a higher perspective that embraces the idea that all interests – of self and others – must merge toward mutuality.

Have you balanced the benefit – integrating your interests with those of others, of the greatest good?

Self	Service
How might your work be impacted if these questions go unanswered? *What is the impact on others if these questions are your ONLY concern?*	*How might your work be impacted if these questions go unanswered?* *What is the impact on others if these questions are your ONLY concern?*
Will I be able to advance in my work?	Where can I do the greatest good?
Will I be recognized for my contribution?	Where are my abilities needed most?
Will I have the opportunity to grow and develop?	What needs can I meet immediately?
Will I receive the resources I need to do my job?	How can I help the group succeed?
Will I receive the attention and direction I need to do my work?	What is expected of me by others?
Will I be fairly treated?	How can I further the common purpose?
Will my financial reward equal my contribution?	How can I be of greatest service?
Will my voice be heard and my opinion count?	What is the greatest sacrifice I can make?
Will I be able to achieve my goals?	How can I provide the most value?
Will I get the support I need?	How can I make others happy?

DON'T FORCE A CHOICE – FOCUS ON BOTH!

Strive to Serve

BECOMING SERVICE-CENTERED

To truly serve others well, you must first adopt a service ethic. This requires you to:

1. Make service to others a top priority
2. Understand what others need and value most
3. Optimize your work methods to meet those needs
4. Consistently exceed any expectations they may have

Exercise:

Examine the key relationships you have in the major categories* of:

• *Colleagues*

• *Employers*

• *Supervisors/Managers*

• *Employees/Associates*

• *Customers (anyone in receipt of what you produce in your work)*

• *Suppliers (anyone enabling you to do your job)*

*(NOTE: Family, Friends and Community may be included!)

To serve well, you will need to arrive at specific answers to these kinds of questions, through discovery and dialogue:

• *Who am I serving?*

• *Who depends on me? On whom do I depend?*

• *What do I owe them? In what form? In what time frame?*

• *What do they need? What do they value most?*

• *What does it take to please them?*

• *What are their goals — what are they trying to accomplish?*

• *How can I contribute to their success?*

• *What do they consider results?*

• *How do their strengths complement mine?*

TRANSCENDENTAL SERVICE

True service spirit transcends the more transactional level of providing service to entering into deeper partnerships characterized by the shared exchange of intangibles: helping each other solve problems, improve situations, gain information, and learn.

Exercise:

1. *Pick one of the key relationship categories from the previous exercise.*

2. *In the center of a blank piece of paper, describe the primary service or product (transactional value) you provide in that relationship. (Example: computer programming)*

3. *Surrounding this word, indicate all those you may provide that product or service to, and all those who may provide value to you in providing that product or service.*

4. *Draw arrows to indicate the flow of value to and from you and your connections.*

5. *Label the arrows: what is the nature of the value? (time, information, advice, etc.)*

Questions:

- Which of the relationships are simply transactional? (exchange of tangibles such as products, services, money, time, etc.)

- Which of the relationships are truly 2-way?

- Which of the relationships transcend the transactional level? (Characterized by shared exchange of intangibles such as advice, guidance, information, knowledge, counsel, support, etc.)

- Which are true partnerships? (Characterized by shared interest, trust, mutual understanding, and honest communication.)

- Where do opportunities exist to strengthen the relationships by further adding and exchanging value?

Foster Positive Feelings

ELEVATING OTHERS

Taking a positive, appreciative approach can be both personally and organizationally transformational. Even small positive gestures such as smiling, warmth, optimism, and compliments have been proven to actually lift performance. Impacting others in such a positive manner sparks a crescendo of reciprocity – resulting in repayment as well as payment forward of the act in greater dimension than it was received.

Warning: Can be contagious!

Exercise:
Run an experiment! For the next two weeks, exhibit the behaviors associated with an appreciative approach – acceptance, affirmation, and accolade. *(Note: refresh your memory of the positive, appreciative approach found in Chapter 4 subchapter "Foster Positive Feelings.")*

Track the impact on others (as well as on yourself) in terms of:

- Levels of trust and respect
- Cooperation
- Performance
- General outlook and attitude
- Happiness
- Reduction in stress and anxiety

Here are some thought starters:

- *Give a little gift, wherever you go, with whomever you meet (can be as inexpensive as a sincere compliment or smile!)*

- *Recognize both the usual efforts and outstanding achievements of those around you (in a manner that is meaningful to them)*

- *Honor the differences in others by acknowledging the validity of their views (shows respect)*

- *Focus on the positive aspects of whatever you're doing, saying, thinking – banish the negative thoughts and doomsday outlook!*

- *Stop negatively comparing, criticizing, competing, and combating!*

Render Trustful Relationships

BUILDING TRUST

Are you building trust in your daily interactions with others?

MISTRUST	TRUST
Ego	Deference
Preoccupation	Listening
Apathy	Action
Selfishness	Sacrifice
Maneuvering	Collaboration
Deception	Candor
Hyperbole	Accuracy
Rumoring	Confidentiality
Sarcasm	Sincerity
Arrogance	Humility
Segregation	Inclusion
Ignorance	Understanding
Anger	Reserve
Defiance	Cooperation
Favoritism	Fairness
Envy	Esteem
Retaliation	Acceptance
Competition	Camaraderie
Secrecy	Disclosure
Critique	Appreciation

Chapter 5: Anchor Your Ambition

GROUNDED ASPIRATIONS

Where are you on the Anchored Ambition Matrix?

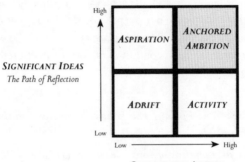

CURRENT REALITY

How clear is your present sense of direction?

	YES	NO
1. I have a clear sense of direction regarding my professional goals. *(e.g. careers, positions, second careers, education, projects, new business startup, retirement)*		
2. I have a clear sense of direction regarding my personal goals. *(e.g. health, fitness, travel, recreation, hobbies, personal growth, adventure, community involvement, lifestyle, spirituality)*		
3. I have a clear sense of direction regarding my relationship goals. *(e.g. family, friends, children, marriage, love life)*		
4. I have a clear sense of direction regarding my financial goals. *(e.g. earnings, income, savings, expense control, building capital, investment, children's education, life insurance, net worth, financial independence, purchases, household)*		

Vest Your Vision

WAVE THE WAND

We are told at an early age that we can be anything we want to be. This more often that not leads to disappointment in life, for we fail to separate pure fantasy from truly achievable dreams that play to our talents and are aligned to our purpose in life. There is almost no limit to what we can accomplish once we are clear about who we are, what we most want in life, and commit ourselves to effecting those dreams.

Exercise:
Reread "Vest Your Vision." It is your turn to envision the future, as the Prince and his Courtiers did!

Pick any or all domains of your life *(see previous activity: "Current Reality")* ***and complete an "I see…" statement.*** *(Hint: Journals are good for this activity. Your vision will be a constantly evolving work in progress.)*

If you are a more visual person, DRAW your vision!

Now, check your vision!

My vision is fully vested, my ambition well-anchored:		✓
Articulate	My ambition is captured in a clear, vivid, and detailed way.	
Appealing	My vision of the future creates a sense of personal urgency.	
Attainable	My dreams are beyond my immediate grasp but within my reach.	
Artistic	My aspirations inspire me to engage my talents fully.	
Adaptive	My vision is flexible enough to accommodate shifts in direction.	
Audacious	My envisioned future requires me to set and meet bold objectives.	
Authentic	My ambition reflects who I really am – it is meaningful to me.	
Affirmative	My aspirations reflect a strong and positive image of my future.	
Abundant	My vision is shared by those most important to me in my life.	
Afterimage	My ambition will leave a lasting legacy of positive impact.	

True the Trajectory

SETTING YOUR SIGHTS

There is perhaps no more motivational practice known to us that leads to higher performance, impact, and meaning than that of setting clear, compelling, mission-level goals. It is through your goals that you will move closer to realizing your ambition.

Exercise:
Review the four major goal categories *(from "Current Reality" Exercise)*
What are your goals in these categories? Are they tied to your vision?

Professional	*Careers, positions, second careers, education, projects, new business startup, retirement*
Personal	*Health, fitness, travel, recreation, hobbies, personal growth, adventure, community involvement, lifestyle, spirituality*
Relationships	*Family, friends, children, marriage, love life*
Financial	*Earnings, income, savings, expense control, building capital, investment, children's education, life insurance, net worth, financial independence, purchases, household*

Classify and prioritize your goals using the following definitions:

PRIMARY: *Big* goals; most important
- Highest level of desire
- Most absolute in impact
- Transformational potential
- Require risk-taking and significant investment

SECONDARY: *Interim* goals, subordinate to primary goals
- Substantial impact
- Important objective supporting a primary goal
- Non-transformational, but necessary

TERTIARY: *Everyday* goals
- To-do list
- Daily fires, tasks

Orchestrate the Opus

MASTER PROJECTS

It's one thing to set goals, it's quite another to achieve them. Your ability to accomplish all you want is dependent upon your skill in turning goals into high impact projects – orchestrating your opus! The following template may help you plan and manage your project.

PHASE	QUESTIONS
Define	What is the proposed project? Why is it important? What is the express purpose? What are the objectives and priorities? How do they support the purpose? What is the scope of the project? What are the key components? Who will be involved? What are the project start and end points?
Design	What are the major phases? What are the project steps and tasks? How are they sequenced? What is the project schedule or timeline? What are the major milestones? What is the critical path (shortest time to complete) of the project? Will there be a small pilot or test run? How much will it cost to execute? What are the resource constraints, if any? What kind of support is necessary? Where does the project take place? What new or additional skills/knowledge are needed? What risks are involved? What contingencies exist to address them?
Deploy	How is progress to be tracked and monitored? What tools or special techniques are required? What is the communication process among all involved? How will resources be controlled and managed to stay within budget? If needed, how are adjustments to the plan to be made? How are adjustments evaluated to determine impact? What activities will conclude the project?
Decode	What did you learn from your project? What was your review process? What "best practices" emerged from the project that you will use again? What "lessons learned" emerged that you will avoid in the future? How was this knowledge captured, documented, stored, shared and disseminated? What were the results? How do they compare to the design or plan?

Figure on Flux

WINDS OF CHANGE

As you consider your ambition and the future, what forces of change have the potential to impact your aspirations as you envision them? What are the uncontrollables? What are the "driving forces in your favor? What are the "restraining forces" that may block your progress?

Exercise:

1.   **Identify the critical issue or important decision regarding your direction.** *(Example: Should I launch my project this year?)*

2.   **"Map" the driving and restraining forces below in the key areas of influencers** *(cultural, technological, environmental, organizational, political, economic, social, demographic, etc.).*

3.   **Number the factors according to relevance (potential to impact) and uncertainty.**

4.   **What are best case, worst case, and probable case scenarios?**

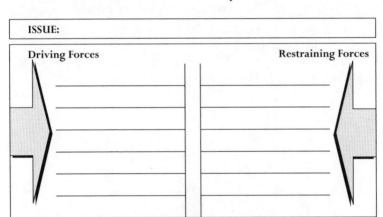

ISSUE:

Driving Forces		Restraining Forces

Best Case	Probable Case	Worst Case

Capitalize on Crucibles

DAILY REVIEW & REFLECTION

Even if five minutes is all you can spare, set aside time each day for thinking and reflecting. When adversity hits, as it surely must, your practice will prove invaluable.

Here's what to do:

- Designate a time and place devoted to daily solitude
- Use this time to reflect on your work, your activities, and planning
- Rigorously critique both successes and failures of the day
- Review all endeavors for potential connections among seemingly unconnected things
- Develop new ideas, fresh approaches, and "what if" hypotheses
- Identify opportunities to try out new ideas and explore scenarios
- Plan a course of action that will initiate your thoughts and provide preliminary direction

Tailor the approach to find what works best for you!

Strange Words

Aevitas – Latin for "lifelong"
Ad infinitum – indefinitely
August – inspiring reverence
Avant-garde – French for modern, trendy
Bailiwick – strong suit; specialty
Between Scylla and Charyldis – double-dangered position
Canon – body of work
Celerity – speed
Charrette – brainstorming session
Clarion – clear
Coffer – treasure chest; strongbox
Conundrum – riddle; puzzle; quandary
Cornucopia – abundant supply
Corporal – bodily; kinesthetic
Courtier – advisor; cabinet member
Dialectic – philosophical or logical debate
Dilettante – amateur
Duomo – distinguishing cathedral dome
Ebullience – enthusiasm; outburst
Élan – vivacity, dash
Ethos – fundamental character or spirit of a culture
Forsooth – in truth; in fact; indeed
Forté – specialty; strong suit
Impresario – producer
Juste-milieu – French for exact middle; perfect balance
Keystone – essence; idea on which all else is based
Languor – lethargy; laziness
Laurels – success; glory
Lexicon – dictionary
Lodestar – guiding light
Logistics – procurement and movement of resources
Magnum Opus – great work; masterwork
Martinet – disciplinarian

Mendacity – falsehood; deception
Meta – Greek meaning "beyond" or "highest"
Métier – French for "calling"
Mettle – strength of character; bravery
Mnemonic – memory aid
Multifarious – complex
Nadir – lowest point
Paladin – hero; icon
Panegyric – praising oratory
Pantheon – hall of heroes and legends
Peloton – main body; majority group
Pentacle – five point
Penultimate – next to last
Perfidy – betrayal of trust
Perorative – forceful argument
Plexus – network
Polaris – North Star
Polemic – controversial argument
Postulate – theorist
Practicum – practical application
Prescience – foresight
Primacy – leadership
Probity – integrity; honesty
Raison d 'etre – French for "reason for being"
Reciprocity – mutuality of benefit or reward
Res Ipsa – Latin for "the matter stands for itself"
Rubicon – difficult, decisive, irrevocable step
Sapient – wise
Socratic – pertaining to logical investigation
Taxonomy – scientific classification
Timber – personal character
Transom – threshold
Vita brevis – Latin for "life is short!"
Vitriol – harsh critique
Vituperation – condemnation
Voilá – French for "there it is!"

Exploring Further

If I have seen further than others, it is by standing on the shoulders of giants.

Sir Isaac Newton

That I can see at all, I owe in part the following giants, whose work has had a profound and lifelong influence on my thinking and approach. In addition to my primary research and consulting with clients over the past two decades, the resources listed here provide secondary support to the strategies in *Absolute Impact*.

A casual perusal of this reading list will reveal a preponderance of classic philosophy and scientific research. These are the enduring resources, lending real insight into the human nature and condition. I urge you to absorb any and all of that which strikes a chord of interest in you. Each is worthy of attention, as each yields at least one pearl of wisdom!

Many of the books are out of print – nothing that a visit to a well-stocked metropolitan or collegiate library won't remedy. Many, though out of print, can be found online by utilizing popular internet search engines.

In addition to general foundational resources, I have arranged the references by key *Absolute Impact* chapter and learning challenge.

General Foundations

Ancient Thought: Plato & Aristotle, edited by Norman Cantor & Peter Klein. Blaisdell Publishing Co.,1968.

The Apology of Socrates and The Crito by Plato, translation by Benjamin Jowett. Bandanna Books, 1993 (©1871).

Dialogues of Plato by Benjamin Jowett. Random House, 1937.

Five Great Dialogues/Plato by Benjamin Jowett. Gramercy, 1995.

The Four Socratic Dialogues of Plato by Benjamin Jowett. Clarendon Press, 1903.

The Great Ideas of Plato by Eugene Freeman & David Appel. Lantern Press, 1952.

A Guided Tour of Five Works by Plato by Christopher Biffle. Mayfield Publishing Co., 1995.

The Laws of Plato by Thomas Pangle. University of Chicago Press, 1988.

Phaedo by Plato, translation by Benjamin Jowett. Golden Cockerel Press, 1930.

Plato's Best Thoughts by Benjamin Jowett. Scribner's, 1883.

Plato's Life and Thought by Richard Bluck. Routledge & Paul, 1949.

Republic by Plato, translation by Benjamin Jowett. The Modern Library, 1941 (©1871).

The legends and myths of Hercules, Prometheus, Croesus, Solon, Janus, Cassandra, Beowulf and other stories can be found in the following classical references. (Interpretations and applications are my own.)

Bulfinch's Mythology by Thomas Bulfinch. Random House, 1987 (©1855). (Includes *The Age of Fable or Stories of Gods and Heroes* [©1855], *The Age of Chivalry* [©1858], and *Legends of Charlemagne or Romance of the Middle Ages* [©1863].)

Greek Gods and Heroes by Robert Graves. Dell Publishing, 1960.

Mythology: Timeless Tales of Gods and Heroes by Edith Hamilton. Little, Brown & Co., 1940.

Old Favorites from the McGuffey Readers. Gale Group, 1969 (©1836, 1857, 1879).

The Parable of Talents *(Chapter 3, subchapter "Lean Into Limits")* can be found in the Bible, at Matthew 25: 14-30.

Chapter One: Questions

Adaptation to Life by George Vaillant. Little, Brown, 1977.

The Appearance of Man by Pierre Teilhard de Chardin, translation by J.M. Cohen. Collins, 1965.

The Blank Slate: The Modern Denial of Human Nature by Steven Pinker. Viking Press, 2002.

The Courage to Be by Paul Tillich. Yale University Press, 1952.

Elements of Knowledge: Pragmatism, Logic, and Inquiry by Arthur Stewart. Vanderbilt University Press, 1997.

The Evolving Self by Robert Kegan. Harvard University Press, 1983.

The Farther Reaches of Human Nature by Abraham Maslow. Viking Press, 1971.

Field of Consciousness by David Herlihy. Dusque University Press, 1964.

The Human Condition by Hannah Arendt. University of Chicago Press, 1958.

Human Energy by Pierre Teilhard de Chardin, translation by J.M. Cohen. Collins, 1969.

Logic, The Theory of Inquiry by John Dewey. H. Holt & Co., 1938.

The Nichomachean Ethics by Aristotle. The MacMillan Company, 1897.

On Death and Dying by Elizabeth Kübler-Ross. MacMillan Company, 1969.

The Play of Man by Karl Groos. Arno Press, 1971 (©1901).

The Presentation of Self in Everyday Life by Erving Goffman. Anchor, 1959.

The Phenomenon of Man by Pierre Teilhard de Chardin. Harper, 1959.

Self-Help by Samuel Smiles. G. Munro, 1884.

Working by Studs Terkel. Pantheon, 1974.

Chapter Two: Guidance

The Achievement Factors: Candid Interviews With Some of the Most Successful People of Our Time by B. Eugene Griessman. Dodd, Mead, 1987.

The Meaning of Life, edited by Hugh Moorhead. Chicago Review Press, 1988.

The Philosophy of Change by Daniel Rhodes. The Macmillan Co., 1909.

The Psychology of Men of Genius by Ernst Kretschmer. Harcourt Brace & Co., 1931.

A Theory of Cognitive Dissonance by Leon Festinger. Row, Peterson, 1957.

To Have or Be? by Erich Fromm. Harper & Row, 1976.

The World of Life; A Manifestation of Creative Power, Directive Mind and Ultimate Purpose by Alfred Wallace. Moffat, Yard & Company, 1911.

Chapter Three: Govern Your Gifts

INTRO

Intrinsic Motivation and Self-Determination in Human Behavior by Edward Deci & Richard Ryan. Plenum, 1985.

Job Attitudes: Review of Research and Opinion by Frederick Herzberg. Garland, 1987.

A Life's Work by Margaret Bondfield. Hutchinson, 1948.
Man Against Work, compilation by Lloyd Zimpel. Eerdmans, 1974.
Motivation and Personality by Abraham Maslow. Harper, 1954.
The Motivation to Work by Frederick Herzberg, Bernard Mauser and Barbara Snyderman. Wiley, 1959.
The Nature of Man by Hippocrates. 450 B.C.
The Soul's Code: In Search of Character and Calling by James Hillman. Warner Books, 1997.
Women's Attitudes to Repetitive Work by David Cox. National Institute of Industrial Psychology, 1953.
Work and the Nature of Man by Frederick Herzberg. World Publishing, 1966.

SOURCE YOUR STRENGTH

Atlas of Men by William Sheldon. Harper, 1954.
Becoming: Basic Considerations for a Psychology of Personality by Gordon Allport. Yale University Press, 1955.
Encyclopedia of Human Intelligence, edited by Robert Sternberg. MacMillan Co., 1994.
The Evolution of Human Nature by Charles J. Herrick. University of Texas Press, 1956.
Foundations for a Science of Personality by Andras Angyal. Harvard University Press, 1972 (©1941).
Frames of Mind by Howard Gardner. Basic Books, 1983.
The Growth of the Mind: And the Endangered Origins of Intelligence by Stanley Greenspan and Beryl Benderly. HarperCollins, 1998.
Human Efficiency and Levels of Human Intelligence by Henry Goddard. Garland Pub., 1984.
Human Intelligence by Jack Fincher. Putnam, 1976.
Human Values and Verities by Henry Osborn Taylor. Macmillan & Co., Limited, 1928.
Human Values from the Greeks to Modern Times: A Continuing Circle by Glenn Visher. Nova Science, 1997.
Intelligence Reframed by Howard Gardner. Basic Books, 1999.
Loose Ends: Primary Papers in Archetypal Psychology by James Hillman. Spring Pub., 1975.
Life in Our Hands: A Study of Human Values by C. Gordon Scorer. Inter-Varsity Press, 1978.
The Nature of Human Intelligence by Joy Guilford. McGraw-Hill, 1967.
The Nature of Human Values by Milton Rokeach. Free Press, 1973.
Please Understand Me II by David Keirsey. Prometheus Nemesis, 1998.
Physique and Character by Ernst Kretschmer. Harcourt Brace and Co., 1925.
The Psychology of Men of Genius by Ernst Kretschmer. Harcourt Brace and Co., 1931.
The Three Sources of Human Values by Friedrich A. von Hayek. The London School of Economics and Political Science, 1978.
The Triarchic Mind : A New Theory of Human Intelligence by Robert Sternberg. Viking, 1988.
Types of Men by Eduard Spränger. Johnson Reprint Co., 1966 (©1928).
Understanding Human Values: Individual and Societal, edited by Milton Rokeach. Free Press, 1979.

PLAY FROM POWER

Developing Talent in Young People, edited by Benjamin Bloom. Ballantine Books, 1985.
The Development of Executive Talent by Werret Wallace Charters. American Management Association, 1928.
The Discovery of Talent, edited by Dael Lee Wolfle. Harvard University Press, 1969.
The Effective Executive by Peter Drucker. Harper & Row, 1966.
Excellence by John Gardner. Harper & Row, 1961.

Executive Talent: How to Identify and Develop the Best by Tom Potts and Arnold Sykes. Business One Irwin, 1993.

How the Mind Works by Steven Pinker. Norton, 1997.

International Handbook of Research & Development of Giftedness and Talent, edited by Kurt Heller, Franz Monks, and A. Harry Passow. Pergamon Press, 1993.

Kinds of Power: A Guide to its Intelligent Uses by James Hillman. Currency Doubleday, 1995.

Out of Our Minds: Anti-Intellectualism and Talent Development in American Schooling by Craig Howley, Aimee Howley and Edwina Pendarvis. Teachers College Press, 1995.

Patterns of Artistic Development in Children: Comparative Studies of Talent by Constance Milbrath. Cambridge University Press, 1998.

Soar With Your Strengths by Donald O. Clifton and Paula Nelson, Delacorte Press, 1992.

Teens With Talent: Developing the Potential of the Bright, Brighter, and Brightest by Ellie Schatz and Nancy Schuster. Open Space Communications, 1996.

The Theory of Polarity by Geoffrey Sainsbury. G.P. Putnam 1927.

Manage What Matters

Affect & Social Behavior, edited by Alice Isen & Bert Moore. Cambridge University Press, 1990.

Big Business and Human Values by Theodore Houser. McGraw-Hill, 1957.

Eupsychian Management; A Journal by Abraham Maslow. Irwin, 1965.

Human Values: An Interpretation of Ethics Based on a Study of Values by DeWitt Parker. Harper, 1931.

Human Values Where People Work by T.G. Spates. Harper & Bros., 1960.

A Source Book of Opinion on Human Values, edited by Kenneth Webb. Tower Bridge Pub., 1951.

The Stress of Life by Hans Selye. McGraw-Hill, 1956.

The Things That Matter Most; An Approach to the Problems of Human Values by Ralph Flewelling. Ronald Press, 1946.

Lean Into Limits

Attention and Effort by Daniel Kahneman. Prentice-Hall, 1973.

Chancing It: Why We Take Risks by Ralph Keyes. Little, Brown, 1985.

The Dangerous Edge: The Psychology of Excitement by Michael Apter. Free Press, 1992.

Flow: The Psychology of Optimal Experience by Mihaly Csikszentmihalyi. Harper & Row, 1990.

Motor Learning: Concepts & Applications by Richard Magill. W.C. Brown Publishers, 1985.

Plans and the Structure of Behavior by George Miller, Eugene Galanter, & Karl Pribram. Holt, 1960.

Risk-Taking in Learning, K-3 by Robert Young. NEA Professional Library, National Education Association, 1991.

Survival Probabilities, The Goal of Risk Theory by Hilary Seal. Wiley, 1978.

Why Man Takes Chances: Studies in Stress-Seeking, edited by Samuel Klausner. Anchor Books, 1968.

Move Toward Mastery

All Our Children Learning: A Primer for Parents, Teachers, and Other Educators by Benjamin Bloom. McGraw-Hill, 1981.

The Closing of the American Mind: How Higher Education Has Failed Democracy and Impoverished the Souls of Today's Students by Allan Bloom. Simon & Schuster, 1987.

Creativity and Learning, compilation by Jerome Kagan. Houghton Mifflin, 1967.

Critique of Pure Reason by Immanuel Kant. St. Martin's Press, 1969, (©1781).

Education and the Larger Life by C. Hanford Henderson. Houghton, Mifflin and Co., 1902.

Freedom to Learn: A View of What Education Might Become by Carl Rogers. C.E. Merrill Pub. Co., 1969.

Greatness by Dean Keith Simonton. The Guildford Press, 1994.

The Ideal Problem Solver: A Guide for Improving Thinking, Learning, and Creativity by John Bransford. W. H. Freeman, 1984.

Ideas: General Introduction to Pure Phenomenology by Edmund Husserl, translation by W. R. Boyce Gibson. Humanities, 1969.

Invented Worlds: The Psychology of the Arts by Ellen Winter. Harvard University Press, 1982.

Invitation to Lifelong Learning, edited by Ronald Gross. Follett, 1982.

Lives of the Most Eminent Painters, Sculptors, and Architects by Giorgio Vasari. Modern Library, 1959 (©1550).

"Motivation Reconsidered: The Concept of Competence" by Robert White, in Psychological Review 66 (1959): 297-333.

The Origins of Intelligence in the Child by Jean Piaget. International Universities Press, 1952.

The Origins of Scientific Thought by Giorgio De Santillana. University of Chicago Press, 1970 (©1961).

The Problem of Knowledge by Ernst Cassirer. Yale University Press, 1950.

Productive Thinking by Max Wertheimer. Harper, 1954

The Social Psychology of Creativity by Teresa Amabile. Springer-Verlag, 1983.

The Structure of Scientific Revolutions by Thomas Kuhn. University of Chicago Press, 1962.

Scientific Elite: Nobel Laureates in the United States by Harriet Zuckerman. Free Press, 1977.

A Theory of Conceptual Intelligence: Thinking, Learning, Creativity, and Giftedness by Rex Li. Praeger, 1996.

Work, Creativity, and Social Justice by Elliott Jaques. International Universities Press, 1970.

Chapter Four: Share Your Strengths

INTRO

On the Application of the Quantum Theory to Atomic Structure, Part I: The Fundamental Postulates by Neils Bohr. The University Press, 1924.

The Tao of Physics: An Explanation of the Parallels Between Modern Physics and Eastern Mysticism by Fritjof Capra. Random House, 1975.

Man's Life Purpose by William Comstock. R. G. Badger, 1915.

Civilization & Progress by John Crozier. Longmans, Green, and Co., 1898.

Mankind Evolving: The Evolution of the Human Species by Theodosius Dobzhansky. Yale University Press, 1962.

Man's Search for Meaning by Viktor Frankl. Beacon Press, 1963.

Humanism: The Greek Ideal and Its Survival by Moses Hadas. Harper, 1960.

The Self and Others by Ronald Laing. Tavistock, 1969.

Science and the Purpose of Life by Boris Sokoloff. Creative Age Press, 1950.

CLARIFY YOUR CAUSE

Life-Power; or, Character, Culture and Conduct by Arthur Pierson. F. H. Revell Company, 1895.

Personal Causation: The Internal Affective Determinants of Behavior by Richard DeCharms. Academic Press, 1968.

The Power of Purpose by William Jordan. F. H. Revell Company, 1910.

The Power of a Purpose by Nenien McPherson. F. H. Revell Company, 1959.

The Power of High Purpose by William Mikesell. Warner Press, 1961.

The Purpose-Driven Organization: Unleashing the Power of Direction and Commitment by Perry Pascarella and Mark Frohman. Jossey-Bass Publishers, 1989.

Scheme Theory: A Conceptual Framework for Cognitive-Motivational Processes by Gudrun Eckblad. Academic Press, 1981.

EXCEED THE EGO

Beyond Self-Interest, edited by Jane Mansbridge. University of Chicago Press, 1990.

The Common Good: Citizenship, Morality, and Self-Interest by Bill Jordan. B. Blackwell, 1989.

Conduct and Constraints: An Introduction to Moral Decision-Making by Robert Hahn. Simon & Schuster, 1994.

Dear Diary: Some Studies in Self-Interest by Brian Dobbs. Elm Tree Books, 1974.

Democracy in America by Sir Alexis De Tocqueville. A.A. Knopf, 1945 (©1835).

Ego Development: Conceptions and Theories by Jane Loevinger. Jossey-Bass Publishers, 1976.

Enlightened Self-Interest; A Study of Educational Programs of Trade Associations by Dorothy Rowden. American Association for Adult Education, 1937.

How Are We To Live? Ethics in an Age of Self-Interest by Peter Singer. Oxford University Press, 1997.

Individualism and Public Life: A Modern Dilemma by Ralph Ketcham. B. Blackwell, 1987.

Individualism Reconsidered, And Other Essays by David Riesman. Free Press, 1954.

Industrial Biography: Iron-Workers and Tool-Makers by Samuel Smiles. Tiknor & Fields, 1864.

Inquiry into the Nature and Causes of the Wealth of Nations by Adam Smith. A.M. Kelley, 1966 (©1776).

Man for Himself by Erich Fromm. Rinehart, 1947.

Morality and Rational Self-Interest, compilation by David P. Gauthier. Prentice-Hall, 1970.

The Morality of Self-Interest by Robert Olson. Harcourt, Brace & World, 1965.

One-Dimensional Man: Studies in the Ideology of Advanced Industrial Society by H. Marcuse. Beacon Press, 1964.

A Pluralistic Universe by William James. Harvard University Press, 1977 (©1909).

Pragmatism by William James. Dover Publications, 1995 (©1907).

The Selfish Gene by Richard Dawkins. Oxford University Press, 1976.

Selfishness, Altruism, and Rationality: A Theory of Social Choice by Howard Margolis. University of Chicago Press, 1984 (©1982).

Shifting Involvements: Private Interest and Public Action by Albert Hirschman. Princeton University Press, 1982.

The Socialized Motive by Marcus Noble. The Acorn Publishing Company, 1934.

The Soul of Modern Economic Man: Ideas of Self-Interest by Milton Myers. University of Chicago Press, 1983.

Stewardship: Choosing Service Over Self-Interest by Peter Block. Berret-Koehler, 1993.

Self-Interest, edited by Ellen Paul, Fred Miller, Jr. and Jeffrey Paul. Cambridge University Press, 1997.

Studies in Self-Interest: From Descartes to La Bruyère, edited by A.J. Krailsheimer. Clarendon Press, 1962.

STRIVE TO SERVE

The Heart of Business: Ethics, Power, and Philosophy by Peter Koestenbaum. Saybrook Publishing Co., 1987.

The Hippocratic Oath by Hippocrates.

How Can I Help: Stories and Reflections of Service by Ram Dass & Paul Gorman. Knopf, 1985.

Servant Leadership: A Journey in the Nature of Legitimate Power and Greatness by Robert Greenleaf. Paulist Press, 1977.

A Theory of Moral Sentiments by Adam Smith. A.M. Kelley, 1759.

FOSTER POSITIVE FEELINGS

Appreciative Inquiry by David Cooperrider and Diana Whitney. Berrett-Koehler Publishers, 1999.

Appreciative Management and Leadership:The Power of Positive Thought and Action in Organizations by Suresh Srivastva and David Cooperrider. Jossey-Bass Publishers, 1990.

The Essays of an Optimist by Sir John William Kaye. Smith, Elder & Co., 1870.

Existentialism and Human Emotions by Jean Paul Sartre. Philosophical Library, 1967.

Hope for Man: An Optimistic Philosophy and Guide to Self-Fulfillment by Joshua Liebman. Simon and Schuster, 1966.

Interpretation and Social Criticism by Michael Walzer. Harvard University Press, 1987.

Learned Optimism by Martin Seligman. A.A. Knopf, 1991.

The Nature of Man: Studies in Optimistic Philosophy by Elie Metchnikoff. Arno Press, 1977 (©1903).

Optimism or Pessimism:Which is the More Reasonable Philosophy of Life? by Henry Frank. Haldeman-Julius Company, 1925.

"Positive Emotions Trigger Upward Spirals toward EmotionalWell-Being" by Barbara Fredrickson & T. Joiner, in Psychological Science 13, 172-175 (2002).

Positive Emotional Power by Stanley Ainsworth. Prentice-Hall, 1981.

The Power of Positive Thinking by Norman Vincent Peal. Prentice-Hall, 1952.

Prophecy, Behaviour and Change by Gerald Smale. Routledge & K. Paul, 1977.

Pygmalion in the Classroom by Robert Rosenthal. Holt, Rinehart & Winston, 1968.

Social Foundations of Thought and Action by Albert Bandura. Prentice-Hall, 1986.

Total Positivity by Samuel Karlin. Stanford University Press, 1968.

RENDER TRUSTFUL RELATIONSHIPS

Beyond Tocqueville: Civil Society and the Social Capital Debate in Comparative Perspective, edited by Bob Edwards. University Press of New England, 2001.

Bowling Alone:The Collapse & Reward of American Community by Robert Putnam. Simon & Schuster, 2000.

Building Trust in theWorkplace by Gordon Shea. AMA Membership Publications Division, 1984.

Elements of Psychophysics by Gustav Fechner, translated by Helmut Adler. Rinehart & Winston, 1966 (©1860).

Executive Integrity:The Search for High HumanValues in Organizational Life by Suresh Srivastva. Jossey-Bass Publishers, 1988.

The Idea of a Civil Society by Bronislaw Geremek. National Humanities Center, 1992.

The Leadership Triad: Knowledge,Trust, and Power by Dale Zand. Oxford University Press, 1997.

Patterns of Culture by Ruth Benedict. Houghton Mifflin Company, 1934.

Patterns of Social Capital: Stability & Change in Historical Perspective, edited by Robert Rotberg. Cambridge University Press, 2000.

Preserving HumanValues in an Age of Technology by Edgar Johnston. Wayne State University Press, 1961.

Social Capital: Critical Perspectives, edited by Stephen Baron. Oxford University Press, 2001.

Social Capital:Theory & Research, edited by Nan Lin. Aldine de Gruyter, 2001.

Social Capital:A Theory of Social Structure and Action by Nan Lin. Cambridge University Press, 2002.

The Silent Language by Edward Hall. Doubleday, 1959.

Trustworthy Government: Leadership and Management Strategies for Building Trust and High

Performance by David Carnevale. Jossey-Bass Publishers, 1995.

Trusting Me, Trusting You by Kim Giffin. Merrill, 1976.

Chapter Five: Anchor Your Ambition

INTRO

Cradles of Eminence by Victor Goertzel and Mildred Goertzel. Little, Brown, 1962.

The Future of Man by Peter Medawar. Methuen, 1960.

Ideas: General Introduction to Pure Phenomenology by Edmund Husserl, translation by W.R. Boyce Gibson. Humanities Press, 1969.

The Phenomenology of Perception by Maurice Merleau-Ponty, translated by Colin Smith. Humanities Press, 1962.

VEST YOUR VISION

Art and Visual Perception: A Psychology of the Creative Eye by Rudolf Arnheim. University of California Press, 1954.

Being and Time by Martin Heidigger. SCM Press, 1962.

Daydreaming and Fantasy by Jerome Singer. Allen and Unwin, 1976.

Daydreaming: An Introduction to the Experimental Study of Inner Experience by Jerome Singer. Random House, 1966.

Gathering the Winds: Visionary Imagination and Radical Transformation of Self and Society by Eleanor Wilner. Johns Hopkins University Press, 1975.

Image and Mind by Stephen Kosslyn. Harvard University Press, 1980.

Mental Imagery and Learning by Malcolm Fleming and Deane W. Hutton. Educational Technology Publications, 1983.

Mind-Play: The Creative Uses of Fantasy by Jerome Singer and Ellen Switzer. Prentice-Hall, 1980.

The Mind's Eye: Imagery in Everyday Life by Rober Sommer. Delacorte Press, 1978.

Roman Stoicism by Edward Arnold. Books for Libraries Press, 1971 (©1911).

Seeing with the Mind's Eye: The History, Techniques, and Uses of Visualization by Mike Samuels. Random House, 1975.

Self-Analysis: Critical Inquiries, Personal Visions, edited by James Barron. Analytic Press, 1993.

Spatial Learning Strategies: Techniques, Applications, and Related Issues, edited by Charles Holley & Donald Dansereau. Academic Press, 1984.

Visualization Techniques by Richard Leinbach. Prentice-Hall, 1986.

Visual Cognition, edited by Steven Pinker. MIT Press, 1985.

TRUE THE TRAJECTORY

Ascent of Mind by William Calvin. Bantam Books, 1991.

Goal Setting; Key to Individual and Organizational Effectiveness by Charles Hughes. American Management Association, 1965.

The Goals Approach to Performance Objectives by Hildreth McAshan. Saunders, 1974.

Goals, No-Goals, and Own Goals: A Debate on Goal-directed and Intentional Behaviour, edited by Alan Montefiore & Denis Noble. Unwin Hyman, 1989.

The Magic of Believing: The Science of Setting Your Goal and Then Reaching It by Claude Bristol. Prentice-Hall, 1985.

Stability and Change in Human Characteristics by Benjamin Bloom. Wiley, 1964.

Teleological Explanations: An Etiological Analysis of Goals and Functions by Larry Wright. University of California Press, 1976.

A Theory of Goal Setting and Task Performance by Edwin Locke and Gary Latham. Prentice-Hall, 1990.

The Throwing Madonna: Essays on the Brain by William Calvin. Bantam Books, 1991.

ORCHESTRATE THE OPUS

The Managerial Choice: To Be Efficient and To Be Human by Frederick Herzberg. Dow Jones-Irwin, 1976.

Managing Creativity by John Kao. Prentice-Hall, 1991.

Managing Innovative Projects by Alan Webb. Chapman & Hall, 1994

Out of the Crisis by W. Edwards Deming. MIT Press, 1986.

Quantum Quality: Quality Improvement Through Innovation, Learning & Creativity by Willam Miller. AMACOM Books, 1993.

FIGURE ON FLUX

Fields of Force: The Development of a World View from Faraday to Einstein by William Berkson. Wiley & Sons, 1974.

Managerial Breakthroughs: Action Techniques for Strategic Change by James Emshoff. AMACOM Books, 1980.

Managing Strategic Change: Technical, Political, and Cultural Dynamics by Noel Tichy. Wiley & Sons, 1983.

Morrisey on Planning : A Guide to Long-Range Planning: Creating Your Strategic Journey by George Morrisey. Jossey-Bass Publishers, 1996.

Planning for Company Growth; The Executive's Guide to Effective Long Range Planning by Bruce Payne. McGraw-Hill, 1963.

Practical Reasoning: Goal-driven, Knowledge-based, Action-Guiding Argumentation by Douglas Walton. Rowman & Littlefield, 1990.

Scenarios and Strategic Management by Michel Godet, translated by David Green and Alan Rodney. Butterworths, 1987.

Scenarios: The Art of Strategic Conversation by Kees Van der Heijden. Wiley & Sons, 1996.

Strategic Interaction by Erving Goffman. University of Pennsylvania Press, 1969.

CAPITALIZE ON CRUCIBLES

Bodily Reflective Modes: A Phenomenological Method for Psychology by Kenneth Shapiro. Duke University Press, 1985.

The Concept of Dread by Søren Kierkegaard, translation by Walter Lowrie. Princeton University Press, 1944.

The Divided Self: A Study of Sanity and Madness by Ronald Laing. Quadrangle Books, 1960.

An Experiment in Mindfulness by E.H. Shattock. Dutton, 1960 (©1958).

The Evolution of Human Consciousness by John Crook. Oxford University Press, 1980.

Focusing by Eugene Gendlin. Everest House, 1978.

The Growth of Self-Insight by John Dorsey. Wayne State University Press 1962.

Mind and Emotion by George Mandler. Wiley, 1975.

Mindfulness by Ellen Langer. Addison-Wesley Pub. Co., 1989.

Mindfulness and Meaningful Work: Explorations in Right Livelihood, edited by Claude Whitmyer. Parallax Press, 1994.

Retrospection and Introspection by Mary Eddy. A. V. Stewart, 1917.

Solitude: A Return to the Self by Anthony Storr. Ballantine, 1989.

The Stress of Life by Hans Selye. McGraw-Hill, 1956.

The Quest of Self-Control: Classical Philosophies and Scientific Research by Samuel Klausner. Free Press, 1965.